Motherhood and the Relationships of the Sexes

Catherine Gasquoine Hartley

PART I
INTRODUCTORY

It is now a well-established truism to say that the most injurious influences affecting the physical condition of young children arise from the habits, customs and practices of the people themselves rather than from external surroundings or conditions. The environment of the infant is its mother. Its health and physical fitness are dependent primarily upon her health, her capacity in domesticity, and her knowledge of infant care and management. Thus the fundamental requirement in regard to this particular problem is healthy motherhood and the art and practice of mother-craft. Given a healthy and careful mother we are on the high road to securing a healthy infant; from healthy infancy we may expect healthy childhood, and from healthy childhood may be laid the foundations of a nation's health.

"Education and Infant Welfare."

Annual Report for 1914 of the Chief Medical Officer of the Board of Education.

CONTENTS OF CHAPTER I
A RETROSPECT—THE POSITION OF WOMEN BEFORE THE GREAT EUROPEAN WAR

The overwhelming events of the Great War—Change in my own views—Primitive conception of the relative position of the two sexes—The war divides the feminist struggle into two periods—The demand of woman to live her own life—The merits and demerits of the Suffrage Movement—The vote gospel a drug swallowed to still the craving for something vitally needed—Women swept out of their own interests into a swirling sea of desire—Emotion the strong guide to action—Militancy—A tremendous adventure—The mob spirit—Sowing a crop of feminine wild oats—What has been gained—Much experience and some knowledge—Experience indispensable as a foundation of a broader feminism—Solidarity of women—War came like a thunderbolt from a clear sky—The clamour and deception of meetings and propaganda.

CHAPTER I
A RETROSPECT
THE POSITION OF WOMEN BEFORE THE GREAT EUROPEAN WAR

"There is one profound weakness in your movement towards emancipation. Your whole argument is based on an acceptance of male values."—Dr. Ananda Coomaraswary.

As I set out to write yet another book on Woman, I find it necessary first to decide whether the primary interest should rest in the eternal instincts, passions and typical character of womanhood, or in women's actions and characters as affected by the unusual conditions of the time in which my work is undertaken. It is a decision by no means so simple as it would seem.

Always the realisation of what is immediately before us tends by its vivid nearness to give an over-estimation of its significance. But to read life in this way is to understand very little. Something must be done to clear our vision so that we may take a wider view. The present, after all, is but the day at which the past and the future meet.

Yet there are times when some overwhelming event so sharply changes the present as to obscure all the shining wonder of life. And at no period in history has this been more true than it has been in Europe in the last two years. Nowhere and never in the world can there have been a period of deeper or more rapid change. War came upon us without warning, like a thunderbolt from a clear sky; and in a day the outlook of life was changed.

Now, this thought of surprising and quick-coming change brings me to something it is necessary for me to say. My book should have been begun many months back, at the very beginning of the war. But here I have to make a confession. The war caused in my mind a confusion that for some time left me extremely uncertain upon many things about which hitherto I have been sure. It has been a war of miracles in so far as it has made real much that seemed outside the world of possibility. Our sluggard imaginations have been stirred by an appeal that has aroused many primitive emotions.

I recall the opening sentence in the last book that I wrote on Woman.[1] "The twentieth century is the age of Woman. Some day, it may be, it will be looked back upon as the golden age—the dawn, some say, of feminine civilisation."

Now, as I read this statement, which, when I wrote it, I felt to be true, it appears so wrong as to be almost ridiculous. That sort of dream is over.

What a fantastic picture it was that Suffrage militancy made for itself before the outbreak of the war. We pictured a golden age which was to come with the self-assertion of women; an age in which most of those problems that have vexed mankind from the dawn of history were to be solved automatically by a series of quick penny-in-the-slot reforms, that would follow on the splendour and superiority of woman's rule. Militants, aflame for the reformation of man, discussed prostitution, the White Slave traffic, and all sex problems with a zeal that was partly pathological and partly the result of a Utopian dream.

Then, at the most crucial hour in the history of women's struggle for power and political recognition, all this dream was arrested. In the stress of war, the promise of an accumulating betterment was swept down, even as a too-bright dawn that passes into storm; the ugly aspects of life sprang upon us with intensifying urgency. Yes, the sudden events of war seemed, for women, to have blotted out the present and the past, and to have made all action uncertain.

So it is always when life is stirred at its depths. The change was almost staggering. Women have had to learn many new and strange lessons; they are more changed than perhaps they themselves know.

There had come a time when, without any preparation, we women were brought back to the primitive conception of the relative position of the two sexes. Military organisation and battle afford the grand opportunity for the superior force capacity of the male. Again man was the fighter, the protector of woman and the home. And at once his power became a reality. The striking and praise-demanding work was done by men. And at the first violent change there seemed to be nothing for women beyond the patience of waiting and the service of sacrifice. Later, women have been called to step in to take the places of men, and there has been work for them to do of all kinds and in ever-increasing amount. But of this work, and the new conditions that have thereby arisen, I propose to speak in the next chapter. Here I am considering only the events that rushed upon women at the oncoming of war. And inevitably they were pushed aside into obscurity; they had to be content with unnoticed work that not infrequently was futile.

It is hard to step so suddenly out of the limelight. And women were acutely aware of this change in their prospects, and many of them expressed the situation with engaging frankness. Let me give a small illustration. I had occasion in the late summer of 1914, a few weeks after the war had started, to visit a friend. Some months had passed since I had previously seen her. At that time she was actively engaged in the suffrage campaign. Now, I found her knitting woollen comforters for the soldiers, and she was knitting them very badly. I expressed my surprise. Her answer to me was, "It is all that there is to do." She then added this significant statement, "We women have had to learn our place."

There was, of course, exaggeration in her remark. But it does, I believe, picture what happened in the thoughts of many women with the sudden ceasing of their active struggle for political recognition. It was a state of resigned surprise.

And may it not be that women had need of some lesson?

In the curious phases witnessed before the war, in that struggle which was but a more violent expression of the eternal effort at adjustment between the sexes, there were many strange signs to give pause and fear to all who think. Women did not, as I believe, realise the possible results of their sex rebellion. They did not sufficiently distinguish between those limitations and hardships which could comparatively easily be removed and those limitations and hardships which are due to the nature of their sex. Old traditions, without any discrimination, were cast aside in a violent seeking, and women broke out in unexpected ways, to fight nervously, carelessly, yet hungrily, as if they were trying to force the pace of progress.

Women are possessed of great elasticity and cleverness; they are, and possibly will always remain, more imitative than creative. And from this follows a very real danger, plainly arising from the quick feminine receptiveness which is at once the strength of women as well as the cause of their pitiable weakness. In every direction the new independence and work capacity of woman was proved in following and imitating men. Thus it was easy for women to externalise their life in every way, and to gain success in many different kinds of work. But the question has never been—could women do this, or do that, kind of work? rather it is—what work is it most worth while for them to do?

Wounded by the narrowness of their lives, women spent immense energy out of which much that is good has been gained. Much that was false has crumbled into ruins, but also much that was fine. What was wanting most was this: the complete absence in the entire programme of reform of any kind of feminine idealism.

Did women forget? I think that they did. The realm of woman was still splendid, still vast. Why, then, this rage against all restrictions? Why this continuous effort to obliterate the wise differences of sex?

In their violent seeking for life, women were ready to spend all to gain something which may well prove to be absolutely unnecessary to them. And to many it must have seemed that they wasted the whole of themselves only to lose something within themselves. There was much heroic fighting. Women robbed life for the sake of what they believed was freedom; yet may it not prove that they have been in love with that which is unattainable for women?

The demand of woman to "live her own life" brought, as it seems to some of us, a slavery not less strong or less evil than that from which an escape was sought. Women, however unconsciously, were suppressing themselves in new ways, and still doing things alien to themselves. This restless seeking was but a further foolish forgetting of the truth that the only freedom worth having is the freedom to be one's self. All that women had promised themselves in a new order of existence must depend on their acceptance of the responsibilities and limitations of their womanhood. And by this I mean a full and glad acceptance of those physical facts of their organic constitution which make them unlike men, and should limit their capacity for many kinds of work. It can never be anything but foolishness to attempt to break down the real differences between the two sexes.

This may be a hard saying to some women: I believe that it is true.

It is necessary to emphasise this fact again, and yet again, because it is the almost complete disregard by women of their own sexual nature and its special needs that is the grave evil that is robbing us of life; this was also the inherent weakness in the Women's Movement, which, so far from fulfilling the promise of its earlier period, had ceased, even before war brought us back to realities, to exert any widely representative or serious influence.

The predilection for wild pranks, which in this country marked the later efforts of women to gain political recognition, may, I think, be traced back to causes bent on crushing and levelling the sex characteristics. Women had not sufficiently valued themselves, and thus they ceased to care to be essentially feminine. Instead there was an insatiable desire to enjoy experience, arising from lack of disciplined culture and from excess of energy and idleness. It is manifest that militancy gave to women excitement and occupation.

And this avidity to know and feel and shine, to establish new contacts with life and affairs, was coupled also with that deeper seeking of the spirit which has robbed peace from the modern woman. Possibly such defects are essential to such a movement, a mere destructive phase in the process of renewing—a clearing of the ground. But the way to gain freedom is long and toilsome; it is a way that permits of no such energetic short cuts as the militant Suffragists would have achieved. Mixed up with all that was fine in their movement was an infinity of glitter and tinsel, vanity and restlessness. There was present always an intense and theatrical egotism, a yearning to make an impression and force applause at any cost.

There was, of course, another side—a side which most gladly I acknowledge. No movement that was founded merely on excitement would have overcome difficulties as the Suffrage movement did, nor could its members have worked and suffered as they did for a common end. There was always much even in the most mistaken militancy that was generous, ardent and wholesome. But these useful qualities were deformed by a want of proportion and sanity; by feelings run riot that made women impatient of all restraints, overweeningly sure of themselves, and incapable of facing troublesome facts or foreseeing the most certain consequences of their own actions. There is nothing here that should surprise us.

In many cases, perhaps in all, emotion is the sole and strong guide of our actions. At least, I am sure this is true of women. What we do is to invent reasons to justify acts to which we are impelled by some emotion arising from an instinctive need. I do not see how this can be avoided, nor do I at all regard it in itself as evil. Reason by itself too often is an excuse for doing nothing; it is the excuse of all those who take infinite care not to see in case they may come to feel. Reason alone never does anything; it is too reasonable. The necessary thing is first to feel. And the only possible method of guiding emotion is to realise its force and to use it successfully; not to take cover fearfully in avoidance of feeling.

There is, indeed, a very deep reason for this human need for emotion. The springs of our actions may be traced back in almost all cases to certain excitements arising from some need or desire of whose existence in ourselves we are in nine cases out of ten quite unconscious, but which (unless dammed up when the fear of an escape is always great and imminent) will find an expression in characteristic instinctive acts. And the most forcible human excitements are fear and anger: these exercise an energising influence on body and mind often leading to the accomplishment of quite extraordinary acts. Periods of intense excitement will yield a consciousness of overwhelming strength, so that the individual reaches a state of self-forgetfulness in which almost anything may be done. Almost every one must at some time have experienced this super-strength. And what is important to note is that at an opportunity for exercising these emotions, the most peaceable people have felt the stir of the primitive instincts of hate and fear, of anger and the desire to destroy and to hurt. They have developed—often to their own surprise—the destructive capacities of the fight-loving, danger-braving animal. And when such emotions seize on individuals in groups, their effect is greatly intensified and is felt by many who would be only slightly susceptible to such emotions when isolated.

This explains, I believe, the surprising revolt of women and how it was they broke out in such unexpected ways. There is in the sex an immense and unrecognised capacity for adventure, due to the surplus of energy unused that was so painfully present in the lives of many women, and to the expression of which the narrowness of their lives had afforded little opportunity. The danger here was strong for women, because in their lives, to a far greater extent than in the lives of men, there had been so many dammed-up channels of emotion. It is the things they might not do that had mattered for women, and not the things they had been allowed to do. Then the fever of this anger caught hold of them, and they became conscious of an obscure travail in their souls. Here, indeed, were causes of unrest; here were the first shadows of some subtle decay.

The suffrage movement was a search—yes, a wild search—for something to bridge the gap, for something to do that mattered, something to open the gates to adventure. The militant revolt to many women proved an exciting game. This may appear strange; but what I want you to mark is that such violence was a necessary thing for women. They felt impelled to get into their lives something that meant movement, excitement, joy, and the stinging of adventure.

And they have been happy.

To many people, and especially to men, it seemed that in adopting militancy women were departing entirely from their womanhood. But it is just here they were mistaken; they did not grasp the fact that women had felt injured, and that this injury aroused in them an excitement of anger forcing wild action. Women, too, I think, have not themselves understood the real causes of their actions. It was impossible to follow the procession of excuses by which the militant apologists attempted to justify their often senseless outrages on the law without realising how erroneously they comprehended their own movement. They honestly thought that they were espousing the cause of Woman's freedom; it never struck them that they were not working for this, at least that this was not the motive which impelled their actions of violence. They did not know that they were taking the quickest way to fill lives left empty, and to express in action the clamorous excitement that surged within them. It is never easy for women to be quite honest even to themselves.

Manifestly this violent seeking was but an outgrowth of woman's fierce race-protecting passion; an unconscious expression of that instinct to give life which rules not only in the body but in the spirit of woman. Many women fought without truly wanting to fight, and merely because their deep hidden instincts demanded something on which to expend themselves.

There was in the Suffrage movement a wise policy of action. And this using of women's stored-up energy, however wastefully it may have been expended, inflamed in them a gladness that made easy all their payments of imprisonment, of forcible feeding, and even of death. In militancy women gained an object and a satisfaction: they were the centre of something that depended on them. Their movement, with all its absurdities, was a live thing in their hands. Thus the members gave to the cause their labour and their enthusiasm, and, because they had given it so much, they came to love it. Their energetic organisation came to stand above them like a big, greedy child, grabbing at anything and everything. It robbed from them the flying hours of life, little by little devouring them. But in so doing new fuel was thrown on the dead flames of women's passions. For they gained that for which they were seeking. A new, strange opportunity for sacrifice was here, supplying the need which, however unrecognised and denied, is the fundamental desire of woman. This was the joy that was gained by the Suffrage martyrs—something vivifying, flooding dead lives with colour, action and emotion. Yes, these women yielded themselves to their movement with joy, just as a woman yields herself to her lover that she may give life to his child.

And then all this audacious, hardly understood movement was brought to an end by war. Militarism put a swift close to militancy. As far as women were concerned, their hope of forcing political recognition fell to confusion. The war came like a great shadow across the whole bright complex problem of the future. So much was this so that writing of militancy now feels almost like referring to a forgotten event that happened in the very far past. It would be easy to pass over the whole Suffrage movement in silence. And, indeed, I should have done this if I did not believe that its inner effect on women had been more lasting than the outward gain.

I wish to emphasise the change that came to women in the period immediately before the war. The Suffrage movement was a collective movement in which the individual had to win honour in self-forgetfulness and in group work. And this co-operation for the gaining of the Vote carried with it also a co-operation of service and a great development of mutual helpfulness. And from this it has followed very directly that many women have turned their backs for ever on petty interests and disloyalties to one another, and have recovered a quite fresh sense of honourable emulations and loyalty.

This concord and unity in duty had much the same quality of joy that sends the soldier to face death. It stirred something very deep in women's nature. Militancy brought a rare chance of happiness: it made women aware of their souls. Through it they first found escape from the deadness of sterile lives and gave up separate little aims that made conflicts between woman and woman. The petty strifes of no issue and no importance were changed into one struggle that must be won; and by expanding from an existence of aimlessness and stagnation into one of common purpose and advance, women gained the chance they were seeking of adventure and sacrifice for body and spirit. No wonder, then, that they gave themselves up to a great holiday of the emotions. This may have expressed itself basely in the wrecking of property and much that was useless, but it was not all base. In the lives of numberless women it has meant something much more than hatred and vanity, or self-deceiving work.

Militancy has been a great as well as a very little thing. As a movement it was foolish and morally perverse, no doubt, but its members were morally passionate. The disorder of purpose, the spectacle of wasted effort and folly, which filled many of us with anger—all this did bring gladness and liberation of spirit to the women themselves. They felt that their fighting was noble and glorious, which it was not, but they felt this with a power that came from the perverse conviction of their whole nature. And we shall need a conviction as passionate as this, but not perverse, before women can in the same way be won again to an equal passion of sacrifice and service.

And this very rapture of escape from an aimless existence was in itself the sign of the failure in women's lives, a proof that there was, indeed, something to be escaped from. We may not claim more than this for the Suffrage movement.

War, such war as is now loose upon the world, came to accomplish its miracles, acting swiftly and almost without women knowing what was being done. The reality of life and of death has shaken up everything, and the quick pressure of events is changing all the conditions of life.

Let us try to see a little more clearly.

It has been a common mistake that amongst civilised peoples intellectual views and peace interests have superseded the primitive fighting instincts. But the cultural period in which wars have been exceptional and peace the normal state has been short, and is, indeed, only a span when compared with the long history when men had to fight in order to live. This violence was a necessary phase in human, as in all animal, development. War is only an organised and specialised replacement of this indiscriminate and blind struggle for life. It is probable that the instinct of battle was once for all developed and fixed; and the question arises, as to whether we shall ever get far away from this deeply rooted stimulus to action. It may even be a condition of life that we should not get too far away from it.

We have had a striking example of the enthusiasm and interest evoked by situations of conflict and danger, in the intense and primitive emotions revived in all of us by the war. War is the thunder and voice of the trumpet without which the wisest moral and political ideas never attract sufficient attention to lead to difficult action. For the world will not listen to a truth until bloodshed and violence have awakened its sluggard imagination.

And in these new circumstances we all, women as well as men, have been caught by a powerful excitement. The war has us in its grip, there is no other thought, no other remedy, no other interest. In many ways war is the most uniting of all forces. We are all joined in one work of service and co-operation. No man or woman can turn away, skulk in the individual garden of their own petty interests, because they do not want to be bothered. Something fresh has come, something that had to come, and all that went before is changed.

We see thus that war has brought to all of us a succession of disturbing revelations of reality. And the lesson has come most severely on those whose lives have been most unreal. Here is a force against which there is no argument. We are involved in a struggle of the most momentous dimensions. No one as yet can mark the limits of destruction, and in the harshness of the war's lesson the struggle of women for sex mastery at once became uninteresting.

For hundreds of centuries and myriads of generations the life of fighting has gone on for men. But women's opportunity waits upon leisure and peace. The savagery of war brings the two sexes back to primitive values. And the truth is forced upon us; we realise the gulf which lies between the man and the woman.

All our days we women have been denying this separation, and, enslaved by male ideals, have sought to break through the barriers of sex. We have been pursuing power, wrapping ourselves up in one garment after another, calling these coverings romance, adventure, work, individual development, and what not; now we have come in our hearts to know the falsity of it all. Somewhere in the confusion of war stark facts awaited us. We had to face life as a reality, not as theories, or movements, or sex development.

For many of us women the lesson has been sharp and sudden. War leapt upon us as it were a beast out of some hidden darkness; leapt upon us, holding us powerless, tearing our illusions into shreds with its blood-stained claws.

And on a sudden women were held by a new, quick-striking, absolute realisation of the truth. They had not seen it nor felt like this before. But this beast of war crouching in front of them said to women, "Always I have been beside you waiting for this hour. I have waited for a long time. You have struggled; you have fought; you have played; you have come to think yourselves important in strange ways, meddling in all the affairs of the world. This you have done, and you have learnt much of the means of life, but you have everything yet to re-learn about life itself.

"In all your struggles for political recognition and in all your work reality has not touched you. You have feared to be yourselves. You have been ashamed of your sexual differentiation. You have gathered power around you to pretend that you were the same as men, your strength as their strength, that your work was the same as their work. You have mocked at those qualities that were your own, that set you apart from men, denying your womanhood. You have suffered. But you will not suffer less by any such efforts to escape. Who can wonder that you have been dissatisfied? For you have wasted in haste the power that is your own. And conscious of, though not understanding, the want in your own lives, you have been deeply conscious of the discords in the rest of the world. The instinct of motherhood has been strong within you, and wasted, it has not ceased to torment you.

"You have gained excitement and applause, much work you have done and had many triumphs. It has seemed a big thing. Yet, after all, has the gain been worth the payment? Have women indeed escaped from their prison? Think, do you not know deep in your hearts that its bars have not been broken?"

CONTENTS OF CHAPTER II
THE POSITION OF WOMEN AS AFFECTED BY THE WAR

The new conditions brought by the war—Seriousness of the position—My object in writing a book on motherhood—The Annual Report of the Chief Medical Officer of the Board of Education for 1914—The condemnation of motherhood shown by the facts of this Report—The greatness of the evil that we are permitting—Women ill-trained as women and incapacitated for their supreme duty—The inquiry into the conditions of working-class motherhood made by the Women's Co-operative Guild—The miserable health of the mothers of our working classes—This one of the greatest dangers and social crimes of the day—The health of women must be safeguarded—The problem greatly increased by the special war conditions—Report issued by the Health of Munition Workers Committee on "Employment of Women" and "Hours of Work"—The danger of overworking women—Woman sows in her flesh for the race—She needs to store energy, not to expend it—The confusion and failure in efficient motherhood—We have got to find what this failure is.

CHAPTER II
THE POSITION OF WOMEN AS AFFECTED BY THE WAR

"To be mothers were women created and to be fathers men."—Sayings of MANU.

I have spoken in the last chapter of the changes that came in the thoughts and attention of women in the first few months of the war. We saw how war spoke with a more powerful voice, and the women who had been snatching at power felt the quickening of a quite new spirit of humbleness. That uplifting was the great opportunity. Women discovered something stronger and more important than themselves.

Our inquiry now is this: What has happened since then? what fresh conditions is war developing or likely to develop? And first it is well to note the strange power of war to stir us into action. Two years ago it would have seemed impossible to feed the hungry and clothe the ragged and to turn all the wasters and slackers into vigorous heroes. Now these things have been done; and much that in peace time seemed a far-off possibility has become a present fact.

War has a terribly effective way of dealing not only with men but with their problems. And one result is that a quite new interest is being taken in motherhood and child welfare.

England can no longer afford to be wasteful of the lives of her citizens. She has been wasteful in the past, and her new mood of caring must be made a conviction and a purpose.

As a result of this world war there has been and will continue to be an immense sacrifice of men, much in excess of any wars in the past history of nations, and it is evident that every belligerent country must lose from her best male stock; and it is not only the physically fittest, but the mentally and morally fittest, that are sacrificed.

For years to come the birth rates will be lowered throughout the greater part of Europe. In our own land the situation is one that must give fear. Our death rate has been very high in numbers and in quality, while at the same time our birth rate has been the lowest on record. Even the civilian death rate has risen; and, worst and most menacing of all, the infantile mortality rate has risen two per thousand above the average of the last two years.

Put these grave facts together, and, with even a fraction of realisation of their meaning, it becomes clear that we have to face a wastage of life unparalleled in the annals of our race. What are we going to do?

Now, I am not one who believes in the advantage, or even in the possibility of any forced excess in procreative activity. Numbers are of less importance to a nation than the moral, mental, and physical superiority of its men. The wholesale waste of these qualities in war is just what must be of such enormous menace to the future. The nation that does nothing to meet this and to ensure as far as possible the superiority of the next generation of her children will gain nothing even from victory, for it will mean only defeat in the future.

The issues of life and death have by the lurid war-light been forced upon our attention. And again I ask, What are we going to do?

The answer is plain. This terrible loss of life and of the forces of life abroad in war must be made good by a more intelligent and efficient care of the young lives at home. This we must do, and we must do it quickly. It is possible for a nation by such increased care of the rising generation of its children to compensate itself for the loss of lives during the war within a comparatively short period after the close of war. Indeed, if we have the will, as we possess the means, we can make it true that because of the war there will be more people—yes, and healthier and happier—in this land of ours in ten or fifteen years' time than if the war had never happened.

This is what we can do. Shall we do it? The answer is with women. We can, within limits, do almost what we please. There has come to us a great opportunity, and out of the gates of death itself we may snatch life.

Much waits to be done, not only in the actual saving of infantile life, but further, by providing effective and prompt remedies to all bad conditions of living, so that the health and the mental capacity and moral character of the children dependent upon these conditions, or related to them, may be raised and maintained at a right standard of efficiency. Then we have to realise that more even than this is needed, and that all our efforts will fail of their full effect unless we go further back than the child, and the problem of the mother be frankly faced. The question of infantile mortality and child welfare is really the question of motherhood. And there is now no ultimate need of the State greater, more imperative, than this of securing a more enlightened motherhood.

This need is the reason for my book. I know that the days of war are not a time suitable either for the writing or reading of long books. Yet I offer no apology, so convinced I am of the urgency of this matter of saving motherhood that I had to write.

The object of my book is twofold. First, to put forward a fresh plea for assigning that high value to motherhood in practice which at present it receives only in words. This would ensure at once right conditions for all mothers and all children; it would also serve better than anything else to do away with many age-old mistakes, misunderstandings and disorder. In the second place (or rather in connection with all that is said), I wish to set forth what seem to me to be the chief causes that hitherto have hindered motherhood and bound my sex from the full enjoyment of life; and to suggest that the reason of this bondage is not, as is so often stated, the aggressive selfishness of men, but is due much more to women's own actions, to their absurdly wrong education and entire misunderstanding of the sexual life; a misunderstanding which has decided the direction in which they believed the freedom they have been so ardently, yet wastefully seeking, was to be found.

So that we may understand our present failures better, I have attempted to seek causes and to suggest reasons. My inquiry reaches back before human parenthood and examines the parental instinct in its making; it shows the way and for what reason this instinct of caring for the young became fixed and stronger in the mother than in the father. It sets out from this beginning, and, after a short chapter on primitive motherhood, passes to the consideration of women and the home, marriage as it affects parenthood, the unmarried mother and sexual relationships outside of marriage, as well as other allied questions. It tries to offer a practical solution to some of the problems involved, in particular the problem of education and new ideals of conduct and sexual health for all girls. It recommends a revolution in our schools and methods of training; changes that must, as I believe, be made, unless we are prepared to accept as inevitable the decay of motherhood, as well as an increasing failure of happiness in marriage, with its resulting antagonism between sex and sex.

But to return to this present introductory chapter. I have upon my study table two documents. The one is that from which I have taken the quotation placed before this opening section of my book. It is the Annual Report for 1914,[2] of the Chief Medical Officer of the Board of Education. The second consists of two pamphlets on the Health of Munition Workers, treating of the Hours of Work and Employment of Women, both prepared by the command of Right Hon. D. Lloyd George, and published in connection with the important illustrated Report, which shows and explains all the numerous and different engineering operations on which women are now engaged in munition work. The object of the Report is to attract more women workers; but it is with the two pamphlets I am concerned. For the present, however, I shall leave them, returning to them later in order to show how closely they are connected with the other Report, which treats of infant mortality, child disease and neglect, and all the wastage of motherhood. It is on the shameful significance of the facts given in this Report that we must now fix our attention.

It would be difficult to find a more complete condemnation of motherhood. The Report is full of condemning facts. For, let us not disguise it from ourselves that, in spite of much that has been done, many efforts and real improvements, motherhood remains very evil; about the lives of little children lurk cruelties, disease, dirt, and neglect that ought not to be permitted.

Let me take one group of facts from this Report; facts that cry out to us all how urgently wrong things are. In the year 1914, 92,166 children died in England and Wales under one year of age. Think of the wanton wastage: in every thousand children born one hundred and five have died. Their number of the year's toll of new lives reaches close up to the recorded deaths for the first fifteen months of war![3] And the evil does not end here, for the bad conditions which kill these babies act also in maiming and disabling, or at least in lowering the health standard, of many of the children who live, and thus add to the number of those who die in the early years of childhood, or survive only with enfeebled bodies and defective minds. And, further, no account is taken here of the lives that are lost before birth takes place: I mean the still births and abortions, the ante-natal deaths of which no record is kept. Our tendency is to assume that life begins at the birth, whereas the life of each child starts at the moment of its conception. Thus the birth rate is really the survival from the conception rate. And the destruction of life before birth from adverse ante-natal conditions is probably larger than the death rate in the first post-natal year.

You will see that the problem is sufficiently grave. And this unnecessary waste—for it is unnecessary—is going on every year, and will go on until we begin to feel it strongly enough to take action to prevent it. It can be prevented. The chief causes of infant mortality are briefly two—

(1) Poor physique of the mother or inheritable disease in one or other parent, causing premature births with weakened constitutions and congenital defects in the children.

(2) Ignorance of mothers in appropriate infant care and low standard of home life; bad feeding and insanitary conditions are accountable for the greater number of child deaths.

We find the infantile death rate is much higher in urban communities than it is in rural England. It is well to give a table to show this—

	Annual Rates per	Annual Rates per 1000 births

	Birth Rate.	Death Rate.	Diarrhœa and Enteritis (under two years).	Infant Mortality Rate.
			1000 LIVING	
England and Wales	23.8	13.7	20.4	105
97 great towns (including London)	25.0	15.0	26.1	114
145 smaller towns	23.9	13.1	19.8	104
England and Wales less the 242 towns	22.2	12.4	12.6	93
London	24.3	14.4	27.6	104

Consider the reason for this difference in the death rates—114 deaths per 1000 in the great towns, 104 in the smaller towns, and 93 in the country districts. Does not this prove that children are killed by the conditions into which they are born. It is obvious that urbanisation, with all that it means of unhealthy living, with factory work and the employment of women, exerts a profound effect on the lives and health of little children.

A portion of infant and child mortality represents, I well know, the removal from life of diseased children who ought never to have been born, and would not have been born under different sexual conditions, for this, above all, is a question of instructed motherhood. I am not forgetting this side of the problem. But these children, doomed to death from the time they are conceived, represent a fraction only of our infant mortality. The vast majority of babies are born healthy; it is we who kill them. Though the fact of the falling birth rate is being shouted aloud with an ever-increasing fear and insistence, the plain, simple fact is neglected; it is absurd to go on having more babies if we can't first care enough to keep alive the babies that we have. There are still too many births for our civilisation to look after; we are still unfit to be trusted with a rising birth rate.[4]

Let us consider now how our neglect acts on the children who fight through the first years of infancy. I can take a few facts only chosen almost at hazard from the mass of similar evidence in the Educational Report. In London, out of 294,000 children medically examined, 101,000 or nearly half, were found to be in need of treatment. In England and Wales 391,352 children of school age were medically attended. A summary of the returns shows a wide prevalence of verminous uncleanness, the percentage being 18.1 per cent. for the heads and 11.8 per cent. for the bodies of the children. Again the figures show unclean conditions to be most prevalent in the towns, in some instances the percentage rising as high as thirty unclean children out of each hundred children examined. I ask you to think what this implies.

The nutrition of the children is equally bad, the different counties varying in percentage between five and twenty. Stockton-on-Tees has the unenviable distinction of standing the highest—thirty out of each hundred of its children showing signs of malnutrition. The same Report shows the fatal prevalence among the children of rickets, eye disease, discharging ears, and diseases of the throat and nose.[5] The proportion of defective teeth is higher than any malady and often exceeds seventy and eighty per cent. of the school entrants.

We should note that insufficient or unsuitable food is the chief cause of malnutrition and illness in children, and investigations seem to show that wrong feeding is the more prevalent. Thus Dr. Gould, writing of the children he examined in Bolton, says, "it is obvious that defective nutrition is due to dietetic ignorance on the parents' part or to parental neglect." Dr. Macdonald of Northampton, reporting on 448 cases examined in 1914, corroborates this view, stating in the course of his report of adenoidal children, "Many are suffering, not from insufficiency of food (that, I think, far from common in Northampton), but from bad food and badly prepared food." Again, Dr. Orr of Shrewsbury writes, "The subject of unsuitable food is a very important one. The women of the working classes often show a surprising ignorance of the proper methods of cooking for family requirements, a want of knowledge of the value and suitability of food stuffs, and too often a general incompetence respecting household management."[6] I may add as corroboration an instance from my own knowledge; one that would be comic, if it were not so piteous. A party of poor workings girls were invited to a meal; they were asked what they would like to have to eat. They answered, "Bread and pickles," and added, "Pickles are so sustaining!"

Who can doubt the greatness of the evil that is going on? I could add many more facts at least equally impressive with the few that I have given, all witnessing to weakness in the constitution of our children, to disease and dirt, and every other painful result of ignorance and neglect. And does not all this speak of unfit motherhood; of women ill-trained as women and incapacitated for their supreme duty? There is failure somewhere. We have to find out where that failure is.

For I wish to make it very clear that I am not blaming the individual mother. What I do blame are the conditions of our civilisation that have called her into being. I have before me the admirable but infinitely distressing book, *Maternity: Letters from Working Women*. They are the outcome of an inquiry into the condition of working-class motherhood made by the Women's Co-operative Guild. Nothing that I can say, or that any other writer could say, can have the reality and the bitter vividness of these letters written by the women themselves. I am able to quote only scattered sentences taken from a few letters just as they come and without special selection.

(1) Mother Injured in Girlhood

"Through being left without a mother when a baby—father was a very large farmer and girls were expected to do men's work—I, at the age of sixteen, lifted weights that deformed the pelvis bones, therefore making confinement a very difficult case. I have five fine healthy girls, but the boys have all had to have the skull-bones taken away to get them past the pelvis.... I wish more could be done to train growing girls to be more careful."

(2) A Wage-Earning Mother

"I myself had some very hard times, as I had to go out to work in the mill. I was a weaver and we had a lot of lifting to do. My first baby was born before its time, from me lifting my piece off the loom onto my shoulder.... If I had been able to take care of myself I should not have had to suffer as I did for seven weeks before the baby was born, and for three months after, and then there was the baby suffering as well, as he was a weak little thing for a long time, and cost pounds that could have been saved had I been able to stay at home and look after myself."

(3) A Mother's Injury To Her Daughters

"I am very pleased to say that, having one of the best of husbands, I suffered nothing during pregnancy, only ailments of my own caused through my mother having to work in the brickyard during her pregnancy with me. That, I am sorry to say, is the cause of my own and my sister's illness ... and that thing will go on until women give up hard work during pregnancy."

(4) WORKED TOO HARD AS A GIRL

"My third child was born nine years after the second.... She lived six hours, and was convulsed from birth. The doctor's opinion was that I had worked too hard as a girl lifting heavy weights, therefore weakening the whole system."

(5) THE RESULTS OF POVERTY

"I think a great deal of suffering is caused to the mother and child during pregnancy by lack of nourishment and rest, combined with bad housing arrangements. The majority of working women before marriage have been used to standing a great deal at their work, bringing about much suffering which does not tell seriously until after marriage, particularly during pregnancy.... I believe that bad housing arrangements have a very bad effect on mothers during pregnancy. I know of streets of houses where there are large factories built, taking the whole of the daylight away from the kitchen, where the woman spends the best part of her life. On the top of this you get the continual grinding of machinery. The mother wonders what she has to live for; if there is another baby coming she hopes it will be dead when it is born. The result is she begins to take drugs.... All this tells on the woman, physically and mentally; can you wonder at women turning to drink?"

(6) ANOTHER CASE OF POVERTY AND OVERWORK

"The first part of my life I spent in a screw factory from six in the morning till five at night, and after tea used to do my washing and cleaning. I only left two weeks and three weeks before my first children were born. After that I took in lodgers and washing, and always worked up till an hour or so before baby was born. The results were that three of my girls suffer with their insides. None are able to have a baby. One dear boy was born ruptured on account of my previous hard work."

(7) THE EVIL OF SEXUAL IGNORANCE

"Judging from my own experience, a fair amount of knowledge at the commencement of pregnancy would do a lot of good. One may have a good mother who would be willing to give information, but to people like myself your mother is the last person you would talk to about yourself or your state.... I have learnt the most useful things since my children grew up. The idea that you impress the child all through with your habits and ways, or that its health is to a great extent hindered or helped by your own well-being, was quite unknown to me."

(8) Another Case

"When I was married, I had to leave my own town to go out into the world, as it were, and when I had to have my first baby, I knew absolutely nothing, not even how they were born. I had many a time thought how cruel (not wilfully, perhaps) my mother was not to tell me all about the subject when I left home.... When my baby was born I had been in my labour for thirty-six hours, and did not know what was the matter with me.... It was only a seven-months baby, and I feel quite sure if I had been told anything about pregnancy it would not have happened. I carried a heavy piece of oilcloth, which brought on labour.... I knew very little about feeding children, when they cried I gave them the breast. If I had known then what I know now my children would have been living. I was ignorant, and had to suffer severely for it, for it nearly cost me my life, and also those of my children. I very often ponder over this part of my life. I must not say anything about my mother now, because she is dead, but I cannot help thinking what might have been if she had told me."

(9) Healthy Motherhood, Given as a Contrast

"Although I have had eight children and one miscarriage, I am afraid my experience would not help you in the least, as I am supposed to be one of those women who can stand anything. During my pregnancy, I have always been able to do my own work.

"With the boys labour has only lasted twenty minutes, girls a little longer. I have never needed a doctor's help, and it has always been over before he came.... My idea is that everything depends on how a woman lives, and how healthy she was born. I had the advantage of never having to work before I was married and never have wanted for money, so when the struggle came I had a strong constitution to battle with it all."

(10) ANOTHER FORTUNATE CASE

"I must be one of the fortunate ones. I have always had fairly good health during pregnancy and good times at confinements and getting up.... I owe my good health to being well nourished and looked after by my mother when I was a growing girl. I think if all young girls of to-day are properly cared for, it will make all the difference to the mothers of the future, and save much suffering during pregnancy and after."

I should like to quote further from these letters, which have filled me with a passion of protest and pity. But why should I go on bringing fresh arguments to prove what already is sufficiently clear?

Give but a moment's attention to the facts that stand out in these eight summarised cases, and at once you will grasp what is wrong. These mothers have not been equal to their task of child-bearing; we have demanded from them too much. We have permitted the weakening of their constitutions from girlhood with unsuitable and too heavy work, and we have allowed them to grow up and marry sexually ignorant. What wonder that so many have failed in their supreme work of motherhood. The women bitterly feel this failure; many of them are convinced of the evils that have resulted to themselves and their children from their own overstrain through work and their ignorance of sexual hygiene and mother-craft.

Take now a few briefly summarised results of all these three hundred and forty-eight examined cases of motherhood. We find the following figures: Total number of live births, 1,396, 80 still-births and 218 miscarriages. These figures speak for themselves. It is probable all miscarriages are not given, but even those that are stated show a pre-natal death rate of 21.3 per 100 deaths. And we have no record of abortions, which, without doubt, are very numerous. According to some medical authorities the frequency of abortion "is believed to be about 20 to 25 per cent. of all pregnancies." Consider the following facts: two of these women each had ten miscarriages; one woman had eight miscarriages and no living child, while a second woman, after suffering seven miscarriages, consoled her motherhood by adopting an orphan boy; another woman gave birth to five dead children; the record of still another woman is three still-births and four miscarriages. The last of these mothers writes: "I had to work very hard to do everything for my little family, and after that I never had any more children to live. I either miscarried or they were still-born."

The post-natal deaths are also numerous. Of the three hundred and forty-eight mothers, eighty-six (or 24.7 per cent.) lost children in the first year of life. The total number of deaths rises to 122, or 8.7 per 100 live births, and it should be noted that 50 per cent., or one half of these deaths, occurred during the first month of infantile life or were due to wrong birth conditions when death was after the first month.

It seems useless to comment further upon these facts; the figures speak with sufficient clearness for themselves. I would ask you, however, to remember them; I would ask you to try to understand all that they mean of our deplorable neglect of motherhood.

For long we have been persistently assuming that the characteristics of the child at birth are genetic or hereditary and therefore can be but slightly affected by a favourable or an adverse nurture. This is a monstrous error. Very few indeed are the defects and the diseases that are inevitable and part of the birth-inheritance, rather they are traceable directly to malnutrition or poison in the mother, and by this means the fresh life is weakened or infected before it is born. So much the greater is the importance of ante-natal nurture. The child can be saved only through the mother. Inferior mothers must result in inferior children. And what we need now for the future maintenance and welfare of our race in adequate numbers and quality, is a speedy and practical recognition of the truth that nothing will avail us if we so educate, train, and work our women that as mothers they fail in their creative hour.

Let us now consider briefly how these matters stand in our land at the present time, and let us examine them in the light of these facts we have established of an over-burdened and, therefore, unfit motherhood. And the first thing we find is that the special conditions brought about by the Great War have greatly increased the problem we have to solve. I have already referred to the Report issued by the Health of Munition Workers Committee on "Employment of Women" and "Hours of Work." They give summary accounts of the conditions of women's labour and what is actually going on. I confess that what is stated has filled me with the gravest fears. I will give a few of the facts as they are set down.

> "The engagement of women in the manufacture of munitions presents many features of outstanding interest. Probably the most striking is the universal character of their response to the country's call for help; but of equal social and industrial significance is the extension of the employment of married women, the extension of the employment of young girls and the revival of the employment of women at night."

With regard to the class of women employed we learn—

> "The munition workers of to-day include dressmakers, laundry workers, shop assistants, university and art students, women and girls of every social grade and of no previous wage-earning experience, also, in large numbers, wives and widows of soldiers, many married women who had retired altogether from industrial life, and many again who had never entered it. In the character of the response lies largely the secret of its industrial success, which is remarkable. The fact that women and girls of all types and ages have pressed and are pressing into industry shows a spirit of patriotism which is as finely maintained as it was quickly shown."

The prodigious efforts of war are employing energies that have never been employed before. And there is something fine in the obdurate courage and determination of women to go through with their work. The spirit of woman does not easily resist. Ah! there is the danger. It is so difficult to induce any woman to recognise the limits of her physical powers. I am certain, too, that this danger of reckless overstrain is greater in England than in many other lands where women are working, for here custom and our habits of curious prudery force a woman to treat her sexual life as if it did not exist. This is the deep root of the danger. Thus, just as I should expect, the report goes on—

> "Conditions of work are accepted without question and without complaint which, immediately detrimental to output, would, if continued, be ultimately disastrous to health. It is for the nation to

safeguard the devotion of its workers by its foresight and watchfulness, lest irreparable harm be done to body and mind both in this generation and in the next."

The necessity of war has revived, after almost a century of disuse, the night employment of women in factories.[7] The report shows the deterioration in the health and energy of the women, due partly to overstrain from want of sleep and proper rest, but also to the difficulty the workers find in eating at night. We read—

> *"In one factory visited at night the manager stated that fatigue prevented many of the women making the effort to go from there to the mess room, though in itself the room was attractive. In another, visited also by night, several women were lying, during the meal hour, beside their piles of heaped-up work; while others, later, were asleep beside their machines, facts which bear additional witness to the relative failure of these hours. A few women of rare physique withstand the strain sufficiently to maintain a reasonable output, but the flagging effort of the majority is not only unproductive at the moment, it has its influence also upon the subsequent output, which suffers as in a vicious circle."*

The report shows plainly the destruction that is taking place in the home life of the workers. It states—

> *"While the urgent necessity for women's work remains, and while the mother's time and the time of the elder girls is largely given to the making of munitions, the home and the younger children must inevitably suffer. Where home conditions are bad, as they frequently are, where a long working day is aggravated by long hours of travelling, and where, in addition, housing accommodation is inadequate, family life is defaced beyond recognition."*

Again, take this passage—

> "Often, far from offering a rest from the fatigue of the day, the home conditions offer but fresh aggravation. A day begun at 4 or even 3.30 a.m., for work at 6 a.m., followed by fourteen[8] hours in the factory and another two or two and a half hours on the journey back, may end at 10 or 10.30 p.m., in a home or lodging where the prevailing degree of overcrowding precludes all possibility of comfortable rest. Beds are never empty and rooms are never aired, for in a badly crowded district the beds, like the occupants, are organised in day and night shifts. In such conditions of confusion, pressure and overcrowding, home life can have no existence."

The overstrain of the women is increased by their difficulty in obtaining living accommodation near to the factories.

> "It is far from uncommon now to find some two or three hours spent on the journey each way, generally under the fatiguing conditions of an overcrowded tram or train, often with long waits and a severe struggle before even standing room can be obtained. The superintendent of a factory situated in a congested district stated that the women constantly arrive with their clothes torn in the struggle for a train, the satchel in which they bring their tea being sometimes torn away. The workers were of an exceptionally refined type, to whom such rough handling should be altogether unfamiliar, but they bore these conditions with cheerful resolution."

What are the results going to be? Women have no right to bear such conditions with cheerful resolution. And it is just this acceptance of so many things that never ought to be accepted that fills me with apprehension. You see, I believe there is a much deeper cause than the urgencies of the war which is causing women to spend their strength in industrial work. Did I not think this, there would be little need for me to write.

I know that women's labour at the present crisis is a matter of necessity. How the work is to be done with the least possible injury to the workers is the question of the present. For it is equally momentous to the future that the standard of health and well-being of the country should be maintained. The problem is, how much work and of what kind can women do combined with perfect health. The health we must have, for it is requisite for the life of the race.

No doubt Nature is prodigal in her gifts of energy to women and provides enough for high-pressure work. But what we forget is this: the total amount of energy is strictly limited, and if women use up in work the energy that ought to be stored for child-bearing, they are preparing the way for an enfeebled race. Thus the problem of women's labour will not be solved until her work no more unfits her to be a mother than man's work unfits him to be a father. Woman sows in her flesh for the race, and because the demands of sex are stronger upon her she has to store more for the future than the man; she cannot expend so much in work in the present.

I have tried now to show in this and the preceding chapter the present and urgent need of an inquiry into the conditions of motherhood. The facts we have considered give, I feel, sufficient proof of our immense failure. Our attempt must be to bring order where we have had confusion. We have got to end this disastrous squandering of women's energies; a bankrupt expenditure which must result in wholesale waste in health and the lives of little children.

And I do not allude here only to the obvious immediate remedies. These will have to be made. The efforts for reducing infantile mortality must be such as will have lasting and substantial effect. Feeble tinkerings with such a question are the deepest foolishness. England can be indifferent to the health and well-being of women no longer, for she cannot afford to lose children by tens of thousands and to let the survivors be maimed and weakened by the million.

This, however, is not all; no legislation or social reconstruction—not any outward change, can accomplish alone what needs to be done. I am very certain of this. The wretched confusion and failure in efficient motherhood, which repeats itself everywhere, again and again, and in all classes of women, must be due to something more than industrialism and the hideous, ugly pressure of work for women, now so startlingly increased by the urgencies of war; it must be due to something stronger and more fundamental, to some inward cause. We must, I think, look to find some general and essential failure in women themselves—some unsoundness in their desires and their ideals, and in the principles they have set down for the conduct of their lives.

We have got to find what this failure is.

Note.—The Annual Report for 1915 of the Chief Medical Officer of the Board of Education has been issued since this chapter was written. The conditions have not materially changed since the previous year. Ten per cent. of all the children attending the Elementary Schools suffer from malnutrition, due largely to unsuitable and insufficient food. There is still a large amount of uncleanliness—the returns show about 16 per cent. of the children have dirty heads, and 15 per cent. dirty bodies.

A further evil has arisen from the greatly increased employment of children of school age; during one year 45,000 children have left school before the usual age, and 15,000 are temporarily employed in agriculture. In addition, more children are working as "half-timers" and as workers out of school hours. This wasteful employment of the young life of the future must, as the Report states, lead to physical and mental deterioration.

PART II
THE MATERNAL INSTINCT IN THE MAKING

"But what is the use of this history, what is the use of all this minute research? I well know that it will not produce a fall in the price of paper, a rise in that of crates of rotten cabbages, or other serious events of that kind, which cause fleets to be manned and set people face to face intent on one another's extermination. The insect does not aim at so much glory. It confines itself to showing us life in the inexhaustible variety of its manifestations; it helps us to decipher in some small measure the obscurest book of all—the book of ourselves."—Henri Fabre.

CONTENTS OF CHAPTER III
INSECT PARENTHOOD

The necessity of beginning the investigation of motherhood before human parenthood—The instinct not fixed but dependent on circumstances and the conditions of life—Experiments in family life—Bewildering diversity in strength of parental instinct—Numerous cases of insect home makers—Domestic economy of bees and ants—Does the word "instinct" explain—Parental devotion of the scarabee beetles—Fabre's account—Important to note (1) connection between form of union or marriage of the sexes and parental devotion, (2) connection between degree of intelligence in the parent and amount of care devoted to the young.

CHAPTER III
INSECT PARENTHOOD

"There can be few people alive who have not remarked on occasion that men are the creatures of circumstances. But it is one thing to state a belief of this sort in some incidental application, and quite another to realise it completely."—H. G. Wells.

This statement of Mr. Wells that I have placed at the head of the chapter will explain the reason why I find it necessary to go back to the grey primeval dawn of life to start my inquiry into motherhood. I want to establish that the instinct of caring for the young is not fixed, that it does not always develop in the same way or in the same parent, but rather that it is a quality, fluid and of indeterminate possibilities, that can be set and shaped by the conditions of life as wax is shaped by a mould. And I know no other way to make this clear. The few scattered facts that I have been able to gather together tell the miracles of the parental instinct. They must, I think, teach us humility. Let us throw aside the garments of conceit and false learning, and recognise that in reality we know almost nothing about anything, if things are probed to the bottom.

In the widest treatment of the maternal instinct it will not suffice to narrow our attention to the function of human motherhood, or to take up our study of the conditions relating to the mother and the child as we find them amongst us to-day. Were I to do this and to attempt at once to bring forward my own views, with the reforms that I wish for in this matter, my work would be as a building without a firm foundation, more or less uncertain, and for this reason valueless.

To get a proper grip of all that is here concerned we must understand that the maternal instinct is the deepest and strongest instinct in woman. It is in the emotions and actions either directly arising from or connected with motherhood that we find the real difference between the sexes. In its essence the parental instinct belongs to woman alone. The male may be infected with its energy—we witness this among birds, as well as in humbler animals, where the duties of caring for offspring are shared and, in some cases, carried out by the male alone; but man possesses, as yet, its faint analogy only. It is the most primary of all women's qualities.[9]

Now, why is this? Why is woman's being so much more strongly infected with motherhood than the man's with fatherhood?

It is a question not so readily to be answered as it might appear. If we find the explanation in the intimate connection between the mother and the child we have not, I think, exhausted the matter. We must not forget that other questions remain behind unanswered, all centring round the one question to which an adequate answer is so difficult to find: How has this arisen? The fact has to be explained that the sharp separation in the parental impulse and the parental duties, so strong amongst us, has not always existed; that there are many examples in the history of life which show an exactly opposite condition.

To find the clue it will thus be necessary to turn our attention to the earlier stages of life where, in particular among insects, reptiles, fishes, and birds, we find the widest possible range of difference in the expression of the parental instinct and the most varied relations existing between parents and offspring. Here indeed, among these pre-human parents, we can study the maternal instinct in the making. There are many new and strange facts for us to learn.

I know well the dangers of such an inquiry. To many, who will allow its interest, it will yet appear as being profitless. There is perhaps some justification for this view. Certainly any attempt to establish the conditions of human motherhood from examples in natural history must be far from conclusive. All comparisons of our own habits and impulses with their earlier expression as we see them in the animals are somewhat unsatisfactory. The lines on which human motherhood has developed and the conditions which have so largely helped to shape its expression, differ vastly from many of the other needs and circumstances which govern the activities of parents in the lower forms of life. Chief among these differences is the more complex character of the human brain, which is correlated with the far greater length of time that the human infant is dependent on its mother.

Yet, allowing for all this difference, I believe that there is much for us to learn from the life-histories of these pre-human parents. At least we find wonderful agreement prevailing between the conduct which we think reason dictates to us and that which we hold instinct dictates to the animals. And the question will be forced upon us: How far back in the record of life did the fierce mother-instinct exist? We shall find many unheeded examples, alike of its operation and of its failure to operate, which, if we consider them, in the light they may possibly cast forward on our own problems, will not fail to bring us to some unexpected conclusions. Life is full of surprises, and this matter of the care of the young affords not the least of them. Nowhere are the links between the present and the past more fascinatingly represented.

I am far indeed from being able to explain many facts I have come to know. I have been puzzled often, and the suggestions I offer I know may be wrong. The early stages in the growth of parental care, even among the animals whose habits are known to us, are often enshrouded in mystery, baffling the penetration of the most patient and careful inquirers. Nevertheless, during recent years a host of facts have been gathered together which throw much new light not only on the theme of pre-human parenthood, but also on the probable action of the parental instinct as it has slowly developed through the ages.

But apart from such more speculative considerations there are yet other aspects to be considered, such as the effect of the environment, the conditions of the home, and the type of union between the male and the female, all of which have their influence on the duration and kind of care shown by animal parents to their offspring. Some explanation must be sought for the almost bewildering diversity which we find in this relationship; for while the young of some animals (and often among low types where least we should expect it) are jealously guarded and cared for by at least one of the parents, in others there is no trace of such sacrifice and solicitude, and the young are thrown on to the world, orphaned before they are born, and left to live or die as chance decrees. Why is this? Why is the parental instinct so actively strong in some cases, so absent in others? Can we, indeed, hope to find the answer? If we can do this, we shall learn much to surprise and also to instruct us.

In the higher types of animals, with the longer period of infancy, some amount of care for the young is always shown by the mother. All the mammals, without exception, nurse their offspring for a longer or shorter period. Among the birds the young in many species are tended by both parents, and we find many beautiful examples of parental fosterage and protection. But we find also species, like the cuckoos, which thrust the parental duties on to others; and there are others, such as the megapodes, where the mother trusts the incubation of her eggs to natural agencies, and after placing them in a position to get the heat generated by decaying vegetation or that derived from hot springs, leaves them, and exhibits no apparent care for the future welfare of the family.

Here is something to give us food for thought. And the same surprises meet us as we descend the scale of life. The reptiles show little or no parental care, but strangely enough the toads and frogs, and many fishes, furnish us with examples of remarkable forethought, or apparent forethought, for their offspring; and, let it be noted, this solicitude is in most cases shown by the father and not by the mother. Even more remarkable are the insects, among whom, though still lower in the scale, we find the most wonderful cases of parental sacrifice to be met with anywhere in life. Some of these little creatures, indeed, seem to be endowed with a devotion to their young so insistent, that their lives can be described only as a passion of sacrifice. In truth they live but to give life and die. And accompanying this parental sacrifice, first in supplying food for embryonic development, and also, in some cases, affording fosterage and protection during the early stages of growth, we meet the most varied and wonderful behaviour which seems to prove an intelligence that thinks and plans; and, whatever explanation we try to find for these acts of devotion, we still are far from understanding them. Life has its secrets, and we shall probably fail to penetrate these mysteries. All that is possible to us is to inquire humbly that we may learn a few truths.

But for the sake of clearness, let me cease from generalising and direct our attention to certain definite examples. I will select first the model household of the *Minotaurus Typhœus* in the order *Coleoptera*—

> "The female digs a large burrow which is often more than a yard and a half deep and which consists of spiral staircases, landings, passages and numerous chambers. The male loads the earth on the three-pronged fork that surmounts his head and carries it to the entrance of the conjugal dwelling. Next he goes into the fields in search of harmless droppings left by the sheep, he takes these down to the first storey of the crypt and, with the aid of his trident begins to reduce them to flour, while the mother, right at the bottom, collects and kneads it into huge cylindrical loaves, which will presently become food for the little ones. For three months, until the provisions are deemed sufficient, the unfortunate husband, without taking any nourishment of any kind, exhausts himself in this gigantic work. At last, his task is accomplished. Feeling his end is at

hand, so as not to encumber the house with his wretched remains, he spends his last strength in leaving the burrow, drags himself laboriously along and, lonely and resigned, knowing that he is henceforth good for nothing, goes and dies far away amid the stones."[10]

Here we have exactly the kind of example we are in search of, and the most important thing to observe is the co-operation of the father with the mother in the work of providing for the family: such male devotion is undoubtedly exceptional.

Some measure of parental solicitude is almost universally common, and even among the lowliest creatures we find convincing proof of this. Among the species of limited resources, where the least care is bestowed and the young are left to look after themselves, the eggs are placed by the mother in a suitable environment so that the young can be sure of a sufficiency of food until they can feed themselves. The numerous caterpillars offer a well-known illustration of this primitive care, where it is common for the eggs to be attached to the food-plant by means of some adhesive covering. More striking is the case of certain weevils, which, in order to endow their young with a suitable home, possess the art of rolling a leaf in which the eggs are laid, thus forming a nursery, which serves as board and lodging in one.

Fabre, in a wonderful account of the most skilful of these workers, the Poplar weevil, states that not far from the scroll, made and laboriously rolled by the mother, we almost always find the male. But do not make a mistake. The weevil father is not moved by devotion to the family interests as was the father in the last case we examined. No, rather he is filled with the egoistic desire of the male. But I must give the history as Fabre relates it, fearing to spoil his beautiful account by my own halting description—

"What is he doing there, the idler? Is he watching the work as a mere inquisitive onlooker? From time to time I see him take his stand behind the manufacturer, in the groove of the fold, hang on to a cylinder and join for a little in the work. This is a means of declaring his flame and urging his merits. After several refusals and notwithstanding advances made by a brief collaboration at the scroll, the impatient one is accepted. For ten minutes the rolling is suspended. The male still looks on. Sooner or later a new visit is paid to the worker by the dawdler, who, under pretence of assisting, plants his claws for a moment into the rolling piece, plucks up courage and renews his exploits with the same vigour as though nothing had yet happened. And this is repeated four or five times during the making of a single cigar."

Here, it may be remarked in passing, we seem to see the first faint expression of the father's interest in the family, which, if I may hazard a guess, may have started in this way as a means of gaining his desire with the female. The correctness of this surmise will receive considerable confirmation as we proceed with our inquiry. And if analogies with animal conduct were not so apt to be misleading, I would venture to suggest the persistence of the same egoistic factor among many human fathers. But for the present I must leave this question.

From the very beginning of life parental sacrifice is more common in the mother; it is in exceptional cases that her devotion is shared by the father. But such good fathers are of special importance to our inquiry. Even more interesting are those species among which the father takes all charge of the young, while the mother spends her time away from the family. Nor is this departure from what we may call the normal order of the family so surprising as at first sight it may seem, if we can account for the necessity under which probably it arose and seek to explain it.

The welfare of the young is a matter of vital urgency; instinct dictates to the animals what reason dictates to us. Nature, as if to show her resourcefulness, her love of successful experiments, is always discovering contrary ways of attaining the same end. And what I wish to make clear is this: when, for some reason that we do not know, the family cares are neglected by the mothers, the work of tending and feeding the young is undertaken by the fathers. I shall have much more to say on this question at a later stage, and I ask you to keep it persistently in the focus of your attention. I desire to emphasise it at once. Whatever groups of animals we survey, we shall find examples of this replacement of the mother by the father, new aspects of the family, which may afford us a better grip of some problems that at present elude us.

The reality of the mother's regard for the young is proved among many insects by the building of a nest to safeguard the family. The Anthidium, or tailor-bee, and the Chalicodoma, a species of wild bee, afford illustrations of this maternal forethought. In the former case the eggs, when laid, are placed in the ground, protected in cotton-felt satchels made by the mother from fibre which she scratches with her mandibles from the cobwebby stalks of the yellow centaury; the Chalicodoma works with cement and gravel carefully selected from some ruined building, and with such difficult material she fashions her nursery. Even more remarkable is the home of the Magachilles, or leaf-cutting bee. The mother bee, using her mandibles as scissors, cuts pieces from the leaves of the trees, wherewith she forms thimble-shaped wallets to contain the honey and eggs; the larger oval pieces which she cuts make the sides and the floor, and the round pieces the lid or door. These leaf-formed thimbles are placed in a row, one on top of the other, sometimes as many as a dozen being used. The cylinder thus formed is fitted into the deserted home of some other insect, such as the tunnels of fat earth-worms, the apartments bored in the trunks of trees by the larvæ of the Capricorn beetles, or, failing these, a reed stump or crevice in the wall is selected. But the choice of the home is always carefully made, it would seem, according to the tastes of the mothers. This structure, in part made and in part borrowed, forms the leaf-cutter's nest.[11]

Numerous cases of home-making might be recorded, and the difficulty rests in the selection. Many spiders and the book scorpion carry their eggs in a silken bag attached to the under surface of the body. There is a case recorded that shows heroic devotion on the part of one spider mother. She was placed (in order that her behaviour might be watched) in the pit of an ant-lion. At once the enemy seized the eggs and tore them from her charge. Then the mother, though she was driven out of the pit, returned and chose to be dragged in and buried alive rather than desert her charge.[12]

A regular process of incubation is practised by the mother earwig, and the young, when hatched, keep close to her for protection. Special food for the young is prepared by many mothers, as, for instance, among the *apidæ*, who prepare a disgorged food in the form of a sweet milk juice. The *Hymenoptera* mothers, upon whom the cares of motherhood devolve in their fulness, provide board and lodging for their family. Stores of insects are caught and preserved in the nursery larder, being cunningly paralysed so that live food may be ready when needed by the children. These clever mothers, as Fabre has shown us, become masters of a host of arts for the benefit of a family which their faceted eyes will never see.

Of the domestic economy of the bees and ants whole volumes might be, and have been, written. The habits of the termites, the so-called white ants, are less widely known, although they show one of the most remarkable developments of the family that I have met. Each colony is really a patriarchal family, in which the members, all the descendants of a single pair, live in a community, and work in different ways. All the individuals are at first true males and females. Some of these develop slowly, but grow up perfect insects able to form new families. But the workers and the soldiers have to pass a period of youthful servitude in the community. These develop quickly, and grow up blind and wingless, and their reproductive organs remain in a condition of arrested development. Some of these are workers, and carry out the duties of the community; others at the same time develop jaws and heads of enormous size. It is their duty to defend the colony. And from this has come about the strange condition of their being so altered and trained for their special work that they cannot pass on to the normal life and normal duties of perfect individuals.

Among the bees and some social wasps there is a further step, and only females are selected to do household work, and modified so that they lose the ordinary personal instincts and devote themselves entirely to working for the community, while the males develop only the instincts and capacities of sex. In some species of wasps, however, the males do some work, chiefly domestic, for which they are fed by their foraging sisters. In the communities of ants, as in the termites, there are individuals modified to serve as workers and as soldiers; but here again they are all arrested females, and the males are used only for the purpose of sex. The colonies of ants last much longer than those of the bees and wasps, which are annual, and this has given the possibility of the elaboration of a very complex and extraordinary community.[13]

We are always being surprised by new experiments in family life which show the ready adaptation of habits to special circumstances. A bald statement of these facts seems to tell very little. I leave untouched a whole series of devices and wonderful behaviour—so much that I should like to record. In all these cases we see the maternal instinct in the making. But so varied and so fitting to the needed purpose are the actions of these lowly parents that much which they do gives an impression of the inexplicable—even the magical.

It is common to explain everything by the word "instinct." But does this explanation take us very far? An elaborate instinctive capacity is probably the result of adding on one contrivance after another to a simpler common habit. And this is surely the same as saying that these little creatures have the power of learning through experience. A beginning of the instinct of caring for the young is exhibited when the mother insect chooses a favourable food position wherein to lay the eggs. Nor is it difficult to imagine how this maternal forethought may have grown out of an earlier habit, for it is but a step, though a great one, from collecting food for self—an instinct that may be traced back and back—to the habit of providing and collecting food for others. Then, this instinct of caring for the future being strongly fixed, it, in some cases and under certain favourable conditions, leads on and on to the specialised maternity and climax of parental sacrifice and devotion, such as may be illustrated by the admirable scarabees, or dung-beetles, of the Mediterranean region and elsewhere.

I have given one case of perfect parents, the *Minotaurus Typhœus*; but I wish to review such conduct more fully. The family qualities of the dung-beetles are so devoted and so striking, they will repay our study.

The late M. Fabre describes in his inimitable way the nursery which makes the centre and life of the scarabees' home. These dung-workers edify us with their morals. Both sexes co-operate in making the burrows which serve as a larder for food and a nursery for the young. They are cavities dug in soft earth, usually in sand, shallow in form, about the size of one's fist, and communicating with the outside by a short channel just large enough for the passage of the balls of dung-food. Both parents work with equal zeal to found a household. "The father is the purveyor of victuals and the person entrusted with the carrying away of rubbish. Alone, at different hours of the day he flings out of doors the earth thrown up by the mother's excavations; alone he explores the vicinity of the home at night in quest of the pellets whereof his sons' loaves shall be kneaded.

"A most careful choice of material is undertaken, and often the devoted husband and father is compelled to search long and far for pellets freshly dropped, for whereas coarse bread crammed with bits of hay is good enough for his own and his wife's food, he is always more careful where the children are concerned. Legful by legful, with slow and most patient labour, the material is heaped up and rolled into a ball. Then the food-ball has to be carried to the burrow; no easy task. Even then the father's labours are not ended; on reaching the burrow, it is his work to shred the dung-food into flour, which he pours down to the mother for her to knead into the children's bread. Finally, when the last task is accomplished, the dung-father goes out alone to die. He has gallantly performed his duty as a paterfamilias; he has spent himself without stint to secure the prosperity of his kith and kin."

The devotion of the dung-father is equalled by that of the dung-mother. More skilled than her spouse in domestic matters, she is occupied always in the home, where she works in the lower floor of the burrow, which she has prepared for the nursery. Here she kneads and forms the cylindrical loaves in which the eggs are placed. In some cases she does more, and we find several species of the dung-mothers anticipating the suckling of the young, the supreme expression of maternal solicitude. These mothers chew the dung-food, and out of it prepare a frothy pap or cream, with which they cover the walls of the nest to form a special first meal for the emerging grub. Throughout her working life the dung-mother never leaves the home. It should be noted that her family is always a very small one: does this, perhaps, explain the parental devotion? From the first fortnight in May, when the eggs are laid, the mother mounts guard over her children. Never does she eat herself, as she will not touch the food prepared and needed for them. She watches through the long months until the coming of the autumn rains in September. Then, when the day of release comes at last, she returns to the surface, accompanied by her family. At once her children leave her; unmindful of her devotion, they go off to find food and begin life for themselves. Thereupon, having nothing left to do, she dies, and ends her sacrifice.[14]

Before I leave this fascinating record of the dung-beetle parents, space must be found wherein to note further certain of their characteristics and habits, which are of special interest to my inquiry as they would appear to be directly connected with the highly developed family qualities of these insects. Fabre tells us that there is no outward difference between the two sexes among the dung-beetles. I call attention to this fact, which I am not able to explain. The scarabees are among the most beautiful of all insects, and the female and male share the same glory. It is my belief that the secondary sexual characters are directly dependent on the occupational activities of the species, as also on the form of union or marriage which pertains and the strength of the parental emotions. Thus, when the male and the female are equally devoted to each other and to the family and its care, many cases among these pre-human parents seem to prove that such devotion and occupational union tends to lessen the ornamental sexual differences in the secondary physical characters. This is a question of profound interest, and demands more attention than it has yet received.

The second fact is of even greater importance to us. The form of union or marriage common among the dung-beetles would appear to be an unusually strict monogamy. These insects, as we have seen, associate in couples, and there is strong evidence that the male remains faithful to his spouse. Such admirable conduct is the more remarkable when we remember that the mother is held in the nursery by her duties during the greater period of the marriage; and meantime the father has to wander far in search of food, making frequent excursions outside the home, but he resists the temptations to which these outings are likely to lead, and always he returns to the home, where he wears himself out for his family.

To test the strength of this conjugal fidelity Fabre made an experiment with the dung-beetles of whose habits I have before spoken, the *Minotaurus Typhæus*. He placed two couples of these beetles in an enclosed space, marking one of the couples. He allowed them to begin the making of their burrows or homes, then he separated the couples and destroyed the half-made burrows. Once, twice, and a third time he did this, causing confusion among these peaceful workers. But on each occasion the couples came together in the same order; the right male and female knew each other, and, taking little notice of the tumult, each time again they began their work of home-making.

Five more times Fabre separated them and broke up their homes. The result I will give in Fabre's own beautiful words—

"Things are now spoilt, sometimes each of the four that are experimented on settles apart, sometimes the same burrow contains the two males or the two females, sometimes the same crypt the two sexes, but differently associated from what they were at first. I have abused my powers of repetition. Henceforth disorder reigns. My daily shufflings have demoralised the burrowers, a crumbling home always requiring to be begun afresh has put an end to lawful associations. Respectable married life becomes impossible from the moment when the house falls in from day to day."

I have now said enough, I think, to show that at many different levels in the insect kingdom the parental instinct is already developed. Pre-eminent in virtue is the behaviour of the dung-beetle parents. And this is all the more interesting as it proves how closely related good parenthood is with the conditions of the home and the form of marriage.

A few more words may here be added to what has been said already concerning the influence of intelligence on instinct. It is a difficult question, but, speaking roughly, intelligence may be said to act in two opposite ways; that is, it may aid both in the making and the unmaking of instincts.[15] Thus the dung-beetles frequently change their conduct, and they do this by modifying their instincts through intelligent adaptation. It is scarcely too much to say that with them intelligence reaches its highest form of originality. Why is this? Fabre gives us the answer. "The more the maternal instinct asserts itself, the higher does instinct ascend."

It would be better probably if the word instinct were used in a more restricted sense: it should not be regarded as being able to explain everything. This mysterious impulse is held to direct all pre-human parents in their conduct to their young. Very well; but what of the directing force behind? The evidence is strong that even the lowliest creatures have their own problems, and are able to solve them. Can we explain otherwise the wide difference in conduct between parent and parent? Do we know what it is that gives a special direction to the instinctive activities in the accomplishment of a design greater than any of these parents know? We cannot answer fully. But instinct has its twin brother in intelligence, and, acting together, they are the guardians of life.

When real things are so wonderful, what can we do but note them and try to understand? Not elsewhere in the insect world do we meet with a devotion more complete than that of both the dung-parents; not elsewhere do we find a finer development of intelligence. These two things are related and closely dependent, the one upon the other. It is this fact that now I am seeking to establish. Sacrifice in the parent does not lead to limitation, but to expansion.

At this early stage of life the care of the young is as a rule very slight, and often is confined, as I have shown, to the laying of the eggs in a favourable position, where the grub can find food. "The higher inspirations of the intellect are banished among these insects." I quote again from Fabre, whose opinion on this question so strongly confirms all that I wish to make clear. He asserts further: "The mother neglects the gentle cares of the cradle, and the prerogatives of the intellect, the best of all, diminish and disappear, so true is it that for animals, even as for ourselves, the family is the source of perfection." And again: "Placed in charge of the duration of the species, which is of more serious interest than the preservation of individuals, maternity awakens a marvellous foresight in the drowsiest intelligence.... The more maternity asserts itself, the higher does instinct ascend."

We cannot get away from this; it is one of the unalterable laws of life.

CONTENTS OF CHAPTER IV
PARENTHOOD AMONG THE REPTILES AND FISHES
A CHAPTER ON GOOD FATHERS

The parental impulse not always fixed in the mother—Among reptiles and fishes, such care as is afforded by parents is given most frequently by the father—Suggested reason for this—Primitive hatching nurseries—Parental care among frogs and toads—Many examples of exemplary fathers—The devotion of the male stickleback—The unnatural conduct of the female stickleback—The emotions of the fish—Fish fathers who guard the nest—Perpetual variety in the actions of even the lowliest parents—Summary—No continuous line of development of instinct in scale of animals—Much baffles our explanations—Suggestions important to my inquiry—Reversal of sex labours—Is it due to failure on the part of the mother—Devoted parents are of high intelligence.

CHAPTER IV
PARENTHOOD AMONG REPTILES AND FISHES
A CHAPTER ON GOOD FATHERS

"Nature is a riddle without a definite solution to satisfy man's curiosity."—MAURICE MAETERLINCK.

In this chapter I shall consider certain examples, which I think are important to establish what we have learnt in our examination of the insects, that the parental impulse was not always fixed in the mother. Among the reptiles and fishes the reverse is true, and what care is afforded to the young is given most frequently by the father.[16]

The bond between the mother and her young is directly dependent on their helplessness and the duration of time during which they require her care and attention. Young reptiles are from birth independent, and, as a consequence, there has been no stimulus to develop maternal solicitude. Between mother and offspring there are no ties of affection save in one or two exceptional cases.

Young alligators, for example, are guarded by their mothers and owe more to her than they can ever know. She prepares a hatching nursery by scraping together a large mound of leaves, twigs, and fine earth, and upon this mound the eggs are placed about eight inches from the surface. Then the mother digs a hole in the river bank, close by, and here she waits and watches to protect her children.

A more advanced form of nursery building is practised by the tortoise, who prepares a sort of nest with considerable care, which she afterwards cunningly conceals. But when once the eggs are safe she shows no further interest in the safety of the nest.[17]

Most snakes bury their eggs and then leave them. But a more enduring maternal interest is felt by the mother python; she coils her body around her future family and jealously guards them during the period of incubation, refusing all food and never leaving her duty.

A similar guardianship is shown to young crocodiles by their mothers. The home is prepared by digging a deep hole in the sand in which the eggs are placed, and during the period of incubation each mother sleeps in guard above her family. The naturalist Voeltzkow, to prove the reality of one mother crocodile's solicitude, built a fence around the nest just before the hatching time. Each night on her return, the mother broke down the fence, though each time it was made stronger than the last. Finally the nest was found to be deserted, and then it was discovered that this intelligent and persecuted mother had dug a hole beneath the fence and thence had led her brood away to safety.

It is impossible to admire sufficiently such a case as this one, where we see so clearly the driving power of maternal solicitude in quickening the intelligence of even the lowliest mothers. Such cases are, however, few in number out of the 2,600 species of reptiles of whom the majority are unnatural parents.

But again surprises await us. Many frogs and toads, both the mothers and the fathers, show a really marked development of the familial instincts.[18] An illustration of this care is furnished by a large tree-frog (*Hyla faber*) of Brazil, commonly known as the *Ferreiro*, "the smith," from its strange voice resembling the mallet of a smith, slowly and regularly striking on a metal plate. This frog prepares a nursery in the shallow waters of the ponds, where a basin-shaped hollow is dug in the mud. The building is done by the mother, the material removed being used to form a wall, circular in shape, which is carried up to the surface of the water. In this cavity the eggs are placed, protected against the attacks of aquatic insects and fishes. A Japanese tree frog (*Rhacophorus schlegelii*) builds a similar nest, but here the mother lines the walls of her nursery with a secretion, a kind of milk food, from her own body, which by rapid movements of her feet is worked into a froth, and in the midst of this foamy mass the eggs are laid. More remarkable is the nursery building of the "Wollunnkukk" frog (*Phyllomedusa hypochondrialis*) of Paraguay, whose habits were noted by Dr. Budgett during the exploration of the Paraguayan Chaco. "Whilst sitting near the water's edge he saw a female carrying a male upon her back. At last she climbed up the stem of a plant, reached out and caught hold of an overhanging leaf and climbed on to it. Both then caught hold of its edges and held them together; and into the funnel thus formed the female poured her eggs, the male fertilising them as they passed. The jelly surrounding the eggs served as a cement to hold the edges of the leaves together. Then, moving up a little further, the process was repeated until the leaf was full, and about a hundred eggs had been enclosed."[19]

A similar leaf nest is made by a Brazilian frog, known as Ihering's frog (*P. Iheringi*), while a home of more elaborate construction, in which several leaves are used, is prepared by Savage's leaf-frog (*P. Sauvagii*).

It should be noted that in these cases the care of the parents is confined to the providing of a nursery; when once this is done the young are abandoned. But many frogs and toads do much more than this, and one or other parents, most often the father, guard their offspring with jealous care. A Papuan frog-father, for instance, takes up the duties of a nurse; and when the eggs are laid, he sits upon them, holding the mass with both hands. And this vigil he keeps during the whole time while the young are undergoing growth, passing through the larval and tadpole stage.

We must own that such a father acts with singular devotion. It should be noted that seventeen eggs only are laid by the mother, a much smaller number than is common among the species where neither parent affords any kind of guardianship. This is what we should expect. Nature has different ways of gaining the same end. Life must be carried on, that is all that matters—an incessant renewal, an undying fresh beginning and unfolding of life. But a species is maintained sometimes by the prodigality of production and sometimes by the expenditure of care and sacrifice on the part of the parents. And here we find again a lesson waiting for us to learn. For it is hardly necessary to point out that the same facts are true of human births; just as the family is unregulated or considered, do we find waste and many births with parental neglect in the first case and restricted births with parental devotion in the second. There seem to be no problems of the family that these pre-human parents have not had to face and solve.

But to return.

"The celebrated Midwife toad (*Alytes obstetricans*) gives us a further delightful example of the father nursing the young. The mother-toad lays her eggs attached to one another by threads so that they form a long chain. The father-toad then twines this chaplet of his wife's eggs round and round his thighs. He has the strange appearance, it has been said, of a gentleman of the court of the time of James I, arrayed in puffed breeches. His devotion is very complete. After having encumbered himself with the coming family, he retreats to a hole in the ground. Here he stays with admirable patience by day, stealing forth at night to feed, and to bathe his egg-burdened legs in dew or, when possible, in water. When his period of service is past and the young are ready for quitting the eggs, he seeks the water. Here before long the young burst forth and swim away, whereupon the father, now free from his family duties, makes himself tidy (cleans himself of the remains of the eggs) and resumes his normal appearance."

With some frogs, as, for example, in certain S. American and African species, the parents take up the burden of caring for the young only after they have reached the tadpole stage. The German naturalist Brauer recently found in the Seychelles islands a small frog (*Arthroleptis Seychellensis*) undertaking the guardianship of the young family. An adult frog (it is not stated whether it was the father or the mother) was carrying nine tadpoles on its back, to which they were attached by a sucker on the belly. Unfortunately, little is known of the habits of these frogs. It is believed that the eggs are laid in some shallow pool, and that later one or other parent returns to the nursery to take up the care of the young tadpoles.

A further remarkable case of care exercised by the father is that of Darwin's frog, the *Rhinoderma darwini*, where the eggs are guarded in a great pouch under the throat, and opening by two slits into the mouth. During the courtship this pouch is used as a voice organ to charm the female, with sharp ringing notes like a bell. But the love-calls end with the birth of the family. There is now serious work to be accomplished. The father takes his wife's eggs into his pouch, which now enlarges and extends backwards under the belly to the groin, and upwards on each side almost to the backbone. In the warm chamber thus formed, the tadpoles live until they become young frogs. They then make their way up through the doorways into their father's mouth, and from that living nursery they swim out into the wide world.

Well, what can we say of this case? We have heard of some animal fathers eating their progeny, but here the father's mouth is turned into the hatching nursery. Did I not tell you we should find very much to astonish us?

I could give many more examples of reptile parents whose family habits are more or less singular. There are the little-known "Cœcilians,"[20] the strange, snakelike amphibians of S.E. Asia and Ceylon; where the mother, with her limbless body, yet contrives to dig a nursery for her eggs, which she jealously guards. I should like to write of the families of the newts and salamanders, among whom the young are never completely abandoned, and whose parental habits present many features of interest. But to tell their life stories with all the vivid facts would take more space than I can allow to this one chapter of my book; and to give a bald record of their habits would afford little interest. I must, however, recount two instances of marked solicitude for the family, shown in each case by a different parent. Take the case of a mother's care first. A captive mother-salamander, of the species known as *Oregon plethodon*, was placed with her eggs in a jar. She at once took possession of them, forming a loop around them with her tail. But, displeased with this unfamiliar house, she moved the eggs repeatedly from place to place till at length she was satisfied, and all the time using her tail for the work of transportation as a kind of maternal arm. In the second case the father most faithfully guards the eggs. A giant salamander in the Zoological Gardens of Amsterdam kept watch over a clump of his wife's eggs for a period of ten weeks. This careful father was seen every now and then to crawl among the eggs and lift them up, apparently for the purpose of aerating them.

From the foregoing examples it may, I think, be taken as established that among the reptiles there are many exemplary fathers. If the question is asked as to why in some species the care of the young is undertaken by the father and in others by the mother, I can only answer that I do not know. It would seem almost that at this early stage of life Nature was making experiments as to which was the better parent. I would suggest that possibly such a reversal of the family duties was started by chance, possibly by the loss of the mother, or even by a specially energetic father, and on being found successful the arrangement was continued and became fixed as a habit. I have not sufficient knowledge to know if this is possible. At any rate, it appears to be plain that, where for any reason the family duties are neglected by the mother, and where the maintenance of the species demands protection being given to the young, the father steps in to take the place of the mother; and by his care and devotion he becomes a truly constituent part —a working member—of the family group. I would ask you to keep this fixed in your attention, as I shall have to refer again and again to this fact that is here suggested.

What obtains among reptiles with regard to the father's care for the young is even more frequent among fish-fathers. The common stickleback of our ponds and streams affords an admirable illustration of intelligent and devoted fatherhood. In this species the rôle of the two sexes is completely reversed; when once the eggs are deposited by the mother, the whole task of guarding them is undertaken by the father. His labours begin with the construction of a nest. This is formed of bits of weed, of fibre and dirt, collected with much care, the whole being held together by a cement produced by the clever father out of a secretion from his kidneys. Having prepared the nursery, the stickleback sets out to find a wife heavy with eggs. His love choice apparently is decided by the capability of his spouse for her maternal function. By means of much persuasion and passionate courtship he woos her and induces her to deposit her burden of eggs in his nest.

I must wait to impress upon you the wonder of this fact. These love-antics of the stickleback, which are unique among fishes, would seem not to be exercised for the gratification of male desire, but for the purpose of inducing the female to lay her eggs,—to do her part in giving him offspring. Vainly do I ask myself the reason of this quite unusual sexual altruism. This is very extraordinary. The father woos the reluctant mother with passionate dances and his glad excitement is apparently intense. At this season the stickleback is transformed and glows with brilliant colours, his scales make silver look dim, his throat glows with flaming vermilion, he literally puts on a wedding garment of love.[21] And did I not fear being tedious by again waiting to point a moral, I should ask attention to this further proof given by the stickleback's love joys to the truth which stands out in these life histories of pre-human parents. I mean this: the parent—the mother or the father—lives in the offspring. You will see how deep is the truth here. The parent is, after all, only the transitory custodian of the undying gift of life.

The conduct of the mother stickleback is in sharp contrast with the devotion of the stickleback father. At once, having rid herself of her eggs, her desire would seem to be to escape any further responsibilities. She forces her way out of the nest by wriggling through the wall opposite the entrance. True, by doing this she renders a service to the nursery, as she thereby furnishes a channel through which a continuous supply of fresh, cool water can be driven, thus keeping the eggs bathed. This is the only work the stickleback mother does for the family. The male, after the first laying, may persuade her to add still further to the deposit of eggs. Sometimes, wearied with her one effort, she refuses. Thus forced, the stickleback seeks a second wife, driven into polygamous conduct through his desire for offspring. I know of no other case that is parallel with this.

And the stickleback's action has often been misrepresented. He is instanced as a polygamist; such is the fate that ever awaits self-sacrifice!

When the nest is full the father stickleback mounts guard over the entrance of the nursery for nearly a month, and he watches by day and by night, defending his precious charge against all comers.

And here another curious fact must be noted: the most dangerous assailants to the safety of the nursery are his own wives; these unnatural mothers would, if they were permitted, devour every single egg. Is it this conduct of the female sticklebacks that explains the devotion of the male? Again I do not know. Certain it is, however, that the safety and care of the young is the stickleback father's constant occupation—the duty to which he sacrifices his life. From time to time he changes the position of the eggs; he is a master in sanitation and keeps them constantly bathed with fresh water. This he does by driving a stream through the nest by means of a fanning motion of his breast, fins and tail. Through all the hatching period he works with unceasing care.

When at length the fry are born, the father's vigilance is even further taxed. The children, vigorous and venturesome, have to be watched by day and by night and protected. Around and across and in every direction the father, as guardsman, continually swims. He drives off all comers with splendid courage. On one occasion a stickleback father was watched while his nest was attacked by two tench and a golden carp; he seized their fins and struck with all his might at their heads and eyes. Truly the stickleback's care of his children is extraordinary. His vigilant eye is everywhere. If any members of the young brood stray too far from the nest for safety, he immediately swims after them, seizes them in his mouth, and brings them back to the safe playwater in the vicinity of the nursery. This continuous watchfulness lasts for about six days after the hatching.[22]

Well, what do you think now of the common view of the parental instinct being stronger always in the mother than in the father? Have we not been taking too much for granted and accepting theory for truth? In the light of our knowledge gained from these examples of the father's extreme devotion, it seems impossible to refrain from thinking that the most intelligent and fit parent is the one who cares for the young. No doubt it is difficult, or even impossible, to decide the circumstances that have contributed to this strange result of the father taking the mother's place in the family. We do not know whether these acts of his sacrifice to the children's welfare imply the presence of the mind element—that is, whether they can be regarded as conscious as distinguished from unconscious adaptation, but this is altogether a separate matter and has nothing to do with the question we are considering.

Fish display, according to Romanes,[23] emotions of fear, pugnacity, social, sexual and parental feelings, anger, jealousy, play and curiosity. Such emotions, he states, correspond with those that are distinctive of the psychology of a child of about four months.

In many diverse species there is clear evidence of some form of parental solicitude. The spotted goby, or pole-wing, for instance, a fish which is found in the Thames, is a nest-builder. An old cockle-shell is skilfully utilised to form the nursery. The shell is placed with its cavity turned downwards, beneath it the soil is removed and then the earth-walls are cemented together with a secretion from the skin of the parents. Access to the nest is gained by a cylindrical tunnel, and the whole nursery is covered and concealed by loose sand. Again it is the father who mounts guard over the eggs; his vigil lasts for about nine days.[24]

There are many instances of nursery building undertaken by fish parents. Agassiz[25] records a case in which an elaborate nest formed of knotted weeds is made by a certain fish, known as *Chironectes*. This rocking fish-cradle is carried by both parents and is a kind of arbour, affording protection and afterwards food for its living freight.[26] A remarkable nest is built by the American bow-fin (*Amia calva*), found in the eastern states of North America. Both the mother and the father work together to construct the nursery, which is formed by a large circular area cleared among the weedy shallows; these intelligent parents actually bite through the stems of all the plants that they cannot break or push aside. In the pool that is thus made the eggs are placed by the mother and fertilised by the father; the young develop with remarkable rapidity and hatch out in about eight days from time of laying. The family is then jealously guarded by the father, who herds the children—often numbering as many as a thousand individuals[27]—by circling around and above them in untiring watchfulness. Another remarkable nest is that of the eel-like *gymnarchus* of the Nile; a huge floating nursery is made of grasses, measuring some two feet long and a foot broad. Within this nest some thousand eggs are laid, and as soon as they are deposited by the mother, the father mounts guard, defending them, and afterwards the young, with great ferocity.

Some fishes' nests, like those made by the frogs, are constructed of foam. M. Carbonnier gives the case of a Chinese butterfly fish in his private aquarium in Paris. The male fish constructed a large nest of froth, fifteen to eighteen centimetres horizontal diameter and ten to twelve centimetres high: this he did by a curious sucking and expelling air which formed the mucus in his mouth into a white foam. When the nest was thus prepared the female was induced to enter. I do not know whether the father's duty was continued after this point.[28]

Even where no nest is made, the eggs and young are sometimes guarded by one or other of the parents, but generally the father. Schneider saw several fishes at the Naples Aquarium protecting their eggs; in one case the male mounted guard over a rock where the eggs were deposited, and swam with open mouth against all intruders. Again, the butter-fish (*Pholis*) of our coasts lays a mass of eggs, and around this future family the father coils his body, just as does the python among the reptiles. Some fishes, as for instance the cat-fishes (*siluridae*), have the curious habit of carrying the eggs in their mouth.

A further interesting case of paternal solicitude is furnished by the male fish of the common lump-sucker. The eggs are deposited in large clumps, and the father's first care is to secure their proper oxygenation. This he does by pressing his head into the centre of each clump, an action which not only prevents the eggs from being too closely crowded, but serves also to press the spawn firmly into the crevices of the rock on which it is always laid. As soon as this is done this fish-father mounts guard over his family. All would-be enemies, such as star-fish and crabs, who make ceaseless efforts to rob the nursery, are driven off. The work of oxygenation is still carried on, and streams of fresh water, so necessary for the young lives, are driven by the careful father into the masses of the eggs. When the young appear new family duties await him, for the fry at once attach themselves to his body and are carried about by him.[29]

There are other instances where the young are attached to the body of the parent. Sometimes it is the mother who gives this protection, and bears her eggs attached to the under surface of her body. The lophobranchiate fish incubate their eggs in pouches in the same way as some frogs, and they show elaborate parental feelings. When the young are hatched out, one or other parent, usually the father, carefully guards them, and the pouch then serves as a place of shelter or retreat from danger.

Dr. Reinhold Hensel states of a little-known Brazilian fish (*Geophagus scymnophilus*) that one of the parents—he does not say which—keeps careful guard over the family, which numbers from twenty to thirty. At a distance he watches his children. When alarmed for their safety, he takes a swift swim towards them, and they, as if at his word of command, collect around his mouth. Suddenly, if the cause of alarm is not removed, the mouth is opened, and the whole family is engulfed. In an adult which was captured while thus laden, the young were seen to be crowded together in the mouth with their heads towards the gills. Here the family is safe, and when the cause for alarm is passed, the youngsters are probably suddenly expelled from their living cavern. Another extraordinary case is recorded by M. Carbonnier, which certainly appears to show anxiety on the part of fish-fathers to have offspring. The males of the grotesque telescope-fish (a variety of *Carassius auratus*) have the curious habit of acting as accoucheurs to the females. On one occasion three males were watched pursuing one mother heavy with spawn. They rolled her like a ball upon the ground for a distance of several metres, and this process they continued, without rest or relaxation, for two days. Then the exhausted mother, who had been unable to recover her equilibrium for a moment, at last evacuated her eggs.

There is perpetual variety in the actions of even the lowliest parents. I might add many further examples more or less extraordinary, of the habits of fish and reptile mothers or fathers; but, even did the limit of my space permit this, it is not, I think, necessary: I have proved the existence low down in the scale of life of marked solicitude for the young, and shown that such care and sacrifice is shown frequently by the father.

Let me summarise now what we have learnt in this and the preceding chapter, so as to establish the lessons that seem to me may be taken from these pre-human parents. The diversity in the expression of the parental instincts must first be grasped. There is no fixed order, nor does there seem to be any continuity of development in this matter of care for the young. We have to give up quite the evolutionary idea of a certain and uninterrupted progress. Throughout our inquiry we have been met with surprises. These things baffle our attempts to find an explanation. What is it that decides and develops the strong instinct of parenthood? A parent in a species that is lower in the scale will often have more parental feeling than a parent in a higher species. Why, for instance, is the stickleback such a devoted father; more self-sacrificing than any other fish-father? and why is the stickleback mother without regard for her children? Why among the dung-beetles is the same parental sacrifice shown by both parents? Again, why is a nursery made in some cases and not in others? why are the young guarded sometimes by the mother and sometimes by the father? We may say that all this wide diversity in habits has arisen through adaptation; the circumstances that have conditioned the life of the species have been different, and this has necessarily caused variety in their behaviour. This is, of course, true, but does it really teach us very much? No sooner do we begin to apply our reasons to any particular case of family behaviour than we find ourselves at a loss. Our reasoning suddenly breaks down, either because our knowledge is incomplete, or because one set of facts we possess seem to be contradicted by other facts of which we are equally sure.

Let us at once acknowledge our ignorance; there is much that cannot be explained.

If, however, we speculate at all on the matter, certain general ideas may be suggested. We are led to the view that when the father undertakes the care of the young, this reversal in the family duties must be primarily due to some failure on the part of the mother in performing the work in the nursery and home which customarily is hers. It is as if the father steps into her place in order that the species may escape the nemesis of elimination. The facts we have learnt are of no little importance. They tend to minimise, in the beginning of the family at least, the importance of the mother in relation to the young as compared with the importance of the father. It is this that I wish to establish.

And what we have learnt suggests the further interdependence, that does seem to exist among all species, between intelligence and good parenthood. Fabre, out of his wisdom and as a result of his great knowledge, says that the duties of caring for the young are the supreme inspirers of the intellect. Wherever we find devoted parents there also do we find lofty instincts. This is the second idea I ask you to accept. I think that we have proved its truth.

I may not stay here to point out the immense importance of these suggestions to the inquiry we are making as to the action of the maternal instinct, nor shall I pause to indicate the lessons that seem to me to await us from the curious transformation found in so many species in the duties of the two sexes. These considerations must wait until we know more. We have, I trust, extended somewhat, as well as rendered more exact, our knowledge on this complex and difficult question of motherhood. In the next two chapters I shall endeavour to extend it still further by a brief consideration of certain striking habits I have met with of parenthood among the birds and higher animals.

I am well aware that there are many people who cannot bring themselves to believe in, or even listen without impatience to, any comparison between the conduct of animals and that which prevails among ourselves. It is absurd, they will say, to try to explain the conditions of human parenthood by references to animal parents. I have no hope of convincing, nor do I much desire to convince, those who thus object. I would merely advise them to leave out this section of my book altogether.

CONTENTS OF CHAPTER V
PARENTHOOD AMONG BIRDS
WITH FURTHER EXAMPLES OF GOOD FATHERS

Recapitulation of facts established—Reversal of sex attributes—Courting females and nursing males among certain birds—Attempt at explanation—Are sex-hunger and parental affection in conflict—A high standard of family life among birds—Few birds who are bad fathers—Examples of varying division of family work—A few birds who are bad parents—Where the mother takes sole charge of the eggs the father as a rule takes little interest in the family—The polygamous gallinaceous birds—Conduct affected by habits of the home—The Adélie penguins—Their co-operative child-rearing—The great emperor penguin—Scrimmage of childless mothers and fathers for possession of chickens.

CHAPTER V
PARENTHOOD AMONG BIRDS
WITH FURTHER EXAMPLES OF GOOD FATHERS

"Prais'd be the fathomless universe,
For life and joy, and for objects and knowledge curious."

WALT WHITMAN.

Two things I have been anxious to bring out prominently in the foregoing chapters: that parental behaviour among the insects, reptiles and fishes presents us with a bewildering diversity of aspects—in particular, that the instinct of caring for the young is not fixed in the mother, but may be transferred from her to the father; and further, that all parental sacrifice, though often unconsciously expended to maintain the well-being of the family, is of direct benefit to the parent who bestows it, and is the surest means of developing and brightening such a parent's individual intelligence.

Now, I wish to elaborate and establish these two propositions with further examples in order that they may be laid hold of and firmly grasped as indubitable facts; and then we may come to see and understand the significance to ourselves of these unusually devoted fathers, which are found, and that not infrequently, among all classes of pre-human parents.

The varied behaviour of bird-parents—more especially of the males—furnishes just the kind of evidence we need. There are several cases known, and I believe there must be others as yet unrecorded, wherein the conduct and, indeed, the whole character of the two sexes is reversed. Here the females, driven it would seem by a fierce sex-hunger, do the courting and fight one another as rivals for the males, while the males undertake all the family duties of incubation and brooding and the feeding of the young.

The phalaropes, both the grey and the red-necked species, which are found in Scotland and Ireland, afford a striking example of these unsexed females. Among these birds the rôle of the sexes is reversed. The duties of incubation and rearing the young are conducted entirely by the male, and in correlation with this habit, the female does all the courting. She is stronger and more pugnacious than the male, and is also brighter in plumage. This is really very remarkable. What has acted in bringing about this reversal in the secondary sexual characters? Can the male nature be transferred to the female? These are difficult questions. In colour the phalaropes are a pale olive very thickly spotted and streaked with black. The male is the psychical mother, the female takes no notice of the nest after laying the eggs. Frequently at the beginning of the breeding season she is accompanied by more than one male, so that it is evident polyandry is practised.[30]

The same unusual family conditions prevail with the rhea and the emu, and also among the painted snipes, cassowaries, tinamous, and some of the button-quails.[31] There are probably instances of other birds, but I do not know of details of their habits; Wallace[32] also mentions several species in different parts of the world, among whom all care of the young falls entirely upon the father. In all these bird families exactly opposite conditions prevail to what we are accustomed. It should be specially noted that these unnatural (I use the word simply to mean unusual) mothers are larger and more vividly coloured than the hard-worked fathers; in all such cases polyandry is practised.

Why is this?

The only attempt at an explanation that I have been able to discover is given by Mr. Pycraft in his fascinating book, *The Courtship of Animals*. He says—[33]

> "The solution of this problem probably lies with the physiologist. We now know that the problem of sex does not rest merely in the complete development of the primary sexual organs; we know that fertile unions do not depend merely on the act of pairing, but on the functional activity of the ancillary glands. And it may well be that some change in the character of the secretions has not only affected the numerical values of the sexes, but reversed the normal rôle of coloration and behaviour."

Mr. Pycraft does not consider that the polyandrous habits of these birds are due primarily to a preponderance of the females in the species over the males, but holds that this condition must rather be regarded as having arisen from a transference to the females, or development in them, of increased sexual hunger, which intensity of passion would tend to lead to an exhaustion of the males. This is exceedingly interesting. Mr. Pycraft continues—

> "Neither polygamy nor polyandry among the lower animals, at any rate, has been brought about or is maintained by the excessive death rate due to combats for the possession of mates, but must be explained as demonstrating inherent changes in the germ-plasm, disturbing the relative proportions of the sexes and correlated with a profound transformation, not only in the behaviour of the sexes during the period of reproductive activity, but also in their physical characteristics."

If I understand this aright, the conclusion seems forced upon us that parental conduct is directly dependent on the action of the sexual appetite: that it may be modified, and in some cases profoundly changed, by any variation in this appetite's strength and expression. This is of profound interest, and such a view, if established, might explain a great deal.[34] But can it be accepted? To say that such changes are due to the action of the "hormones," or secretions of the sexual glands, does not help us very much. What we want to know is what induces the changes. There is much that cannot yet be explained. If I may venture to speculate on so difficult a question, it would seem that when the intensity of sex-hunger becomes for any reason stronger in the females than in the males, the result may be a diminishing of the instincts of motherhood. It is as if the egotistic desires of sex were in opposition to the racial duties. This would explain the female phalaropes, whose maternal instincts are completely atrophied. Does it not suggest also a possible explanation of some failures in human motherhood? This opens up questions that reach very far. I am tempted to wait to enlarge on the immense significance of these unnatural bird-mothers in the analogy their conduct bears to one of the most difficult cases of human motherhood—the strongly sexual woman who bears children but is quite unfit and without any desire to rear them. I shall have more to say in the later part of my inquiry about such women, who are driven by passion to be mothers without having any instinct for motherhood.

But now a return must be made to the birds' nurseries. It is a matter of common knowledge that birds display a marvellous solicitude for the welfare of the young, and their family life presents a beautiful and high standard of conduct.[35] There are very few examples of birds who are bad fathers. Often the male rivals the female in love for the young; he is in constant attendance in the vicinity of the nest; he guards, feeds, and sings to the female, and often shares with her the duty of incubation. The cock ostrich, for example, watches by night over the hole in which the eggs have been buried, and the hen takes this duty by day. The screamer birds, again, work in shifts of two or three hours each. When they bred in the London Zoological Gardens, it was noticed that the cock-bird acted as timekeeper, and at the end of a watch used to come and push the female off the nest.[36] These examples are delightful. It would seem almost that the males, when infected with paternal passion, were more ardent and regular in the performance of nursery duties than the mother.

Among many birds it is usual for all family work to be performed quite irrespective of sex, and the parent who is free takes the task of feeding the one who is occupied with the nest.[37] The male hornbill is a family despot; during the breeding season he walls up his spouse within the trunk of a tree. He feeds her with great care, but he allows her no liberty. As soon as one family is reared many birds at once burden themselves with another. The Californian quail affords an example. In this species the father takes sole charge of the family as soon as the young birds attain the age of three weeks, when the mother begins the labours of rearing a second brood. More curious are the habits of the water hen, among whom the young of the first family assist in the work of feeding their brothers and sisters of the later broods.[38]

The labour of feeding the young family is a heavy task in which both parents commonly share. There are no cases of unsuitable feeding of nestlings by careless or ignorant parents. A regular course of nursery dietary is practised, in particular with nidicolous species, where the young are born in a helpless condition; often a special infant food is prepared by a process of regurgitation, or food partly digested and thrown up. Thus baby finches are fed on food made of digested insects; parent parrots also prepare a digested vegetable food; storks break up worms and frogs and pieces of little fishes and mix it with partly digested matter and throw it out on the edge of the nest for the family meals. Young pigeons thrust their beaks into the mouths of their mothers to absorb the so-called pigeon's-milk, which is really digested food mixed with a secretion from the crop; little cormorants thrust their bills right down the neck of their mother and help themselves to food out of her stomach. The petrels secrete oil from the fish they eat to feed the young: this oil is used also as a weapon of defence both by the parents and the nestlings, who squirt it out from their mouths and nostrils at any unwelcome intruder on the privacy of the nest.[39]

When the young are fed entirely on insects the work entailed on the parents is enormous. A pair of blue tit-mice, for example, have been seen to make no less than four hundred and seventy-five journeys to the nest during a day's foraging extending over seventeen hours. Again, the male of the common dabchick works untiringly, and has been seen to take as many as forty journeys, with food, in the space of an hour, back to the nest, where his wife waits with the children, which commonly perch on her back and are protected by her wings. Small wonder is there that the labours of both parents are needed to keep the young families from starvation. In some cases a practical division of work is arranged; and the father will bring a different kind of food from the mother. With the stow-chat, for instance, the mother brings small prey, generally spiders, but sometimes butterflies and moths, while the father selects and carries large caterpillars. Even where the young are precocious, fairly active at birth, and soon able to feed themselves, one or both parents for a considerable time guard, teach and protect them. Great bravery and intelligence are displayed in the face of any danger, not only will many parent-birds savagely attack an enemy, but in some cases, as, for instance, the plover or the partridge, the mother will feign to have a broken limb or to be lame, to draw off from the young the attention of the intruder. No parental duty is neglected. Daily lessons are frequently given to the nurslings on the right kind of food and the best way of feeding. Thus young birds of prey are instructed, first in the art of breaking up their food, and later in the best methods of its capture. Young swallows, again, receive a carefully graduated course of lessons on the difficult work of catching the insects which form their food, while they are flying. The parents of the woodcock carry their children to the feeding ground, to and from the nest, supporting the precious little ones with their beaks, and pressed close within their feet, which are used as maternal arms.
[40]

A delightful incident was witnessed during the feeding-time of a red-backed shrike—[41]

"The male had brought to the nest a young bird, and, pulling off its head, proceeded to ram it down the throat of a very unfortunate youngster. But the morsel was too big, and had to be readjusted, not once, but many times; and finally it was forced home with such success that the wretched bird was in imminent danger from choking. At this the female, who had been sitting on the opposite side of the nest, making, apparently, very sarcastic comments on the awkwardness of her lord, and males in general, suddenly seized the offending head and, dragging it forth, proceeded to tear it into small pieces, giving each of the brood a piece. And during this time the male looked on in what appeared to be a very subdued fashion."

Almost all birds take great trouble to ensure the sanitation of the nursery, and are diligent in their care of the health of the young. All the excrements are removed from the nest, a task that is rendered easy, as the droppings of the young are enclosed in a white, film-like envelope or capsule. A most careful search is made at the bottom of the nest for these capsules by the parents whenever they come to feed the young. Do they fail to find the expected capsules, one or other of the parents after the feeding will tap, tap on the anus of the young birds as if to remind them of a duty neglected.[42] This is, perhaps, the most extraordinary example of parental care that I have been able to discover. One wonders how far this apparent recognition of the necessity of regular habits and cleanliness is instinctive, or how far we may grant to these parents some direct realisation of the dangers arising to their children from neglect and a dirty nursery.

It must not, however, be thought that all birds are good parents. In some species there would seem to have been a revolt against family ties and the duty of caring for the young. The common cuckoo and some other cuckoos are well-known examples. Among them, the mother, as every one knows, always lays the eggs in the nest of some other birds, and the young cuckoo, when it is hatched, would seem to have some knowledge of its precarious position as a stranger. It creeps under the nestlings of its foster-parents, and, by a violent effort, raises them one by one on its hollow back and jerks them out of the nest, so securing undivided attention in its alien nursery. A similar parasitic habit, not yet so firmly established, is found among the cow-birds of the Argentine. Mr. W. H. Hudson has seen the mothers trying to build nests and failing to do this, as if they were struggling to regain a dying instinct. The females flutter about the mud-nests of the oven-birds, and whenever a chance presents itself will dart in and lay their eggs. Other cow-birds make no effort at all in nest-building, and always lay their eggs in the occupied nests of other birds, and, as their eggs develop very quickly, the intruders hatch out before the true children of the nursery and rob them of their parents' care.

What do we learn from this? That neglect on the part of the mother—any shuffling out of her duties, thereby placing the care of her children on the shoulders of other parents, leads to crime and disorder in the social organisation.

Some birds are content with very little care for home-building ready for their eggs. Birds belonging to many different species make nurseries in hollow trees, caves, burrows or natural cavities, sometimes lining them with leaves and feathers to make them soft, but sometimes even neglecting this care. The New Zealand kakapo or ground parrot, to take one instance, hides in any hole it finds and lays its eggs there without any preparation; the kingfisher, again, digs out a hole in the ground, or occupies one that it finds. Emus scrape a shallow hole in the ground and do not cover the eggs. The cassowary scrapes together a rude pile of leaves and mould on which she lays the eggs. Some of the megapodes or bush turkeys bury their eggs in the sand, and then take no further trouble about them, leaving incubation to the chance warmth of the sun. Others build enormous heaps of decaying leaves, forming a hot-bed from natural fermentation, by which the chicks are hatched out with no trouble to the parents. The young of the megapodes are the only living birds that are hatched out able to fly at once and ready to take care of themselves. It would appear that neglectful parents foster self-development in the children.[43]

Where the mother broods alone over the eggs it sometimes happens that the father-bird takes no interest in the family. The polygamous gallinaceous birds appear to be without, or to have lost, the paternal instinct. Peacocks, pheasants, turkey-cocks, and barn-door cocks do practically nothing for their families, and while the mother-birds' care in feeding and guarding the young is untiring, the fathers are running after amorous adventures. The conduct of the male turkey is even worse, for, prompted by jealousy, he will often attempt to devour the eggs, and the young are protected from his attacks only by the mothers uniting together in troops. Here we see the exact opposite conduct in the two sexes from that in such a family as the sticklebacks, where good fathers replace bad mothers. But the same result follows. In either case the neglect of parental duty by one or other parent is a source of weakness to the family and increases the risks to which the young are exposed.[44]

I must insist on how strongly conduct is affected by the conditions of the home; and any change of habits will directly modify parental behaviour. Thus an animal habitually domestic may easily change under the pressure of external causes. Thus wild ducks, though good parents and strictly monogamous, and very highly developed in social qualities when in the wild state, become indifferent to their offspring and loosely polygamous under domestication.[45] Civilisation, in this case, depraves the birds as often it does men. But the examples of bad parents among birds are few in number.

I will end this chapter by relating, with as much detail as is possible, the curious family history of the Adélie penguins;[46] as these birds have developed some interesting and startling experiments in nursery care and parenthood. The penguins live in large social colonies. It should be noted first that the death rate among the young birds is enormously high, as happens invariably where the single family is replaced by great breeding colonies.

Yet the penguins are self-sacrificing parents. Year by year in the month of October they return to the same breeding-ground, having travelled many hundreds of difficult miles, and urged by a mysterious nostalgia that their children may be born in the same home. The first duty is to take possession of one of the old stone nests, or to scoop out a new hollow in the ground. Here the hens sit by the future home, and wait for proposals from the cocks. The advance is made by what appears to be a symbolic action and the cock places a stone at the hen's feet. But often the hen answers never a word. Bloody duels are fought between rival suitors to arouse her passion and prove the vigour of her mate.

Both birds work at the home-making, repairing an old nest or forming a new one, which is made of rounded stones. The cock collects these, and it is interesting to note what would seem to be an æsthetic taste in these bird-builders; certain painted pebbles, provided by the explorers for the use of the birds, were in great demand, the colour red being preferred to green.

During the first days of wedded life the conflicts between the cocks continue, and the chosen cock maintains his rights by driving off all interlopers; but later, when the pair settle down to the serious duties of the family, they live in peace and are perfectly faithful to each other. Not until the eggs have been laid does either parent go to feed; the shortest period of total abstinence from food being about eighteen days and the longest about twenty-eight days—a fine example of parental sacrifice. Then one of the birds marches off to the water for a holiday, which may last from seven to ten days, after which it comes back to give the other bird its turn. When the young penguins are hatched the parents share in the work of feeding and guarding them, and relieve each other at frequent intervals. The bird who goes to feed always returns heavily burdened with provisions, and its always quaint shape becomes grotesque, when so laden with crustaceans that it has to lean backwards to keep its balance. Sometimes a bird will try to carry too much, with the result that it tumbles over and loses the entire load. The young chicks feed in the same way as the young cormorants, by thrusting their heads into the parent's gullet.

Though both birds work together and with the same zeal, it must be noted that the mother's guard over the young is more strict than is that of the father. When the mother is sitting, nothing, not even a wrangle with her next-door neighbour, will induce her to move from her post. Whatever happens, there she stays until her turn for relaxation comes. But the cocks are more easily led astray. Their combativeness causes them to forget family affairs. Often much harm is done by these quarrels in the crowded rookery, which occur frequently and in spite of the protests of anxious neighbouring parents, who are seen trying to make peace.

The most curious habit of these delightful birds has still to be recorded. They have developed a taste for games, such as leaping, diving and boarding the ice-floes. These amusements are indulged in by the adults, who band themselves in large companies, and play occupies much of their time. To gain the necessary freedom for this fun from their homes, and without leaving the chicks to perish, a most instructive device has been evolved by the penguin parents. The birds with young families "pool their offspring" in groups, which are left in charge of a few conscientious birds, both cocks and hens, who act as nurses; they ward off the attacks of the sukas, and keep, or try to keep, the chicks from wandering. The holidaying parents bring food at intervals—when their consciences smite them—and they remain faithful to their own crêches.

This is, I think, the earliest example of what must be regarded as a premeditated experiment in co-operative child-rearing. For the parents it doubtless has many advantages. These remarkable birds certainly appear to find a quite unusual joy in life: we read of the ecstatic attitudes they will frequently assume and the weird "chant de satisfaction" which they utter during play when all is well with their world. Yet the fact, already noted, must not be overlooked that the death rate in the rookery is enormously high; indeed, a frightful mortality often overtakes the young chicks when left by their parents. The children pay for the escape on the part of the parents from the sacrifice parenthood must entail.

I have a further case to record of a different experiment in co-operative parenthood, in this case necessitated through the severities of the struggle of life. In the same antarctic regions where the Adélie penguins make their home there dwells another penguin, the great emperor penguin. This bird has a sad history; never, during the whole course of its life, does it touch dry land; the vast ice-fields form its only home, and it has to brave the perils of the open water in its search for food. Under such circumstances the struggle for life is severe, and the parent-birds have the greatest difficulty to rear the young. In these ice-nurseries, incubation in the usual manner in a nest is impossible; a new and curious method is adopted. Each mother lays but a single egg, which is placed for warmth and safety in a "brood-spot" situated at the back of the feet, where it is covered by the overlapping feathers of the abdomen. Even this care is not rewarded always, and many of the eggs perish.

Owing to the difficult incubation, a large percentage of brooding birds are left without eggs and young. And the curious thing is that this loss seems to increase the desire for offspring, until the parental instinct becomes a tormenting passion. This is what happens. Each childless bird strives to adopt a child from the more fortunate parents; and this leads to a competition in parenthood, which of its kind is without parallel.

Not only the duty of incubation, but afterwards caring for the young chicks, is carried out not by one bird only, but by a dozen or more, which stand patiently round for a chance to seize either a chicken or an egg. Nor is it, as might be expected, the mothers alone who are seized by the passion of thwarted maternity; the fathers help their childless wives in their efforts to steal offspring. Every bird, male as well as female, has developed the "brood-spot," and has the same bare patch of skin at the lower part of the abdomen against which the egg, when possessed, is pressed for warmth.

"What we actually saw, again and again," states Dr. Wilson, "was the wild dash made by a dozen adults, each weighing anything up to ninety pounds, to take possession of any chicken that happened to find itself deserted on the ice. It can be compared to nothing better than a football scrimmage, in which the first bird to seize the chicken is hustled and worried on all sides by the others while it rapidly tries to push the infant between its legs with the help of its pointed beak, shrugging up the loose skin of the abdomen the while to cover it.… The chicks are fully alive to the inconvenience of being fought for by so many clumsy nurses, and I have seen them not only make the best use of their legs in avoiding so much attention, but remain to starve and freeze in preference to being nursed. Undoubtedly, I think that of the 77 per cent. that die before they shed their down, quite half are killed by kindness."

It is from such an example as this that we may come to realise the extraordinary power of parent-hunger. Consider these penguin mothers and fathers clamouring and fighting for the possession of a child. With them the parental instinct has gained fierce strength from being thwarted. Is there not here yet another lesson for us to learn?

CONTENTS OF CHAPTER VI
PARENTHOOD AMONG THE HIGHER ANIMALS

THE FIXING OF THE PARENTAL INSTINCT IN THE MOTHER

Retrogression in fatherhood—Among mammals no examples of devoted fathers—Egoistic desires increase in the males and interest in the family decreases—Probable reason—Method of birth and circumstances of life of infant mammals force mothers to monopolise nutrition and care of young—Parenthood more automatic—The father pushed out of his earlier position of service to the family—Instead of a working partner with the mother he becomes a member apart—His character appears to change—He becomes masterful, pugnacious and jealous—This general among mammals—Number of young among mammals usually reduced—Varied forms of sexual association practised by different species—Polygamy frequent—The matriarchal family—The clue we are seeking—The egoism of the males acts for the advantage of the females—The maternal instinct fixed in the mothers—Self-sacrifice becomes once and for ever the supreme joy and privilege of the female—Objections that may be raised—Resumé—General conclusions to be drawn from pre-human parenthood.

CHAPTER VI
PARENTHOOD AMONG THE HIGHER ANIMALS
THE FIXING OF THE PARENTAL INSTINCT IN THE MOTHER

"The universe throbs with restless change. Everything that we know is becoming rather than being."—P. CHALMERS MITCHELL

One of the difficulties that has met me in my studies of the family among the animals is that, as we ascend the scale of life, there is a moral retrogression in fatherhood—at least, that is how it appears to me. There are, as far as I have found, no examples among mammals, the highest and last group of the animal kingdom, of devoted fathers undertaking the sole charge of the young, and few where the father even shares with the mother to any extent in the work connected with the upbringing of the family. The egoistic desires seem to increase in the males, with a corresponding weakening of their interest in the family and willingness to participate in its duties. The young are carried by the mother alone, they are protected chiefly by her; the father takes no part in the nursery cares, and rarely does he help in providing food for the children. The family is maternal, the female—the mother—its centre; the male is bound sexually to the female, but apart from this his connection with the family is slight; we find him most frequently following personal interests.

In contrast with the conduct of the fathers in the families we have so far examined among the birds, reptiles, fishes and insects, with whom the father's solicitude and sacrifice for the young equals and, in some cases, rivals that of the mother, this complete paternal indifference is really very startling. It demands our attention.

What factors have brought about this reversal, which at first sight appears so strange? Why is it that the parental instinct diminishes in the father and is now fixed in the mother? It is, however, easy to understand this change if we consider what now happens, and the changed conditions under which the young are born. The mammals do not lay eggs like bird and reptile mothers, but each mother retains the eggs within her body, and so secures for the young warmth and protection far more certainly than would be possible in the best-contrived nest or home.[47] But this has led to changed habits. No nest or brooding-home has to be made, and the same preparations for the family, which hitherto have united in work the father with the mother, are unnecessary. Again, food has not now to the same extent to be collected and stored in readiness for the future needs of the children. The embryo, living within the body of its mother, gains the food for its growth directly from her blood. The connection between mother and child now is closer; her condition and health become of direct importance for the welfare of the young. At the same time the importance of the father is sharply lessened. This is plain. The early stages of mother-care, instead of being conscious and external acts regulated by special circumstances and often modified to meet different needs, now become part of the unconscious functions of the body of the mother—the child is an extension of herself. The advantage to the offspring of this change from external to internal protection is great, in the added safety thereby gained from fixed functions over the habits that might be slurred over, bungled or forgotten. I think, however, that there is a corresponding loss—that parenthood becomes more possibly irresponsible and, at the same time, individualism becomes stronger. Birth, with narrowed opportunity for intelligent adaptation, is more of an unconsidered incident; I mean that before it occurs it demands much less from the parents in sacrifice and in work. This is certainly the case with the father, whose part in gaining offspring is reduced to a single momentary act, and one, moreover, that is prompted by the fiercest egoistic desire.

But I think, too, there is a deterioration, though much less in degree, in the quality of motherhood. The preparation made for the birth of her children by the mammal mother is very slight, indeed, in many cases the mother appears to be unaware of the approaching event until the actual birth begins. Here is an account of a langur monkey, whose first baby was born in the London Zoological Gardens, at which event the mother seemed to be utterly surprised. The birth took place at night, and the mother, from the marks in the cage, must have dragged up and down the new, astonishing object. But by the morning she had grown accustomed to the baby, and held it pressed closely to her breast, from time to time thrusting the head outwards and eagerly looking at it. For several weeks the baby never left her, and she showed endless curiosity and pleasure in it, ceaselessly examining it, turning it over, stroking it and keeping it clean with her hands. She was jealous of visitors, and when they came near to the cage she would turn round so as to hide the baby from them. The father, in case of accidents, had been taken away and put in the adjoining cage, which was shut off by a piece of canvas. He made a hole in this, and from time to time, especially when the mother or baby made any noise, he would raise the torn flap and peep through.[48]

It must be remembered that among the mammals it is the rule for the young to be suckled by the mother, a mode of feeding already foreshadowed by many bird parents and some insects. But with them the special nursery food is prepared from their own food by incessant work, undertaken, as a rule, by both parents. The act of suckling, on the other hand, occurs without conscious work, and is a function in which the father has no concern whatever.

I have no facts to trace the steps whereby this function of maternal feeding was developed and established, but I would suggest that, apart from the advantage to the young of a special diet, the immense labour entailed on the parents in obtaining food—the foraging over wide areas and the carrying of the provisions back to the nursery—made it a question of economy; and that the mother, as more usually being with the young, was the parent who came without conscious effort to prepare for them in her body this early nourishment.

It is plain that the bond between the mother and offspring would be greatly strengthened; they would be dependent upon her alone, and drawing life from her body, she would become increasingly conscious of them during a much longer period. The emotional quality of affection really develops now. The suckling is a continuation of the organic relation by which the child is born of the mother's body; now the child exists through her, and becomes, so to speak, a habit which grows up out of her own individuality. I lay stress upon this fact: the maternal feeding is the beginning of a new period in the growth of motherhood, and is the foundation of the indestructible bond between mother and child.

We see, then, the reasons for the curious and sudden deterioration in fatherhood; the father has, as it were, been pushed out of his earlier position of service. Now that there is no nursery to be built, and the mother is the sole feeder of the young during their period of greatest helplessness, the father loses his interest in the family. Our interests and our habits are fixed by whatever occupies our attention. Freed from the first and most important care of the young, the male is severed from the family and its duties, and his attention, thus set free, turns in new directions and centres upon himself. In this connection we have, I would suggest, an explanation of the greater variability of the male as well as of his more violent passions. Instead of a working partner with the mother, sharing in her sacrifice for the welfare of the family, he is a member apart; he grows larger than the female, becomes masterful, pugnacious, jealous of her and of the young: a fighting, egoistic specialisation. He is still attached to the female, but he seeks her to satisfy his sexual needs, he less frequently remains with her as a domestic partner, relieving her in connection with the rearing of the young.[49]

This is the general condition among the mammals. It is the rule that the young are tended by the mother during the period of their youth. At birth they are usually helpless, and often are born before the eyelids have opened and while the body is yet naked, or but scantily clothed. But there are degrees of helplessness, determined, it would seem, by the conditions of the environment and habits of the parents. The maternal care is greater or less in accordance with the needs of the young. The period of youth is much longer, and increases as we ascend in the scale of life. The great apes, for instance—the gorilla, the orang and the chimpanzee—take from eight to twelve years to grow up, while baboons and common monkeys take from three to eight years, and the little South American monkeys and lemurs two to three years.[50] In connection with this longer childhood we find an increased mental growth; the years of youth are the time in which the brain cells increase in size and co-ordinate with the rest of the body. And the longer the period of youth the more perfect is the brain. Thus the helplessness of the young stands in direct relation to the increased vitality shown by the adults. It is also the strongest factor in developing and fixing the maternal instincts.

The young do not leave their mother until they are well ready to start life on their own account; then they are thrown into the world. Till then they are cared for. Freed of any duty of finding food, and very seldom having to defend themselves, they have time to experiment and learn from experience. The instincts in this way become educated, their rigidity is destroyed, and more and more they are controlled by memory and experience—the stored-up results of experiment. The purpose of youth is to give time for this.

The number of the young is now very greatly reduced, and the small families are protected by the mothers, in some cases assisted by the fathers. The maintenance of the species by the production of enormous families has ceased. Some of the small rodents, it is true, breed several times in the course of the year, and there are other fecund mammals, such as pigs, which give birth to many young in one litter. But these are rare exceptions. The usual number of young is two or three at a birth, and the higher in the scale of mammalian life the smaller is the family.[51]

There is a fact that must be noted here. A curious perverted instinct is not uncommon among mammal mothers, though rare with the monkeys. In the first day or two after birth a mother will kill and eat her young. I had a bitch who once did this: the first time she had a family she ate all her puppies in the first night; afterwards (I mean when for a second time she had puppies) she was a good and fond mother. I think this habit of maternal infanticide must be connected with that change, of which I have spoken, whereby the early stages of brood-care are carried on without the direct consciousness of the mother. The children do not enter into her experience because she has not had to work for them. She eats them as she would eat any other helpless thing. In a carnivorous mother especially this habit is not surprising; it happens almost always with young and inexperienced mothers. And I think it shows that maternal care is not so instinctive as we are led to believe, but is the result of, and directly dependent upon habit and the attention being fixed on the family.

In all the carnivores the young are born helpless, usually blind, though new-born lions can see; they remain with their mother for a period varying from a few weeks with the smaller creatures to even more than a year. Sometimes the father stays loosely attached to the family. The large predaceous creatures cover great distances in search of prey. There is, however, a stationary home lair in a well-concealed place, to which the mother always returns with food. She takes scrupulous care to keep the nursery clean, and she carefully looks to the needs of her young family, licking them with her tongue, until they are old enough to perform their own toilet or lick and clean each other. Before they are weaned they are allowed to scrape off fragments of flesh from the mother's food, so that they may become accustomed to their future food. At the same time they are taught the elements of stalking, in play-lessons with the mother's tail and paws. Later they are taken out by the mother, sometimes by both parents, on foraging expeditions. Family parties of lions, for instance, often have been seen by African hunters.

The fathers do little for the young families. Sometimes they afford protection in fighting and driving off enemies; it is important, however, to note that this service to the family seems to be prompted by jealousy and aggression, and must be considered as an expression of the egoistic instincts rather than connected with parental solicitude.

Among the mammals polygamy is frequent, and there are cases of the most brutal promiscuity, where the males and females unite and separate at chance meetings, without any care for the family arising in the mind of the male. Polygamous unions are especially common among species with sociable habits who live in hordes. Sociability probably arises through individual weakness. Animals that are badly armed for fierce combats, and that have, besides, difficulty in obtaining food are glad to live in association. Thus the ruminants live in hordes or polygamous groups, composed of females and young subject to a male who protects them, expelling his rivals, and being a veritable chief of a band.[52]

The conditions of the nursery and early life of the young are changed necessarily by these different habits. In the first place, the ruminants are wanderers, and travel long distances in search of food and water. Thus there is no permanent home and no nursery, and the mothers make no preparation beforehand for the young. They retire for a few minutes to a thicket, where they drop the calves or lambs. Families are small, and one is the usual number at a birth. The young are not born helpless, as is the case among the young carnivores where there is a settled nursery, but are clothed, have their eyes open, and their senses are very alert. In a very short time, almost as soon as their mother has licked them clean, they are ready to follow her; and they join the herd, if the animals are gregarious. The mothers show marked affection to the young, but it would seem to be the business of the young one rather to follow and stick to the mother than for the mother, as amongst the carnivores, to take the lead in the affections. There is no real training of the young by the mother. Sometimes, if there is a herd, the males will combine to defend the group of the females and their young; but more frequently there is a family party, consisting of one or possibly two males, with their several wives and children.[53]

Many different animals live in this manner in familial groups. The moufflons of Europe and of the Atlas, for instance, form polygamous social groups in the breeding season.[54] Among the walrus, the male, who is of a very jealous temperament, collects around him from thirty to forty females, making altogether a polygamous family sometimes amounting to a hundred and twenty individuals.[55] Again, the male of the Asiatic antelope is inordinately polygamous; he expels all his rivals, and forms a harem numbering sometimes a hundred females. It should be noted that polygamic régime does not appear to lessen the affectionate sentiment in the females towards their tyrant lord. There are many examples of the most oppressed females being faithful wives. And so much is this so that the conclusion is almost forced upon us that the female animal likes servitude.[56]

There is a wide range in the form of sexual association practised by different species. The carnivorous animals, as a rule, live in couples; this is done, for example, by bears, weasels and whales. But this is not an absolute rule, for the South African lion is a polygamist, and is usually accompanied by four or five females.[57] Sometimes species that are very nearly allied have different conjugal customs; thus the white-cheeked peccary lives in social groups, while the white-ringed peccary lives in couples.[58]

Permanent unions are formed, especially among the anthropoid apes. Thus strictly monogamous marriages are frequent among gorillas and orang-utans, and any approach to loose behaviour on the part of the wife is severely punished by the husband.[59] The ouanderoo (*Macaque silenus*) of India has only one female, and is faithful to her till death.[60]

But polygamy is frequent. Savage tells us that the *Gorilla guia*, for instance, forms small hordes, consisting of a single adult male, who is the despotic master of many females and a certain number of the young. We find both the matrichate and the patrichate family; but whatever the form of sexual relationship practised, the father has always much less affection for the young than the mother. Among the mammals this is universal.

The females among the mammals being smaller and less powerful than the males, no sexual association comparable to polyandry is possible. Yet in justice it must be noted that the desire for sexual variety is not always confined to the males. A female will sometimes take advantage of the moment when the attention of her lord and master is entirely absorbed by the anxiety of a fight to run off with a young male. Even among species noted for their conjugal fidelity this will happen. The male animal has no monopoly in sexual sins.[61]

The polygamous families of monkeys are always subject to patriarchal rule. The father is the tyrant of the band—an egoist, who spends his time in fighting and in love adventures. Any protection he gives to his wives is in his own interest and to keep them bound to himself. He neither makes the home nor feeds the young. Often he is a disturber of the family peace. He will, on occasion, show jealousy of his own sons, whom he expels from the band as soon as they are old enough to give him trouble; his daughters, in some cases, he adds to his harem.

Even in monogamous species, where the male keeps with the female, he does so more as chief than as father. He takes little interest in the nursery. At times he is much inclined to commit infanticide and to destroy the offspring which, by absorbing the attention of his partner, thwart his amours. Thus among the large felines the mother often is obliged to hide her young ones from the male when he stays with her, in order to prevent his devouring them.[62]

Again, among the even-toed ungulates (pigs, peccaries and hippopotami) we find marked maternal affection and care. Little pigs are feeble at birth, and are sedulously guarded by their mother. A hippopotamus baby (the family usually consists of one only) stays with its mother for a long time, probably several years, and when the mother goes to and fro to the water to feed, the little one rides on her back. The fathers take no notice at all of the young. The odd-toed ungulates (horses, asses and zebras, and the tapirs and rhinoceroses) live in herds. The young are active soon after birth and able to follow their mothers, who have great affection for them. The males will protect the females and young when the herd is attacked if a fight is unavoidable, but they prefer to seek safety in flight. The fathers do not appear to have any affection for the young.[63]

Among the numerous classes of rodents, where the young are born naked, blind and helpless, the whole duty of their upbringing is undertaken by the mother. "I do not know of any instance," states Mr. P. Chalmers Mitchell, "in which the male takes care of the young; generally they either neglect them altogether, or attack them and persecute them."

From such pictures as these the position of the father in the family will readily be seen. No longer bound by domestic ties to the young, he knows no duty to the family except the rule of jealous ownership. How complete is the change in the family organisation. How sharp is the contrast between these indifferent males, jealous and fighting, and the devoted fathers among the birds, fishes, reptiles and insects, uniting with the mothers as working partners in the home-making, food-providing, and all the care of the young. The father is now alone—separated from the family, banded with other males. And do you not see how this change, and the indifference of the males to any interests but their own, have forced the mothers into closer union with the family? The male strength, the gorgeous display of sex-charms, the fierce fighting for prey and for love, are now markedly developed. But this polygamous jealousy and egoism acts really for the advantage of the females. It is the egoistic male conduct that forces altruism upon them. I attach great importance to this. I maintain that the forcing out of the father from his service and earlier important position of a worker in the circle of the family served as a means to the end of deepening and fixing the maternal instinct in the mothers. What was lost for fatherhood was gained for motherhood. Self-sacrifice became once and for ever the supreme joy and privilege of the female.

We have found the clue we were seeking.

Further than this I must not go. The first part of my inquiry has come to an end. There is little more that I need to say. It may seem to the reader that the animal family, in a book written to establish the duties and rights of human motherhood, has received too much attention. To those who hold this view I can say only that I do not agree with them. In forethought and sacrifice for the well-being of the young—the devotion of the father as well as of the mother—these pre-human parents do not yield precedence to many human families. They deserve our attentive study. But I have no hope, nor much desire, to convince those of an opposite opinion, who hold that we are so much higher and different from the animals that we can learn nothing from them. To all such I would recommend again that they leave this section of my book unread.

There is, however, another objection that may be raised. It may be thought that too much stress has been laid on the father and his connection with the family, that my choice of illustrations has been biased, and cases taken in which the father's devotion is unusually prominent. This I have done. And I have done it of fixed purpose. In the first place, I desired to prove the error in the common opinion that the parental instinct has at all times been the endowment of the female, stronger in her than in the male. I wanted it to be known that in the beginning of the family the father was as true a parent as the mother, his devotion sometimes being greater than hers. Then, secondly, I hoped, by means of the insight that the many and great changes in the past conditions of the family afford us, to establish the close connection which does at all times exist between parental devotion and the duties performed in feeding and caring for the young. The parent who sacrifices most is the parent who loves most. Some of the suggestions I have made may be more or less open to question, but not a few, I think, are true in the light of the facts that cannot be questioned. I am fully aware of the omissions and inadequacy of my summary; probably I have made mistakes. I think this could not have been prevented. Much ground had to be covered. The illustrations I have been able to give of each stage in the history of parenthood are few, compared with the rich number that might be studied. I have made no attempt at completeness, nor have I tried to set up any exact order of behaviour. Life is too full of surprises for such arbitrary theories. I have, however, tried to make clear certain ideas that have forced themselves very strongly upon my attention during my own studies.

We have seen the maternal instinct in the making, and we have come to understand the strong force of this impulse, which finds its expression in so many diverse ways. There is much that we cannot understand. But this is largely because we know so little. We have, I hope, gained a clearer view; we have learnt many things that may cast forward suggestions for the solving of our own sexual, domestic and social relationships. The facts which I have recorded are, I trust, sufficient for this purpose: I hold that the following general conclusions may be drawn from them—

Regarding the care of the young as the moving force in developing the intelligence of the parents, I have accepted the truth, which it is the chief purpose of my book to make plain, that the individual exists for the race. Other personal things may be important, they may be profoundly important, but they are not primary—not one with the forces that do not change. The individual is primarily the host and servant of the seed of life. Birth is the essential fact underlying all experience.

From this service to the future arises the family and the home. And with the appearance of the family, new habits are necessarily formed, and these act in developing the higher sides of mental and emotional life. Co-operation, friendship and love which is not sexual attraction find their first beginnings in the limiting by the parents of their desire to look after themselves, to satisfy their own appetites and provide for their own needs. The mere toleration of the young is the start in a new life. There follows a mutual joining in work with the necessity and opportunity of modifying instinct by practice. In this way a direct push forward is given for the development of intelligent conduct. An immense advance, then, is gained from the association of the young with the old in the family tie.

In the cases we have examined, we have seen that the same end is not gained always in the same way. Nature has no fixed rule for the family. The contrasts and paradoxes of animal family life are numerous. We have watched the development of the parental intelligence in many family groups; we have seen that there is no fixed order in the relations which exist between parents and offspring. All arrangements are good on the one condition that they succeed in serving the family and preserving its life.

To produce large families, making little provision for them, is a wasteful and improvident way of maintaining life. This spendthrift fashion of reproduction was the early method. To limit the number of the family and to cherish and protect the young, not throwing them upon the world until they are well fitted to make a brave fight against its dangers, is the later, wiser and safer way. We have noted devices of this kind in each group of the animal kingdom, but parental care becomes more and more complete as the scale of life is ascended. Not only are the numbers in the family reduced, but the period of youth becomes longer. The protected young are permitted a longer time in which they have the opportunity of learning to live.

The importance of the form of union or marriage between the parents and of the kind of home must be considered. We have found that polygamous fathers and polyandrous mothers care little for the young. The withdrawal of the interest and care of either parent is a source of weakness which can be compensated only by an added devotion on the part of the remaining parent.

We have noted the withdrawal of the father from active work for the family. This came with the greater importance of the mother, which itself was not the result of any conscious act. It was a necessary step, following the change from external to internal protection, whereby the young are retained within the body of the mother. Animal parents do not teach us that mothers are always more devoted and self-sacrificing than fathers. Sometimes, indeed, the contrary would appear to be true. Even the mother's instinct to protect and serve the young, which seems to increase as we ascend the scale towards human parentage, must, I think, be regarded as an extended egoism. Formed in her body and fed from her sustenance, the young are a part of her individuality, and her solicitude for them is but a wider caring for herself.

There are many surprises in animal parenthood. The conduct of the parents may vary within very wide limits, and all kinds of devices are employed by different parents to ensure the well-being of the family.

Solicitude and sacrifice for the young are common, but indifference also occurs; and there are unnatural parents of both sexes who shirk family duties. We have found, indeed, the suggestion of all the virtues of human parents as well as many of their sins, every form of devotion and intelligent parenthood as well as examples of folly and neglect.

We have observed the greatest difference in particular in the conduct of the father as regards his participation in the work of building the home and in feeding and rearing the young. Thereby we have learnt that a psychic metamorphosis of the male may occur, causing him to fulfil the duties of the mother, and that accompanying this is an alteration in the character of the female which completely transforms her sexual nature.

An attempt was made to solve this riddle of sex. It seems probable that changes in function, by which is meant changes in the form of union and conditions of the family—as when one sex, for some reason or other, performs the duties usually undertaken by the other sex—may profoundly alter the sexual nature of the individual and modify the differences which tend to thrust the sexes apart. We cannot know with any certainty. Yet I can see no other interpretation of these curious instances of sexual transformation, and, if I mistake not, it may be possible in this way to cast a light on one of the most difficult problems with which we are faced to-day.

I have asserted again and again that the strength of the parental instinct is dependent directly on the opportunities for its expression; which is to say that the parent who tends and feeds the young is the parent who loves the young. We may go further than this. There is no such thing as instinctive motherhood. The emotional quality of affection comes later than the birth of offspring, and is not dependent on any instinctive feeling in the mother. It is the consequence and not the cause of parental care. So true it is that sacrifice and forgetfulness of self is the basis of affection.

The most important result that we have gained from our inquiry is a knowledge of the close connection which exists between the care of the young and the character and conduct of the parents. You will see what this implies. The essential fact for the male and the female—for the mother and also for the father—is a development of responsibility in fulfilling duties to the family. Neither sex can keep a position apart from parenthood. Just in so far as the mother and the father attain to consciousness and intelligent sacrifice in their relation to their offspring do they attain individual intelligence, development and joy. To me, at least, this is the truth that stands out as the lesson to be learnt from these pre-human parents.

PART III
THE PRIMITIVE FAMILY

"Round the fundamental facts of parenthood and the dependence of the breeding mother woman has built up the tissue of customs and conventions called 'home,' which expanded in ever widening circles became society."—E. Colquhoun.

CONTENTS OF CHAPTER VII
THE MOTHER IN THE PRIMITIVE FAMILY

The importance of the customs of primitive peoples—Such knowledge necessary to an understanding of our present family system and form of marriage—My earlier book, *The Age of Mother-Power*—This work a necessary part of my present inquiry—Re-statement of my own views—An attempt to group the matter to be considered—The early period in which man developed from his ape-like ancestors—Parenthood more fixed, fewer experiments—The probable conditions of the primordial human family—Customs of brute male-ownership—This the pre-matriarchal stage of the family—Progress—The second stage—The growth of the communal clan—The increasing influence of the women—Reasons why this view may be accepted—Mother-descent and mother-rights—The importance of this early matriarchate—The maternal form of marriage—Visiting husbands—Communal dwelling houses—Contrast between the customs of the patriarchal individual family and the maternal communal clan—The power of the wife and the mother—The alien position of the husband and father—The assertion of the male force in the person of the woman's brother—The communal clan a transitional stage—The re-establishment of the individual patriarchal family—The fixing of paternity and the rise of the father's power—Lessons to be learnt from this past history of the family.

CHAPTER VII
THE MOTHER IN THE PRIMITIVE FAMILY

(*A chapter which may be omitted by the reader who has no interest in the customs of primitive peoples.*)

"The clan exists on account of the struggle for existence, the family seeks for the enjoyment of that which they have obtained."—STARCKE.

And now having finished my preliminary study of the maternal instinct in the making, having given examples of its varied manifestations in the animal kingdom, and made clear certain general ideas on parenthood and the family, I may hope to go on to consider human mothers and fathers with a surer knowledge and less misunderstanding. The fitting method of inquiry, and the one I should like to employ would be to begin with the lowest forms of the human family. I myself am always greatly attracted by the customs of primitive peoples, for I was born amongst them. I hold that some knowledge of the family and the domestic and social conditions still to be found among uncivilised races, in all parts of the world, is essential to a complete understanding of our own social and sexual problems.

In an earlier work, *The Age of Mother-Power*,[64] I have given my views on the past history of the family. I have attempted to establish the existence of a Mother-age civilisation, the so-called Matriarchate, described in detail the privileged position of the mother, and noted, with many examples, the family conditions, sex-customs and forms of marriage among primitive peoples. That book should form the historical section of this present work. It is, indeed, a necessary part of my inquiry. I am convinced that the only way to estimate the value of our present family system is to examine the history of that system in the past. We find suggestions of primitive customs in many directions; they are shadowed in certain of our marriage rites and direct many of our sex habits; they have left unmistakable traces on our literature, in our language and in our laws; indeed we may find their influence almost everywhere, if we know what to look for and how to interpret the signs. The close connection which links the present with the past cannot easily be neglected. We often say: This or that custom belongs to the present era: yet nine times out of ten the thing we believe to be new is in reality as old as the history of mankind. Often what we think is a step forward is not so at all; we are going back to a custom and practices long discarded. We are less inventive and more bound than we know. No period stands alone, and the present in every age is merely the shifting ground at which the past and the future meet.

I would therefore ask all those among my readers who care to follow in detail the history of the family through the long, early, upward stages of its growth, at this point to leave this work in order to read *The Age of Mother-Power*, therein to learn what I hold to have been the family conditions in the period known as the Mother-age. But as such a course may be impossible, or be disliked, by the reader, I will now for our present guidance re-state very briefly the main conclusions arrived at by that investigation.

And first it should be noted that the history of human parenthood from its earliest known appearance shows an orderly progress from the start to the end. There is no difficulty even in fixing the beginning. Man, the gorilla, the orang and the chimpanzee had a common ancestor, and for this reason the parental stages of the great apes and of man have an almost startling resemblance. Professor Metchnikoff was so impressed by this likeness that he has suggested that the human race may have taken its origin from the precocious birth of an ape. We thus find no gap that has to be filled: we take up our inquiry of the family at the exact place at which we left it. There are, of course, changes to fit the parents and the young for their new stage of life; more and more instincts are modified by experiment and experience. Intelligence grows. New habits afford possibilities of advance, and suggest the directions in which the family may move. There are, however, far fewer experiments, less sharp differences in the conduct of the different parents; the family shows less flexibility, and the maternal instincts settle down, as it were, to an average character, with average limitations and an average expression.

Our most primitive ancestors, half-men, half-brutes, lived in small, solitary, and hostile family groups, composed of an adult male, his wife, or, if he were powerful, several wives and their children. In such a group the father is the chief or patriarch as long as he lives, and the family is held together by their common subjection to him. His interest in the family is confined to fighting to drive off rivals, and, for this reason, he drives his sons from the home as soon as they are old enough to be dangerous to his interests: his daughters he adds to his wives, unless they are caught and carried off by some other male.

It was doubtless thus, in a family organisation similar to that of the great monkeys, that man first lived. Here was the most primitive form of jealous government of the family by the male. Such conduct, prompted by the egoistic desires of sex, mark the continuation of the degradation in fatherhood, which we noted as occurring among the mammals as soon as the father was freed from the duties of providing a home and the first feeding and tending of the young.

In the primitive families the idea of descent is feeble so that the groups are small and readily disrupted. But though originally without explicit consciousness of relationships, the members would be held together by a *feeling* of kin. Such feeling would become conscious first between the mothers and their children, and in this way mother-kin must have been realised at a very early period. The father's relationship, on the other hand, would not be forced into conscious recognition. He would be a member apart from this natural kinship.

Such were the probable conditions in the primordial human family. The important thing to note is that in each family group there would be only one adult polygamous male, with several women of different ages, and the children of both sexes, all in more or less complete subjection to his rule.[65]

These customs of brute-male-ownership are still in great measure preserved among the least-developed races. This may be called the pre-matriarchal stage of the family, and its existence explains how there are many rude peoples that exhibit no trace at all of mother-descent. In the lowest nomad bands of savages of the deserts and forests we still find these rough paternal groups, who know no social bonds, but are ruled alone by brute strength and jealous ownership. With them development has been very slow; they have not yet advanced to the social organisation of the maternal family clan.

From these first solitary families, grouped submissively around one tyrant-ruler, we reach a second stage, out of which order and organisation sprang. In this second stage the family expanded into the larger group of the communal clan. The change had to come. With the fierce struggle for existence, the solitary family-group became impossible, association was the only way to prevent extermination.

How did the change come?

Now, it is part of my conviction that the earliest movements towards peace and expansion of the family came through the influence of women. I must state briefly my reasons for this view.

In the first place it certainly would be in the women's interests to consolidate the home and the family, and, by means of union, to establish their own power. What we desire and fix our attention upon, as a rule, is what we do. In the early groups the mothers with their adult daughters and the young of both sexes would live on terms of association as friendly hearthmates. Such is the marked difference in the position of the two sexes —the solitary jealous unsocial male and the united women.

The strongest factor in this association would arise from the dependence of the children upon their mothers, a dependence that was of much longer duration than among the animals on account of the pre-eminent helplessness of the human child, which entailed a more prolonged infancy. The women and the children would form the family-group, to which the male was attached by his sexual needs, but he remained always apart—a kind of jealous fighting specialist. The temporary hearth-home would be the shelter of the women. It was under this shelter that children were born and the group accumulated its members. Whether cave, or hollow tree, or frail branch shelter, the home must have belonged to the women.

It is clear that under these conditions the female members of the group-family must necessarily have been attached to the home much more closely than the man, whose desire lay in the opposite direction, and whose conduct by constant jealous fights tended to the disruption of the home. Moreover this home attachment would be present always and acting on the female members, as the daughters—unless captured by other males—would remain in the home as additional wives to their father; on the other hand, it could never arise in the case of the sons, whose fate was to be driven out from the hearth-home as soon as they were old enough to become rivals to their father. Such conditions must, as time went on, have profoundly modified the female outlook, bending the desire of the women to a steady settled life, conditions under which alone the family could expand and social organisation develop.

Again, the daily search for the daily food must surely have been undertaken chiefly by the women. For it is impossible that one man, however skilful a hunter, could have fed all the female members and children of the group. Further than this, we may, I think, conceive that much of his attention and his time would be occupied in fighting his rivals; also his strength as sole progenitor must have been expended largely in sex. It is, therefore, probable that the male was dependent on the food activities of his women.

The mothers, their inventive faculties quickened by the stress of the needs of their children, would try to convert to their own uses the most available portion of their own environment. It would be under their attention that plants were first utilised for food, seeds planted and nuts and fruit stored, birds would also be snared, fish caught, and animals tamed for service. Primitive domestic vessels and baskets would be fashioned and clothes have to be made. All the faculties of the women, in exercises that would lead to the development of every part of their bodies and their minds, would be called into play by the work of satisfying the physical needs of the group.

In all these numerous activities the women of each group would work together. And through this co-operation must have resulted the assertion of the women's power, as the directors and organisers of industrial occupations.

As the group slowly advanced in progress, such power, increasing, would raise the mother's position; the women would establish themselves permanently as of essential value in the family, not only as the givers of life, but as the chief providers of the food essential to the preservation of the life of its members.

And a further result would follow in the treatment by the males of this new order. The women by obtaining and preparing food would gain an economic value. Wives would become to the husband a source of riches indispensable to him, not only on account of his sex needs, but on account of the more persistent need of food. Thus the more women he possessed the greater would be his own comfort, and the physical prosperity of the group.

And again, a further result would follow. The greater the number of women in the group the stronger would become their power of combination. I attach great importance to this. Working together for the welfare of all, the maternal instinct of sacrifice would be greatly strengthened in the women so that necessarily they would come to consider the collective interests of the family. Can it be credited that such conditions could have acted upon the males, whose conduct would still be inspired by individual appetite and selfish inclination? I maintain such a view to be impossible.

Another advantage, I think, would arise for the women. From the circumstances of the family their interest in sex must have been less acute in consciousness than that of the male. They must have gained freedom from being less occupied with love, and from being less jealously interested in the male than he was in them. Doubtless each woman would be attracted by the male's courageous action in fighting his rivals for possession of her, but when the rival was the woman's own son such attraction would come into strong conflict with the deeper maternal instinct. Thus the unceasing sexual preoccupation of the male, with the emotional dependence it entailed on the females, must, I would suggest, have given the women an immense advantage. They would come to use their sex charms as an accessory of success. And if I am right here, the husband would be in the power of his women, much more surely than they would be in his power.

From the standpoint of physical strength the male was the master, the tyrant ruler of the family, who, doubtless, often was brutal enough. But the women with their children, leading an independent life to some extent, and with their mental ingenuity developed by the conditions of their life, would learn, I believe, to outwit their masters by passive united resistance. The mothers and daughters may even have asserted their will in rebellion. I picture, indeed, these savage women ever striving for more privilege, and step by step advancing through peaceful combination to power.

Such conditions as those I have briefly pictured could not fail to domesticate the women. They must have acted also in strengthening the bonds between the mothers and their children and in making more conscious the strong instinct of maternal sacrifice.

But mark this: I do not wish to set up any claim for, because I do not believe in, the superiority of one sex over the other sex. Character is determined by the conditions of living. If, as I conceive, progress came through the mothers, rather than through the father, it was because the conditions were really more favourable to them, and drove them on in the right path. Collective motives were more considered by women, not at all because of any higher standard of moral virtue, but because of the peculiar advantages arising to themselves and to their children—advantages of peaceful family association which could not exist in a group ruled by individual inclination.

During the development of the family, we may expect to find that the males will seek to hold their rights, and that the women of the group will exert their influence more and more in breaking these down; and this is precisely what we do find. And for this reason the clan system, which developed from these solitary hostile families, must be considered as a feminine creation, which had special relation to motherhood.

The sexual egoism by which one male, through his strength and seniority, held marital rights over all the females of his group had to be struck at its roots. In other words, the solitary despot had to learn to tolerate the association of other adult males.

It is impossible for me here to follow step by step the means whereby this change was brought about. I would, however, assert my strong belief that it was the mothers, acting in the interests of their children, who tamed the jealous desires and domesticated the males. The adult sons, instead of being driven from the home by the father, were permitted to remain as members of the family group and to bring in young wives captured from other families. At a later stage, daughters received husbands, young males from other groups, who came first as temporary lovers, visiting their brides by night, but afterwards remained with them as permanent guests in the home of the mother. Under these new conditions, the marital rights of the male members were restricted and confined. A system of taboos was established, which, as time advanced, was greatly strengthened by the use of sacred totem marks, and became of inexorable strictness.

In this way peace was established, and association between the jealous fighting males was made possible.

Here, then, are the reasons which led to the formation of the maternal family and the communal clan. It depended, in the first place, on the development of mutual aid between mother and offspring, based on the much closer relationship of the children to their mothers than to the father. As soon as the women of the family-group by combination were able to outwit and curb the jealous rule of the father, the matriarchal clan developed from the primitive patriarchal family.

The contrast between the family and clan seems to me of great importance. Individual relationships became of less importance; the clan did not consist of groups of families but of individuals. I have stated that the sexual relationships between the young people began with the reception by the daughters of temporary lovers in the clan-home. A connection thus formed would tend under favourable circumstances to be continued and would be perpetuated as a marriage. Thus it came to be the custom for the husband to live temporarily or permanently in the wife's home and among her kindred. Here he was compelled to work for the general good; he was without property or any recognised rights in the clan; he was not permitted a separate home, and was left with no—or very little—control over his wife and none over the children of the marriage. He occupied, indeed, the position of a more or less permanent guest in the maternal hut or tent.

Under such an organisation the family—the first group of the father, wives and children—is swallowed up in the larger clan. The male has no position of mastery over the female. As time goes on, the clan becomes more and more a free association for mutual protection, ruled over by the ablest and most capable members. Not only does the father not stand out as a principal person from the background of the familial clan; he has not even any recognised domestic rights in connection with his own wife and children. This restriction of the husband and father was clearly dependent on the form of marriage.

The later modifications of the communal clan and the social customs that grew up, in most cases—and always, I believe, in the complete maternal form—were favourable to the authority of the mothers. Kinship was reckoned through the mother, the totem name was taken from her, since in this way alone could the undivided family be maintained. The continuity of the clan thus depending on the women they were placed in a position of importance; the mother was at least the nominal head of the household, shaping the destiny of the clan through the aid of her kindred.

All the members of such a compound family were responsible for the offences of any individual member; and in the same way the clan exacted blood vengeance or compensation collectively for any offence committed against its members. But the men belonged to their own clans, that is, to the clans of their mothers; they did not belong to and had no rights in the clan of which their wife and children were members. As husbands and fathers they were without power. This is very important. The woman's closest male relation was not her husband, but her brother, who acted as father to her children.

A pure type of matriarchal family fully preserved is rare. There are scattered tribes in different parts of the world where descent is still reckoned through the mother. Some features favourable to women are found in one community, some in another. The sexual relationships, in particular, are interesting. The girl is frequently the wooer of the man, and in certain cases she or her mother imposes the conditions of the marriage. After marriage, the free provisions for divorce (often more favourable to the wife than to the husband) are, perhaps, of even greater significance.

There are many traces of discipline exercised in the bringing up of children and more or less systematic training of boys in endurance, speed, courage, etc. This task falls to the mother's brother. The daughters are instructed by the mothers and the matrons of the tribe in all that concerns their duties as wives and mothers.

The woman is subject to the authority of her eldest brother, and sometimes as well to that of her other brothers, her uncles and male relations. But descent being reckoned in the female line, and the fact that she is the conduit by which property passes to and from the men, gives the woman a position of very considerable, though varying, importance.

In all cases the power of the wife is clearly dependent on the maternal form of marriage. I must insist upon this. Where this custom of the husband living in the home of the wife was practised for any long period, the women often established their own claims and all property was held by them; conditions which, under favourable circumstances, developed into what may literally be called a matriarchate. Elder women among some tribes are the heads of kinsfolk, they even have a seat or voice in the tribal council, and there have been exceptional cases of female tribal chiefs. Religion is in some periods in the hands of women, and goddesses are more reverenced than gods. Here is certain proof of the favourable influence mother-descent may exercise on the authority held by women. In all circumstances the children's position was dependent on the mother and her kindred.

Such a system of inheritance may be briefly summarised as mother-right.

Other forms of marriage are found; indeed, every possible experiment in family and sexual association has been tried and is still practised among barbarous races, often with very little reference to those moral ideas to which we are accustomed. It is, however, very necessary to remember that monogamy is frequent and indeed usual under the maternal system. When the husband lives with his wife in a dependent position to her family, he can do so only in the case of one woman. For this reason polygamy is much less deeply rooted under the conditions in which the communal life of the compound family is developed than in the single patriarchal family. Polygamy is an indication, if not always a proof, of the subordination of women to the headship of the husband. In the complete maternal family it is never common and is even prohibited.

It was quite otherwise with polyandry, and though less usual than monogamy, this form of association is in some cases connected with the conditions of the maternal clan. I do not believe it can be regarded as due to a licentious view of the sexual relations, but arose as an expression of the communism which was characteristic of such an organisation.

The whole subject of primitive sexual relationships—which, of course, involves the family, the position of woman and the welfare of the children—is a very wide and complicated one. If I differ on several important points from learned authorities, whose knowledge and research far exceed my own, I do so only after great hesitation, and because I must. Almost invariably the writers on these questions are men, and perhaps for this reason the position of women has not received the attention that it claims. My own studies have convinced me that in the early beginnings of the human family women exercised a more direct and stronger influence than is usually believed. This is no fanciful idea of my own, as I claim to have proved in my earlier book,[66] where it was possible to bring forward in detail the evidence I have collected on the subject.

But even in this brief summary enough has been said to give in rough outline some picture of the family under the conditions of the maternal communal clan. We have marked the steady strengthening of the tie between the mother and the child, with the corresponding movement in the opposite direction in regard to the father's position in the family. All the chances for success in parenthood rested with the mother, rather than with the father. The male was driven out from the holy circle of the family. This degradation of fatherhood is a fact that must be kept before our attention.[67]

There is, however, another side to the matter. In the face of what we have established, it must, I think, be accepted that women held considerable power in this period of mother-descent and under the maternal form of marriage. The mother was dominant in the family in this second stage of its development. This is still denied by some authorities. There are many facts of the early power of women which the great world does not know.

How, then, are we to come to a decision? Shall we look back to the maternal stage as the golden period of the family wherein were realised conditions of free motherhood, which even to-day have not been established? It is a question very difficult to answer, and we must not in any haste rush into mistakes. And unfortunately the limitation of my space can allow only the briefest consideration of the matter.

We find that the mother-age was a transitional stage in the history of the growth of society, and we can trace the stages of its gradual decline. There is nothing to show that the customs of maternal communism, dependent on descent traced in the female line and the maternal form of marriage, have ever been permanently maintained in any progressive society. The enlarged family of the maternal clan is thus proved to have been a less stable social system than the patriarchal single family which again succeeded it, or it would not have perished in the struggle with it. I think this must be accepted.

Within the large and undivided group-family of the clan, the restricted family became gradually re-established by a reassertion of domestic interests. In proportion as the family gained in importance (which would arise as the struggle for existence lessened and the need of association was less imperative) the interests of the individual members would become separated from the group to which they belonged. As society advanced and personal property began to be acquired, each man would aim at gaining a more exclusive right over his wife and children; he would not willingly submit to the bondage of the maternal form of marriage.

We find the husband and father moving towards the position of a fully acknowledged legal parent by a system of buying off his wife and her children from their clan-group. Then the payment of a bride-price was claimed from the bridegroom by the bride's relations, and an act of purchase was accounted essential before marriage; it was, however, regarded as a condition, not so much of the marriage itself, but of the transference of the wife to the home of the husband and of the children to his kindred. The change was, of course, effected slowly; often we find the two forms of marriage—the maternal form and the purchase-marriage—occurring side by side. What, however, is certain is that the purchase-marriage in the struggle was the one which prevailed.

This reversal in the form of the marriage brought about a corresponding reversal in the position of the woman in the sexual relationship. This is so plain. As the patriarchate developed, and men began to gain individual possession of their children by the purchase of their mothers, the father became the dominant power in the family. Women no longer are the transmitters of property and of the family name, but are themselves property passing from the hands of their kindred to those of a husband. As purchased wives, they reside in the husband's house and among his kin, where they occupy the same position of disadvantage in the family as the husband and father had done under the maternal marriage. The protection of her own kindred was the source of the wife's privileged position. This now was lost. The change was not brought about without a struggle, and for long the old customs contended with the new. But step by step the man became the father-master in the home.

It is, however, very necessary to remember that this reversal in the marriage custom may well have been brought about as much by the desire of the women as by the action of the men. I believe that the change to the individual family must have been regarded favourably by primitive women. An arrangement which would give a closer relationship in marriage and the protection of a husband for herself and her children may well have been preferred by the wife to the position of subjection in which she was frequently placed to the authority of her brother and her own relatives. Nor do I think it unlikely that she, quite as strongly as the man, may have desired to live apart from her mother and her kindred in her husband's home. We have to remember that the reassertion of the father within the family-group was a necessary step, and one that had to be taken. The mother is bound to the family by her children in a much closer way than the man ever can be bound. And for this reason any conditions which separate the father from the home and liberate him from his responsibilities to his children are certain not to act in the direction of progress. The male needs to be held to the family. This is a fact much too often forgotten.

The social clan organised around the mothers carried mankind a long way—a way the length of which we are only beginning to realise. But it could not carry mankind forward to the closer family ties and family life from which so much was afterwards to develop. The clan system was essential to the conditions of primitive life, owing to the fierce struggle to exist, and it could then limit and interfere with the family on every side. But as soon as life was easier, men wanted to establish a home with wife and children and to enjoy the possession of property. And women wanted this too. It was not possible for the family to be permanently absorbed. I must insist upon this again. The individual family—that is, the trinity composed of father, mother and child—is the older and the more lasting institution.

I affirm, further, that of the two forms of the family, the individual limited form is the one that is the more natural and happy. Special circumstances may make necessary the enlarged social family, but such conditions are not really a step forward.

With all the evils and restrictions that father-right and the individual family-group may, throughout the ages, have brought to women, we have got to remember that the woman owes the individual relationship in love and the protection of the man for herself and her children to the patriarchal system. The father's right in his children (which, unlike the right of the mother, was not founded upon kinship, but rested on the quite different and insecure basis of property) had to be re-established. Without this being done, the family in its fairness and complete development was impossible. The survival value of the patriarchal family consists in the additional gain to the children of the father's to the mother's care. I do not think this gain can ever safely be lost.

PART IV
MOTHERHOOD AND THE RELATIONSHIPS OF THE SEXES

"For the great majority of mankind at least it can be held that life resolves itself quite simply and obviously into three cardinal phases. There is a period of youth and preparation, a great insurgence of emotion and enterprise centring about the passion of Love; and a third period in which, arising amidst the warmth and stir of the second, interweaving indeed with the second, the care and love of offspring becomes the central interest in life.… Looking at this with a primary regard to its broadest aspect, life is seen essentially as a matter of reproduction; first a growth and training to that end, then commonly mating and actual physical reproduction, and finally the consummation of these things in parental nurture and education. Love, Home and Children, these are the heart-words of life."—H. G. WELLS.

CONTENTS OF CHAPTER VIII
THE FAMILY AND THE HOME

Attacks on the family not likely to destroy it—Dominance of the male may be changed without altering the fundamental ideal of the family—Bernard Shaw ignorant of human needs—Two statements by H. G. Wells—The inhuman ideals of intellectual reformers—Trained hands to replace mother's love—Foolish egoism the basis of the whole argument—The sweated victim of an industrial age is the ideal emancipated woman—The power of the mother in non-industrial societies—Modern uncertainty and want of a fixed standard of conduct—The extension of women's work during the war—Is it of benefit to the coming generation—Can the mother both work outside the home and give sufficient care to her children—Woman's subordinate qualities are man's dominant qualities—Hence the wastefulness of rivalry in the same work—Early experiments in communist families—The child's need for a home of its own—We must insist on conditions that will make home life possible—Types of mothers—The personal rights of the child—The position of the father—The father can be detached from the family—This harmful—The child's need for the care of both its parents—The home exposed to danger—It awaits a fresh inspiration to turn back and hold the desires of women.

CHAPTER VIII
THE FAMILY AND THE HOME

"The ideal which the mother and wife makes for herself, the manner in which she understands duty and life, contain the fate of the community."—*Amiel's Journal.*

There are some who hold that the family rests on a trembling quicksand, and state that its supporters are compelled to weave a network of lies to sustain its foundation. We hear much wild talk, and a great deal is said about the restrictions imposed by the family, and very little about its duties and its joys. There is, and I think its existence must be faced, a growing tide of discontent which would seem to render the stability of the home more and more precarious—the faint-hearted cry to us that everything is coming to an end. It is not so, but rather, everything is about to be renewed.

Institutions as vital to life as the family will continue. From the most distant period of life, among the animals as among mankind, the history of the family has been a long series of regenerations. We have found witness to this again and again in the past records of pre-human and primitive human parenthood. And, indeed, the most important result we have gained from our long inquiry is the abundant proof it has furnished of the indestructible character of the family.

Wherever the individual family (the lasting union of the male with the female for the protection of the young) has been departed from for some other and perhaps freer form of sexual association a return has followed. Special conditions have called forth experiments, new family arrangements, but in no case have they become universal and permanent. We cannot argue against all that the past teaches us. And assuredly the history of the family turns into foolishness many reforms that, in our blindness, we are seeking to-day. We believe they will bring progress and freedom to women. But what sure ground have we for such a belief? In truth we have much to learn.

Institutions have this in common with rivers, they do not readily flow backwards. If they sometimes seem to retro-grade, it is generally only a mere appearance, and though tributary streams break away in experimental courses the main river flows on. You will see what I mean by this. The changes that will take place, and have for long been taking place, have been changes not affecting the fundamental qualities in the ideal of the family—its permanence, the fidelity of its partners in thought and deed, its sentiments and its obligations of joyous sacrifice in united parental care. Attacks have altered (and it is well that they have altered) the dominance of the male. The patriarchal customs of proprietary ownership are gradually disappearing both for the wife and for the children. The family has broadened. The feeling of hostility to the outer world, the self-centredness—much that limited the family is being changed. But the idea of the family, and its value as one of the most essential forms of social life, remains unaffected.

And mark this: *No ideals whatever have been produced by even the most progressive and enlightened persons to replace the family group.*

The wild reforms contemplated by some among us, who talk, but fortunately do not act, are fog and nonsense.

The home, in particular, has been spoken of with contempt. Thus, Bernard Shaw, who in the reforms he advocates fails so frequently to see the real human needs of life, cries: "Home is the girls' prison and the woman's workhouse." Again, W. L. George in *Women and To-morrow* (a "To-morrow" which, by the way, I trust I may never live to see) states: "The home is the enemy of Woman. Purporting to be her protector, it is her oppressor. It is her fortress, but she does not live in the state apartments, she lives in a dungeon."

Mr. H. G. Wells, in a much more recent utterance, wherein he professes to forecast "What is Coming," speaks even more strongly, and all the present conditions are estimated. He states: *"Now, to be married is an incident in a woman's career, as in a man's."* (The italics are mine.) "There is not the same necessity of that household, not the same close tie; the married woman remains partially a freewoman and assimilates herself to the freewoman. There is an increasing disposition to group solitary children and to delegate their care to specially qualified people; and this is likely to increase, because the high earning power of young women will incline them to entrust their children to others."

And again, at the conclusion of his article on "The War and Women," Mr. Wells sums up the situation as follows: "To sum all that has gone before, this war is accelerating rather than deflecting the stream of tendency, and is bringing us rapidly to a state of affairs in which women will be much more definitely independent of their sexual status, much less hampered in their self-development and much more nearly equal to men than has ever been known before in the whole history of mankind."

Now, if these two late pronouncements of Mr. Wells are compared with what he wrote a few years back, with the quotation from *Mankind in the Making* which I have placed before this section of my book because it so well expresses my own views, I think the harm that of late years has been working is strongly evident; harm that is incredibly active in our consciousness.[68]

Such talk of my sex as "freewomen" and of a liberation from the sexual life, as if that could be possible, fills me with impatience. I would not wait to notice it did I not believe that the hurt done to women had been deep and far-reaching. It has increased for them the difficulty of unifying life. And this uncertainty of desire is, as I believe, the modern disease which has worked such havoc in the souls of women. I would like to silence all useless, impious negators; those who, seeking to be clever, really are blinkered, and unable to see the results that would follow from their destructions. The error in all these outcries is the error of blindness, of getting into a condition of confused intellectual excitement, and because some women are dissatisfied and have been unhappy, saying, therefore, and usually with passion, that they would be more satisfied if all the sex were freed from its own duties. As if freedom were ever gained by running away. The intellectual reformer is so very far from understanding the real human needs. There is, for instance, a significant omission in the quotations I have given—no mention is made of the results of all this to the child, and no suggestion is offered except that it should be trained and cared for by experts and apart from its parents. The home is to go because it restricts the liberty of women and will hinder their earning power, as if this were all that had to be considered. I can hardly find a more striking example of how far the apparently simple and elemental things escape the attention of the intellectual reformer.

In the society in which we are living, the only use that can be made of modern progressive teaching about the family—the only ounces of practice to be derived from pounds of precept—will lead, as I believe, to a very undesirable course of action. The programme for the abolition of the home has been outlined for us by reformers of both sexes. Communal houses and kitchens, and the intervention of armies of experts, are to solve the problems which now keep women tied in the individual home. The parents are to be supplanted by "born educators." Successive institutions are planned for the bottle-period, kindergarten, school age, and so on. The children are to stand on visiting relations to the individual home and their parents, while their bodies and souls are to be cared for by specialists. And we are asked to believe that this will be a gain to the child! "It is the trained hand that the baby needs, not mere blood relationship … personal love is too hot an atmosphere for the young soul."[69]

Now, if I wanted a general term to express the state of mind of these reformers, I do seriously think the word *inhuman* would be as near to it as any. Some people talk as if there were no emotional quality to decide these questions; they are dry-minded and quite unable to grasp the true values in life.

And the essence of all such folly is an insupportable egoism. The whole argument against the home is based on the claim of woman to lead an independent life. Independent of what? It is not easy to answer. It is asserted that the ideal of the home as the special care of woman has tied her to material things; it is urged that her emancipation from the fetish of the home is essential for her soul's freedom. The feminists ask us to make the wage-earning woman our ideal, instead of regarding her, as I do, as the unfortunate victim of industrial life and industrial ideals—and this is a very dangerous attitude and one which cannot fail to affect very seriously the fate of the home in the future. It is this that causes me such grave fear. The ideals that we set before us do exercise an influence greater than we know.

Now, I am not much moved by this modern cry for liberty. What is this freedom for which women have been clamouring? In what tyranny are they held other than that in which their womanhood holds them? Is the new liberty to be found as sweated workers? Will it come even now when women's industrial work is being sought for and well paid? Can it ever come from the fevered effort to live the same lives as men live and do the same work that men do?

But this kind of view is of a most superficial sort, and one that, comparatively speaking, is new. Before the coming of industrialism the ideals of women were far different and were centred in the home. The family was then firmly established on the patriarchal system.

I have just read a Russian book[70] which gives a perfect picture of the patriarchal home. The scene is described by a child: the head of the house has died and the new male-head comes from the death-bed. He is thus received by the women of the house—

"Suddenly the door opened, and my father came in. He looked thin and pale and sad. Instantly all rose and went to meet him; even grandmother, who was very stout and could not walk without some one supporting her, dragged herself towards him, and all his four sisters fell down at his feet and began to 'keen.' It was impossible to catch all they said and part I now forget, but I remember the words, 'You are our father now: be kind to us poor orphans.' My father with tears lifted them all up and embraced them; when his mother advanced towards him, he bowed to the ground before her, kissed her hands, and vowed that he would always submit to her authority, and that no changes would be made by him.... They then sat down to eat so heartily—my mother did not—that I watched them with astonishment. My Aunt Tatyana helped fish-soup out of a large tureen, and, as she put bits of roe and liver on the plates, she begged all to do justice to them: 'How poor father loved the roe and the liver!'"

Now, to the self-assertive, feminist mind, imbued with industrial ideals, this scene may make no appeal. Its peace is too quiet. Here is none of the modern unrest, the boredom, the moving about in worlds unrealised. But I do not think this will be noted. The one suggestion that will leap to the thoughts is the dependent position of the women. This is true, but it is equally true that the power of the women is far greater than it is in any industrial home. And we find that such power is not exercised by the young women and on account of any sexual attraction, in the way to which we are accustomed and have come to expect, but the power is held by the mother, whose desires through life are a law to her son. I can hardly emphasise too strongly this power and influence of the mother at all times when the family is firmly established. I think it must be granted that the mother has lost her position of influence in the home wherever industrial views of life have penetrated. She has little power over her grown-up sons or even over her daughters. Self-assertion is also the desire of the children; they want to break away from the mother. Perhaps this is inevitable, and maybe it is right. It is very difficult to be certain.

I will not dwell on this question. I would, however, ask you to keep fixed in your attention this hesitation that has entered as a disease into our modern consciousness. We are without purpose, and have no absolute standard of conduct. And the result for most of us is a life of confused aims, restless and seeking, achieving by accident what is achieved at all.

There have been, of course, many separate causes and influences uniting to bring this unrest, but the disorganisation of the patriarchal home, with the change in the ideal and desires of women, has acted very strongly as a disturbing force. We have lost, especially, that harmony in life which woman alone is able to create.

Within the patriarchal family-group women lived a life that was complete in itself, the home was self-contained because it included all the elements necessary for the carrying on of a useful and healthy life. True this home life, complete as it was in itself, was not life in the fullest sense of living, for it lacked some of the larger elements that only freedom of action can give. It was for women a restricted, and, in later times, even a stunted life: in the end it came to be a parasitic life. But for long it was a natural and satisfying life and it was always entirely feminine, because motherhood embraced it all, inspiring every motive and guiding every act.

What we want is the family reconstructed, with all its historic bonds of unity and sanctity preserved and yet fitted to meet modern needs. It must be a home where life can be lived in its fulness and its depth. It is clear that this reconstruction is not going to be easy. Such a task must even be held to be absurd, if we view life from the modern standpoint, which can only be that of the doctrine of self-assertion. Where the Self is so insistent, there can be no consciousness of duty as something fixed and of life as being purposive, consecrated to an end, which may not be left or taken up. And the first thing necessary is to break through the separate aims that cause such confusion in women's thoughts and desires. No standard of action can be fixed until we know what we want. Separation must arise from self-assertion. Nothing worth doing can be done until the collective consciousness of women has found itself and regained a unifying ideal.

Life at the moment is in a state of too violent instability for any attempts to reconstruct the home to be of any avail, and, in any case, it is difficult to believe that any new form of the family can in modern times exercise the sway that the patriarchal system wielded in times gone by. And yet some standard we must have, or the confusion in women's lives will go on, and all feminine idealism must perish through the very number of its varieties.

Now, it may be that the forces which acted against the family in its past history are acting again to-day. Communal living and group homes have been tried already in the beginnings of civilisation. They were developed on account of conditions of danger which threatened the primitive family-groups, forcing them to unite with one another for mutual protection and help.[71] To-day again the home is threatened. Industrialism has steadily undermined its foundations, and changed the desire of women. Industrial workers have departed far indeed from the ideal of absolute self-dedication and service to the home that once was the supreme conception of woman. And now a further step has been taken. War has made necessary conditions that industrialism first taught women to desire. For the first time in our industrial history a demand has arisen for women's labour as pressing and large as the supply. Hundreds and thousands of women and girls have been called from their homes to carry on the necessary work of the country. There are already 195,000 women employed in munition work, while 275,000 more women are engaged in industrial occupations.[72]

Women have shown that there is hardly any work of men that they cannot do. They are driving motor-lorries, they are working on the railways, acting as conductors on trams and buses; they are doing the postman's round and carman's deliveries; they are ploughing and sowing the land; they are standing long hours at the mechanic's lathe. Women are everywhere.

And day by day the country is calling for more, and yet more women workers. They are wanted on the land, they are wanted in the factories, they are wanted in the shops, in offices, in schools, they are wanted in every kind of industry. Women will answer the call; they will take the places of those who have gone to fight, for their patriotism is as strong as the patriotism of men. That women should work to-day is unavoidable: it is war.

Yet necessary as this working of women is for the duration of war, it is equally necessary that the conditions of their labour should be regulated to meet the special needs of their feminine constitution. In all cases where women are doing men's work they should work shorter hours, have longer rests and more holidays. Do we understand what the results of overwork may be? It is racial suicide to allow adolescent girls and young women, who are, or who will be, mothers, to do work which may break into or overstrain their reserve strength, using up now what ought to be given to the next generation. A nation's wealth and future depend directly on the health and nerve reserve of its women. It is deplorable that these forces of life are being used so wastefully. I know well that in the confusion of the times it is not easy to get public attention for the needs of women workers. Yet the importance of this matter is such that delay may be disastrous.

A further consideration arises, and one, too, that is vital. After the war, what will happen? Peace is the normal state of the world and we shall return to it—some day. Are these conditions of continuous work for women to go on then? There is much to cause grave fear. Women—and I have spoken to many of them on the subject—seem to regard this taking on of men's work, not as a temporary thing forced on them by the necessities of war, but as the gaining of a goal for which for long they have been fighting.

Here is some of the talk that I have heard at women's meetings or read in recent articles by feminist writers: "New fields of action lie open to women on all sides, the opportunities are coloured with splendid possibilities"; or "The need for workers is woman's opportunity, and as such she recognises and will use it." Again, "The path lies open and clear before women, their hour has come to establish a rooted and solid foundation for the woman worker of the future." And yet again, "Woman has done more than any man could have imagined to win this war. At the same time she has won a new station for herself."

Now to me all such talk is the visible sign of the deplorable failure in women's lives. Feminists tell me that the breaking up of the individual home with the institutional rearing of children will liberate women. By this plan of reform they will be free, able to have children and also to devote themselves to gainful work. They will gain the economic independence for which they are so loudly crying. Motherhood will be but a short interruption in the professional or industrial career—mother-care a superstition of the past.

What can I say to show how misplaced and how mischievous is the outlook of those who thus turn away from the long experience of the past? It is not so that the problems of the future can be solved. The past gives us proof enough that woman's creation, the home, has been her great contribution to civilisation. No transitory needs or seeming personal gains can counterbalance the loss that must come to us as a people from woman's neglect of positive duties. There has been neglect under industrial conditions. Escape was impossible. And in our homes there has been urgent need for reform. Here I am in agreement with those who discredit the value of the home. I, too, am certain that our family and home life, in many directions, have been as bad as they could be. A radical change is needed, but I hope it will be in the opposite direction from the plan of institutional upbringing of the children, and the substitution of the communal dwelling-house for the individual home.

I know well, as every woman must know, that the creating of the right kind of home is no easy task, but one that demands the continuous presence of the mother, with an unceasing giving of herself in body and in soul.

And the trouble is that under industrial ideals of restless discontent and of pulling down the barriers, the majority of women have become more and more unfitted for efficient home-making. Of one fact I am certain. Things cannot go on as before. Here is the reason. The supervision of the home and the maintenance of any true form of family life is not compatible with the regular outside occupation of married women. Such a duplication of a woman's energies can be undertaken only by her using for herself and her work the reserve of physical, mental, and spiritual energy that should be stored and given to her children. To deny this is foolishness. Are women possessed of inexhaustible stores of energy? Do the ordinary rules of arithmetic and subtraction not hold good in their case? It would seem so. For women are maintaining that to divert so large a proportion of their energies in fresh directions will not involve any diminution of the strength available for their own affairs. Women are oddly blind.

Yet modern experience makes it daily more evident that to do any work well requires the employment of one's whole time with a complete concentration of attention. Now the woman is rare who can put the best of herself both into professional work and into her home. One or other must suffer, and since the standard required in the outside work is fixed and cannot, as a rule, be lowered, if the position is to be retained, it is the home that is certain to suffer. A wife's and a mother's duties cannot be accomplished in stray hours snatched from professional work. I speak from my own experience. I know that the attempt to do this results too often in failure, together with an intolerable overstrain.

The case is much worse with the industrial worker, the conditions of whose existence make any kind of home life impossible. What, then, is the remedy? The answer that will be given by many is the raising of women's wages to the same level as the wages of men and the improving of the conditions of labour. This will do something, but it will not do what I want. Conditions that at bottom are continuously wrong need revolutionising, not patching up. The change must be a different one, if the ideal of the home for which I am pleading is to be saved. There is one way out, and only one. The socially wasteful, racially suicidal, and body and soul withering consequences of the working of mothers outside the home must cease.

I know well the difficulties. Self-centred professional women, worldly women who have never found their souls, cultured intellectuals chasing the new, dreamers who think to reform society—all these and many other women are preaching the doctrine that the economic independence of woman is essential for her own well-being and equality with men. This, as I believe, is a profound mistake that is dependent on industrial values. But on this question I have spoken already, and I shall speak again in a later chapter.

Let us clear our thoughts absolutely, or at least as far as we humanly can, from personal standards of value. The home is not a bygone contrivance to be given up as useless in the march of humanity. Each home that is established in love will burn in its children an ineradicable impression that no folly from those who have missed its protection will be strong enough to destroy.

The demand that women shall prepare for competition with men at all costs will fall into foolishness under wiser conditions of life. This must surely be. For women's qualities and capacities are different from those of men. What is paramount in woman is secondary in man; her dominant qualities are not the same as his, but different. And by using her subordinate qualities, as she must do, in competition with man, she is up against the dominant qualities in him and will be beaten by him: on the other hand, if woman develops her dominant qualities with a wise education in youth and afterwards by training herself in the right performance of her own work, she cannot fail increasingly to occupy a position of power. And this is only another way of saying that woman can achieve her highest position only as a woman. As a worker she has at all times and in all races occupied a secondary place, as woman she is the strongest force in life. We cannot escape from nature, and no matter how seemingly urgent it is for women to train themselves to act like men on account of prevailing economic conditions, it is always wrong at the bottom to yield to those conditions: the results will not fail to bring evil in the future.

Let us know where we are going.

War conditions have rushed women forward at a racing speed on the paths which their desire previously had made them seek. If after the coming of peace the desire of women is not turned back to family duties and the home, if it still seems better and happier to them to do men's work than to do their own—then the individual home may be swallowed up and replaced by some form of communal living. This may be necessary; it can never be an ideal.

And further, let us remember that it will not be a step forward in progress; rather will it be a sign of failure, a step made necessary by the confusion and conflicts of our industrial civilisation. We delude ourselves for want of knowledge when we think that we are thus advancing to something that is new. The long houses of Iroquois Indians, the joint tenement houses of the Pueblo peoples of New Mexico and Arizona, and the village communities common among the Panang Highlanders of Sumatra are a few instances of the many early experiments in communistic life. Even Garden Suburbs have been tried by the Creek Indians of Georgia, where the natives live together in groups of associated dwellings.[73] Did I not tell you that many of the reforms we are seeking in the belief that they are new discoveries, giving proof of our progress, are really worn-out forms that are as old as mankind? They are even older. I would recall the curious experiments in co-operative child-rearing made by the Adélie penguins, noted in Chapter V. These pre-human parents would seem to be troubled with a strongly developed egoism. Craving liberty for play, they pool their families in what I may perhaps call "the primordial co-operative nursery scheme"—a plan of child-rearing much advocated by advanced feminists. Among the penguins the results are not satisfactory. True, the penguin mothers have liberty to play with the penguin fathers, but the price thereby paid is an excessively high mortality among the young birds.[74]

I recognise that co-operative nurseries and proposals for freeing mothers to work outside the home have interest for some women, and consequently have their use: they will help, no doubt, those women who while desiring and physically fit to bear children, yet have no capacity or wish to care for them. There are many such women to-day. I regard this as a great evil.

It has been left to modern intellectual women to fail utterly to understand the primary value of the home. Its first service is to immerse the child in a *protective environment of its own*. I wish to emphasise these five concluding words. They will make clearer why I believe so firmly in the patriarchal individual family. Each child needs to feel in personal connection with its surroundings—that what is nearest to him belongs to him and is his own. And this connection can be established only by love, and maintained by a lasting tradition of duty on the part of both the parents bound to each other in service to the child.

It is often objected that children are happier and healthier away from their parents, and that no conditions could possibly be worse than those which exist in countless homes. I know this. But it is no indictment against the home as an institution, rather it is an indictment of the kind of home and of the mother and the father.

I can hardly express too strongly my own want of faith in the expert child-trainer. I have found always that they regard the child, mainly, if not entirely, as something to be improved and instructed on a definite plan. The expert is never human, and the child has need of all the human element that it can get. It has absolute need of a mother and of a father. And it is impossible to be parents in the complete and right sense apart from the individual home. All experience shows us that the home, with its sympathetic relationships of mutual affection, cannot be replaced. We must insist on conditions of society that will make home life possible. The child has to accept the arrangements we make as a sacred thing, that is why this question is of such immense importance. If the matter could be fixed by the will of children, I should have no fear. The child has not lost the true values of life.

We have grown careless of the home under the blighting effects of industrialism. And the problem of the child is much more difficult in the case of modern mothers, who have few children and no strong traditions— no fixed standard of child training and of home life. Each mother is continually making personal experiments, a course of conduct that is not only harmful to the individual child, but one that must lead to collective confusion. Under such conditions excessive ardour may be as dangerous as neglect. One of the most unfortunate children I have known was an idolised only child with most conscientious modern parents, who kept a record in many large volumes of its every act and every saying. This child was trained out of childhood. There may be too much care and attention given by the parents as well as too little.

Motherhood in theory much praised, poetised, and hailed as a wonderful thing, often in actual expression is the strongest deterrent influence in the life of the child. The mother cannot realise the young life that has come from her life apart from herself. The child is too near to her. And it follows from this that her instinct and her love are not primarily concerned with the child, rather she is interested in it chiefly as its mother, that is, the birth-giver and possessor of the child. Most mothers bind their children to them much too closely with an egoistic love which is the most poisonous form of selfishness. Therefore the mother often is the real enemy in the home, the most self-centred and conservative member.

There are, of course, exceptional mothers who have the knowledge and the will to avoid such danger; mothers who as need arises are strong enough even to push their children from them at any personal cost; who insist on the freedom of each child, and see it has the opportunity to grow up harmoniously, unhampered and unspoilt, and according to its own nature. But such wise mothers to-day are few. And the average mother is like the hen with her brood, for ever fretting about her chicks if they venture away from her. In such conduct there is a terrible infringement of the personal rights of the child. Indeed, the mother too often enslaves with kindness, a bondage harder to bear and even more difficult to escape from than the brutal fist of a father.

Now, this mother-egoism will not be changed easily. It is a quality that reaches far back before human parenthood, and is instinctive and not conscious. You will recall that I referred to this in Chapter VI,[75] where I tried to find an explanation. We saw then the manner in which the maternal instinct was fixed and strengthened. The mother became chief parent, as soon as the early stages of mother-care were changed from an external to an internal process. This strengthened immeasurably the relation of the mother to the offspring, who now became an extension of her life. Before, the mother's relation to the family was not very different from the relation of the father, and was dependent on parental sacrifice and the amount of care bestowed. And one result of the change was a deepening of egoism—of the self-feeling, if I may so call it—in the mother's love, a quality which has a much deeper significance that is commonly recognised. In my opinion it is stronger in the love of the mother than it ever is in the love of the father. Mother-love is not quite the unselfish thing we have been accustomed to believe. Even the care which is bestowed so lavishly upon the child is often but the outward sign of a self-fussing anxiety, and serves no true purpose, but is a hindrance to the child's health and happiness.

I would emphasise this difference between the two parents, a difference which may be marked in the father's attitude to and affection for the child. It seems to me to be of great importance. It is the popular view among women who are too idle to think—it saves them the trouble of detecting their own faults—that all good women have an instinctive understanding of a child and of its needs. This is very far from being true. And, indeed, there are good grounds for believing—though I own I do not like to acknowledge it—that the father's guidance and sympathy are of even greater importance to the spiritual well-being and happiness of the child than the excessive care and too-absorbing love of the mother.

Here, then, is yet another reason why we must regard with profound mistrust the modern movement to break away from the tried and fixed institution of the patriarchal home. We have seen again and again in our examination of the past history of parenthood, that wherever the father has been cut off from the family and the duties in caring for the young, a deterioration has followed. The development of the individual family is most intimately connected with patriarchy. It was under this system that the father's position in the family and his right to his children were established. Nature sees to it that the tie between the mother and the child cannot be set aside; the case is different with the father, and his position in the family has to be made secure in another manner. We need to remember the degradation of fatherhood which must be connected with any matriarchal programme. And my own faith in the patriarchal family-group and the individual home, a faith that has only recently been fixed and made strong, is based upon this: I am convinced that it is the natural and, indeed, the only way of securing the loving care of both parents for the upbringing of the children.

In these days of destruction and of the pulling down of barriers, the home is exposed to peculiar danger. Much, incalculably much, depends on women's attitude. The maternal instinct, or what I would call the mother-sense, has surely lost in quality. When I think about this, I feel as if I would like to found an order for motherhood. Everything to be truly done must become a religion. And motherhood should have its ritual no less than faith. There is not a single act of duty in the home and in care given to the child which the mother may not make into a spiritual exercise of her soul. The child should be the mother's creation. She is the potter with the power to mould the clay, and she should know the rapture of the artist. I want to bring back to motherhood the quality it has lost.

The home awaits a fresh inspiration to turn back and hold the desire of women. We have to find again the right way. If we get our ideal fixed, it will be translated later into the acts of our life.

CONTENTS OF CHAPTER IX
MONOGAMOUS MARRIAGE AND WOMAN

The false view of woman's being instinctively monogamous—The Adam and Eve myth and what it symbolises—Woman's inevitable power over man—The beginnings of marriage—The maternal form—The personal relationship in marriage dependent on patriarchy—Its advantages in fixing the father to the family and the service of the home—Polygamy the most ancient form of marriage under father-right—Polygamy tends to disappear as social life develops—Monogamy the permanent form of marriage—Its supreme advantage over all other marriage forms—Our preference for monogamy goes beyond laws and religion—It is the best way we have yet found of men and women living together—The stupidity of profligacy—False intellectual views of life and of right and wrong—The sexually masterful lover—Misuse of the word love—The function of passion—Women regard love from a standpoint of unreality—The Christian view of marriage too materialistic and too ascetic—How this has reacted disastrously on marriage—The immense disturbing power of the sex emotions—We need the limiting safeguards of legal marriage—The ideal of faithfulness—The refixing of moral standards.

CHAPTER IX
MONOGAMOUS MARRIAGE AND WOMAN

"It should be remembered that the progress of a nation is stimulated and the stability of society is increased by the most humanising of all institutions, marriage."—WALTER HEAPE.

It is commonly asserted—I am not sure whether it is really believed—that woman is instinctively monogamous, whereas man by his sexual nature is bent towards polygamy.

Now, my experience and desire for truth forces me to doubt the reality of this view. I believe that the woman's superiority in this matter of constancy, even when it is present, is not fundamental to the female character any more than it is fundamental to the character of the male, and, indeed, I am inclined to think that it is the man who in his desire is more bent than woman towards complete faithfulness in the sexual partnership, and if it is the wife who more often is apparently and outwardly constant in marriage than the husband, it is because such conduct is expected of her and has been forced upon her by the conventions of her life. We must see things a little more as they are. Compared with woman, man is a comparatively constant creature, romantic, and not readily moved from his love when once it is fixed. I am very certain that I am right in this. No man leaves a woman till she sends him from her: while she wants him, and *lets him feel that she wants him*, he is hers.

What is symbolised by the myth representing Eve as first eating of the fruit and then offering it to Adam: the representation of the man in subjection to the woman, the bending of his action to her will through his need of her; the active rôle being here rightly attributed to the woman which man in the blindness of his masculine conceit has pretended to hold himself: this piece of symbolism has left deep marks throughout the entire history of marriage and is active in all the relationships of the two sexes.

Maybe woman is what man has made her; but this is an outside thing, a social tag, having reference only to her position in the world. Man has not touched woman's soul. He cannot. There are many things which a man must learn that woman knows from the beginning. To love is one of them.

Woman teaches man that, and he does not learn easily. And it is in these trials, these efforts of his to find himself, that woman contributes in so great a measure to the making or the marring, of the man. The soul of a man passes from the hollow of one woman's hand to the hollow of another's. He loves first that extension of himself called "mother," and from her he passes on to other less individualised relationships. And each woman, with cruel hands or with kind, presses deep the imprint of her hold upon his plastic clay.

Yes, it is women who mould the lives of men as it is women who give them birth.

It is strangely difficult to induce in good women to-day a practical understanding of their almost limitless power over men. Each woman is able to create perpetually in the man she loves the qualities she desires; a power infinitely greater, as I believe, than can be ever gained through individual self-assertion.

And if woman feels this power of being the source of creating energy to man (and it belongs to all women, although many of them have lost the consciousness of their gift), this knowledge is the very centre of her being, the flame which feeds life; and she is intensely and supremely happy just in so far as she is steeped in sacrifice. I do not hope, however, to convince any woman who does not know within herself already the gladness of this service to man, and I diverge a little from my main subject in making these remarks.

A glance back at the beginnings of marriage should teach women a little modesty, for there we see that the wife's constancy was directly dependent on the conditions of her marriage. Under the maternal form, where the husband lived in the home of the wife, her sexual liberty was in many cases greater than his. And there is abundant proof that full advantage was taken both by unmarried and married women of such freedom wherever it was allowed.[76] Woman is not instinctively inclined to virtue. And an inherent desire towards faithfulness in marriage has not, I am certain, always acted more strongly in women than it has in men; indeed, I am not sure that the opposite is not true.

The development of the personal relationship in marriage is intimately dependent on patriarchy. Again I am compelled to assert this truth. The establishment of paternity as a working and acknowledged fact was comparatively a late achievement. Under the conditions of the maternal clan, the family was incomplete; it consisted only of the mother and children. This was not a natural condition, and therefore was not permanent. The new stage was ushered in by what may perhaps be called "the social annunciation of paternity." And this led eventually to the establishment of marriage in the form in which we understand it to-day.

Now for the first time the home was firmly founded. The father was the head of the domestic hearth: he was the priest of sacrifice at the domestic altar. His ancestors were present in the spirit and all the members of the family honoured them. And in their presence nothing unclean was tolerated. The wife at the moment when, as a bride, she crossed the threshold of the home, or was carried across it, gave up her own kindred and her own gods. Her husband's home was now her home, his gods were her gods.[77]

So strong an insistence has been made on the evils of the wife's subjection to the husband, which arose under this system of marriage, that we have lost sight of the enduring benefits that from the beginning to the end must be connected with it. There is much nonsense talked and written about the patriarchal home. Its conditions and rules were slowly established for the workable happiness of all its members, not, as is too often assumed, arbitrarily imposed by the will of men. The duties of the husband and the wife were regulated by tradition, and all the service in the home was a holy service. By fixing the father to the family and securing his protection and toil for the children a future stability as well as fuller happiness was made possible. I do not see that this advantage could have been gained, or can now be maintained, under any other form of marriage. Nature herself seems to condemn man in his capacity as father. So delicate is the bond which binds him to the child compared with the bond which binds the mother, so readily can he be pushed outside the circle of the family, where, as a member apart, he will inevitably seek his own interests and pleasure.

The most ancient form of marriage under father-right was polygamy. Wives and children were a source of wealth in primitive communities. As a rule there was a principal wife for the procreation of legitimate children, but in addition a wealthy man had several subordinate wives or concubines. Polygamy has always been dependent on the possession of property. The position of each wife and that of her children was fixed by custom, sometimes enforced by law; in no case was a man free from obligations in regard to any woman who had "been to him as a wife"; even an unfruitful and childless woman could not be cast aside without provision being made for her. It is important to remember this. However distasteful the idea of legalised polygamy must be, and I believe it is distasteful to the majority of women and men (and this not from ethical reasons, but on account of deep and instinctive desires), it is certain that an open recognition of unions outside of marriage does prevent an escape from sexual responsibility on the part of men. I shall consider this question in fuller detail in a later chapter,[78] just now we are concerned with the development of marriage.

Out of this patriarchal polygamy monogamic marriage gradually arose. The long upward process by which the change was accomplished cannot be stated here. One factor I would emphasise, as its force has never, I think, been sufficiently recognised. Polygamy tends to disappear with the development of the conception of fatherhood. As I have asserted already, the child is bound to its mother and belongs to her whatever the form of marriage, but the same force does not act in the case of the father. The child belongs to him much more closely under monogamy than under polygamy or any other form of marriage. Now men do want the possession of their children. Thus a desire to have many children by several wives gives place to the desire to have a closer connection with fewer children born of one loved wife. As the marriage relations become more firmly established the partners in each union are held more closely to each other and to their children, and are pledged to greater purity of life.

There were, of course, many causes that contributed to this result. Chastity, first imposed upon the wife because she was the property of her husband and might transgress this rule only with his permission, came in time to bind men, though for a different reason. For the limits set to the sexual freedom of women acted also on them, since they were thus deprived of the means of obtaining women for themselves, without violating the rights of other men.

In this and other ways we find that polygamy was threatened on many sides. As an accepted and legalised form of marriage it tends to disappear with the conditions under which social life is developed. Like the maternal marriage, and other primitive experiments in sexual associations, polygamy is not a form of marriage that can be regarded as a permanent expression of the marriage law: that is, it is experimental and suitable to special conditions; it is not a final form, growing up by custom from earlier practices, or one which strives for mastery and will not tolerate other co-existent forms. On the other hand, monogamy has always been characterised by the strongest self-assertion, and from the earliest times we find it triumphing, and more and more seeking to exclude other forms of marriage.

These facts of the past history of marriage need to be considered by those who seek to bring discredit on monogamous marriage. Various reformers, too frightenedly concerned with the present shortage of men, increasing as it will enormously the disproportion between the number of the two sexes, have jumped to the conclusion that polygamy is likely to be legalised in the near future. I do not believe it. At least, it will not be polygamy under the form we have known it in the past. Polygamy has always been connected with the property value of woman and is dependent upon wealth. For this reason, even if for no other, polygamy will not replace monogamous marriages. Such a marriage system could not be supported by war-impoverished countries. The remedy must be a different one, as presently I shall show.

There is a strange idea among some people that sexual happiness can be gained by breaking away from the traditional bonds; it is the visible sign of our confusion as a people and the want of happiness in our lives. We should not set at naught the experience of the ages. Polygamy is an institution which in the growth of civilisation belongs only to primitive or non-progressive states. No race or nation has ever risen to front rank, or even secondary rank, under this marriage system. Our preference for monogamy goes beyond laws and religions. It is that deeply rooted thing—a matter of racial experience and desire. It is the best way that we have yet found of men and women living together.

The individual household, where both parents share in the common interest of bringing up the children, is the foundation on which monogamy has been built up and on which it must stand. If the conditions of the home are seriously changed, and the duty of providing and caring for the children is taken out of the hands of either or of both parents, a change in marriage practice will follow. I do not think you can hold the one if you let the other go. For Westermarck is right, and children should not be regarded as the result of marriage, but rather marriage is the result of children. And love between parents implies duties and sorrows on each side; without this, love, even of the most passionate kind, loses its quality and tends to become an ephemeral or even a corrupt thing.

There is much stupidity in the view of many reformers of marriage who fail to see that, however hard it is to live faithfully as man and wife, the monogamic ideal of marriage does so appeal to our emotional nature, that men and women are seriously unhappy in trying to destroy it. Fortunately it is easier to talk of "love's freedom" than it is to act as if it ever could be free. In spite of what advanced people say, some feeling of duty will always exist as long as it at all hurts us to hurt others. The immorality that says, "Do what you desire irrespective of others," is as yet beyond most of us.

Attempts to solve these problems quickly are bound to fail. Intellectual revolutionists are, I think, too hopeful with regard to what may be done to produce a harmony of sexual needs. The optimism that once prevailed in economics is being transformed to sexual matters. Once people supposed that if every one followed his own interests, a harmony would automatically establish itself in the economy of society. Now they tend to say the same about sex. They put forward many solutions, but they do not as a rule make use of these solutions, even when they could, in their own lives. They say what they do not believe, either with conscious insincerity, or because they are ignorant of life and are used to trying to get effects with words.

Intellectual views of life and of what is right and wrong always tend to break people into groups, each struggling to explain everything according to one theory, built on a single principle. And as the result of caring so much for one thing people seem quite unable to grasp any facts that do not refer to their own one particular reform, they are not even able to consider it as part of a world in which there is anything else. All the evil in marriage is due to too large families and population pressing on the food supply, we are told by one class of enthusiasts, while others point to men's tyranny over women. Votes for women would have a magical effect: men are all bad, say some. The father is a parasite, unnecessary except for his share in begetting the child; the mother is the one parent. All would be well if legal marriage were abolished and motherhood made free, is the view common among one class of reformers. Eugenical breeding and the sterilisation of the unfit is the remedy brought forward by others. Many suggest economic changes and the endowment of motherhood.

But the matter is not so simple as these reformers seem to believe. And I doubt if any outward change is really capable of producing the prompt kind of penny-in-the-slot results that its supporters claim that it can. The complexity of marriage, in particular, the occurrence of sexual disharmonies so present and active for misery to-day, are ignored by all intellectual reformers. It is because they have no emotional hold of life as a whole that they find it easy to squeeze all life into their magic theories. For myself I can see no sure remedy: and were I asked to state one, I could say only: "A few thousand years more of development: a growth towards consciousness and a fuller understanding of the meaning of life."

Marriage is not a matter of abstract principles: it will always be difficult. If it is anything that can be stated, it is a social practice, preserving unity and order amongst those who find these qualities of service in the art of living. We should humble ourselves to accept the lessons of life, then we should be more careful of simple human needs.

A very slight knowledge of existing marriages is sufficient to convince even the most optimistic believer that true mating is hard. I do not believe that most marriages are unhappy, but I do know that only the very few are happy. With many partners, and even those who are passionate lovers, the attraction of sex always seems to fall short of its end; it draws the two together in a momentary self-forgetfulness, but for the rest it seems rather to widen their separateness; they are secret to one another in everything, united only in the sexual embrace.

And the man who has not found his way already to the soul of a woman by some other means, will not do so through the channels of sex. For a woman wants to be loved for what she is, not for what the man wants from her. And for this reason those men who have in them no faculty for friendship will be likely always to meet with coldness on the part of their wives in response to their continued ardour. Such men do not understand that despite all their sexual proneness they are psychologically impotent.

The word love is used in so general and indiscriminate a way to denote sometimes the most transitory impulse, and sometimes the most intimate and profound feeling, that a mass of misunderstanding arises. Love comes from the senses as well as from the soul, and the one emotion often is mistaken for the other. And what this serves to bring home to us is the dualism inherent in the marriages of a civilised age, in which the element of sexual masterfulness, being a natural expression of masculinity, is unintentionally active, a survival of very primitive instincts, which to-day struggle for mastery with newer emotions and sympathy, flaring up in a late expression to justify the need for sexual contrast.

It is, however, very necessary for me to guard against my meaning being mistaken, in case I should be thought to be supporting the view that men are less capable than women are of unselfish love, and feel only passion. I do not understand such a distinction. Possibly it is true that affection can exist without passion, though if by "passion" sex-feeling is meant, it certainly is not true; and assuredly passion is the great and important part of love—nay, rather, it is Love itself.

The truth is this: Women have been taught for generations to look on love from a standpoint of unreality, and when in marriage they are forced to face some great fact in life, they are shocked and disillusioned. It is useless for women to go on acting as if sex desire was something of which nice people ought to be ashamed. Marriage is really a contract in which the woman undertakes certain sexual duties as well as the man, and the woman has the advantage, for she possesses all that the man most wants.

We may not safely ask too much or too little from marriage or take too high or too low a view of it. But the Christian view of the nature of marriage is at once too materialistic and too ascetic. The ancient world looked on marriage as a religious duty. "To be mothers were women created, and to be fathers men." Christianity permitted marriage, but only as a necessary evil against the temptations of lust. "It is better to marry than to burn."

This is, of course, a long past story. But such hateful view of marriage has left in every Christian land an inheritance of evil. The sexual life was considered impure and a concession to the lower nature in man; true purity of life was to be attained only in celibacy. Small wonder that marriage, thus regarded as an escape from worse evil and a cover to laxity of sexual conduct, is often so immoral. We see at once that the main evil of this gross misunderstanding of love must have fallen upon women. The woman was there just to keep the man in condition and from sin. I can hardly over-estimate the disastrous consequences both to marriage and to women of this unholy view of the sexual relationship.

The false glorification of asceticism, which denies the true nature of marriage while at the same time professedly regarding marriage as a sacrament, has involved a corresponding and unhealthy classifying of love into higher and lower, the spiritual and the physical; and the action of this double standard in the sexual life has led, on the one side, to the setting up of a theoretical ideal of conduct which, as few are able to follow it, tends to become an empty form, and this, on the other side, has led to a hidden laxity, within marriage and outside it.

I have emphasised this question of the unholy ascetic view of marriage because of its unspeakable evil, not only for women, but for the waste it entails to the race. It is the basis of most of the failures and diseases in our sexual life. As you know, our moral and religious systems regard the body as the prison of the soul, and pay consequently no attention whatever to the body from the moral point of view. I desire a regeneration of all the instincts of the body through consciousness. I desire this much more for the health and happiness of women themselves than I do for the enjoyment of men.

But it is not going to be easy. The education of the senses is quite a new thing, and it is not even allowed to most women to possess them. The principle of "re-discovery" will have to be begun. We must teach woman that she wants love for herself; the man must not claim it from her as a right he has bought by marriage.

Most women and some men do not realise (at least, they do not openly acknowledge) the immense disturbing power of sex and the claims the sexual life makes at some time on us all. To hear many people talk you would think it were possible to free ourselves at will of all those troubles and prejudices of sex that are our heritage from an uncountable past. Love is something fiercer than hand-holding in the darkness of the cinema, or moon-gazing in the parks.

In fear we try to keep the blinds down so that love may be decently obscured. Yet how can we ever begin to understand and deal with these problems of sex unless we will admit all the instincts and tendencies which ever lead us backwards to the more elemental phases of life? The deepest of the emotions is sex, and its action, like all the emotions that are fundamental, may be traced into a thousand bye-paths of the ordinary experience of each of us; it exercises its influence on every period of our development, and works subconsciously to control our actions in endless ways that we refuse to acknowledge.

Hence the conflicts which manifest themselves so strangely and so fiercely in our lives. The emotional self refuses at times to be controlled by the reason self. Restraint cannot do much, and indeed, often brings deeper evil. For our unconscious selves are stronger than all the pretences we have set up by our conscious wills, either as individuals to encourage our own deceit or collectively as a nation in the hope of controlling conduct.

This is why so much that is said to-day about sexual conduct is so foolish. The real question is not what people *ought to do*, but what they *actually do* and want to do, and, therefore, are likely *to go on doing*. It is these facts that the reformers of marriage almost always fail to face.

Having said this much, you will readily understand why I regard as necessary for the morality of marriage some public recognition of the relationship, and some accepted standard of conduct in it. We cannot, remembering the inherent defectiveness of our wills, safely hesitate and experiment in the liberties we can allow and the limits we must set to a force so strong as sexual love. Still less can we allow to be done in secret and in shameful darkness things that we will not face in the light. The unregulated union in any form does not seem to me to be practicable. Our sexual relationships are, or ought to be, so hedged about by duties, obligations, and consequences, that sexual conduct can never be considered as a personal question, and any society that permits such a view, whether openly acknowledged or secretly accepted, opens the way to real immorality and great unhappiness.

Not all who cry "It is useless," can do without the limiting safeguards of legal marriage. We still feel the serpent's sting of jealousy, and the old questions, "Where do you come from?" "What have you been doing to-night?" "Who handled your body till daytime, while I watched and wept?" "In what bed did you lie and whom did you gladden with your smile?" are still felt in the heart, even if not uttered by the lips, of the most advanced and emancipated husbands and wives. For often we are forced into acts over which reason has no control. And our sex judgments are not merely moral, not just questions of understanding and forgiving, but also physical questions of the nerves, of the blood, of the fiercest instinct.

And marriage, I say, the old patriarchal marriage that the advanced people and the idealists alike scoff at, is necessary for most of us—it does through its checking influence help us, and, by setting clear limits and prescribing a fixed code of conduct, it certainly hinders, if it cannot destroy, irregular manifestations of love. Moreover it does, by its ideal of faithfulness and duty to one mate, turn the imagination to desire fidelity. It is not so much that we could not love others, but that we shall not want to do so. Our desire is the first necessity: all else will follow. It is the seed of everything that can grow up in marriage: it is the true magic power. And this desire is always active, every real marriage is a continual renewing of interest through love, and, if the partners are not interested in each other, they will seek for something else.

If we try to be faithful to one another in marriage, instead of outside of it, there will be for most of us a greater chance of enduring happiness than is likely under conditions where each individual couple sets up a standard of sexual conduct for themselves.

Our minds to-day are certainly in conflict, and, in my opinion, it will be impossible to make much change in all that is wrong without the refixing of moral standards. There is no kind of unity in our desires: we do not know what we want. We have broken down without building up. And when traditional rules for conduct are absent there must be confusion. For the existence of many standards, each with its own theory of what is good, is an evil which opens a clear way for license and unhappiness.

As I have tried to show, the two great faults of the modern reform movements connected with marriage and sexual conduct are their instability and externality. These faults are the direct result of too much intellectualism and too much individualism. We have gone astray because we have thought chiefly of our own immediate wants and been over eager for experience, without considering what the result of our action must be to others in the future. We have had no clear vision of evil and good. I feel almost that a mistaken vision—so long as it was a vision common to us all—would be better than no vision at all, which really is the result when each one of us gazes at our own particular star. This has been the blasting modern disease. And our inability to set up plain standards of right and wrong, with no ideals to strive after, has left vacant room for false ideals.

For I hold that the broad direction of our conduct follows straight from our faith. To believe in marriage is to want to do right in marriage. Then do we fail, and our own union comes to disaster, it will be a personal failure, not a collective failure; we shall blame ourselves, not the institution of marriage. And to have this faith in marriage as a people—not as a law imposed upon us, but a necessary binding that we accept of our own wills—will bring us again to be unified by a comprehending idea: an ideal of purpose and duty to one another and among us all in our sexual conduct, and in this way we shall be helped in right-doing. Carried onwards by a ruling motive, we shall find unity of desire, with its value to life of an absolute standard. It is for this reason I care so deeply that the monogamic ideal of marriage—the living faithfully to one mate in thought and deed—should be held sacred by us all: held sacred, however greatly we may fail as individuals to attain to this ideal. Our failures in faithful living may bring disaster to ourselves. But the institution of marriage can be hurt much more by the fading and loss of our belief in the duty of faithfulness.

CONTENTS OF CHAPTER X
MONOGAMOUS MARRIAGE AND WOMAN: A CONTINUATION OF THE PREVIOUS CHAPTER, WITH SOME REMARKS ON THE CHARACTER OF WOMAN

Some men and women unfitted for faithful mating—The enforced continuance of an unreal marriage—This leads to immorality—The real controlling power in marriage is our desire—The need for honourable divorce—The immorality present in many marriages—We accept monogamy but tolerate hidden extra-conjugal relationships—This worse than regulated polygamy—The necessity of distinguishing between sex passion and the desire for a child—All women do not want to be mothers—The sins that follow the binding of such women in the bonds of monogamous marriage—The child born against the will of its mother—A contrast between two types of women—The siren woman and the maternal woman—An attempt to explain such difference—The pleasure factor in sex—Our ignorance in all matters relating to sex—An instance of the siren type of woman as a mother.

CHAPTER X
MONOGAMOUS MARRIAGE AND WOMAN: A CONTINUATION OF THE PREVIOUS CHAPTER, WITH SOME REMARKS ON THE CHARACTER OF WOMAN

"That the first decade of the child life of all mankind age after age passes continuously through the hands of woman seemed to him one of the most significant facts in the whole range of human affairs."—*Life and Letters of Edward Thring.*

I trust from what I have said already on marriage in the previous chapter that two things have been made plain: on the one side, my own strong faith in monogamous marriage as the most practical and happiest form of association for the great majority of women and men; and my further opinion that sexual relationships must be regulated by law. I am, however, deeply conscious of the ignominious conditions of many marriages, and thus, on the other side, I am forced to the opinion that for the whole of sexual conduct there cannot safely be one only rule. I know well there will always be exceptions: men and also women who are unfitted for faithful mating. It is this fact we do not face that makes the problem so difficult to solve at all and to solve completely impossible.

Regarding companionship as essential in any true union, the reform most likely to produce a balance of good in marriage is such an alteration in the basis of marriage and increased spirituality in the way of conceiving it as will make incompatibility of temperament, resulting in inability to maintain companionship, justify honourable divorce. To consider sexual infidelity as the only valid ground for divorce is to take a limited and wrong view of marriage. Spiritual unfaithfulness may be a far greater sin, and one bringing much deeper unhappiness in marriage, than sexual unfaithfulness.

It may seem that this view is a contradiction of what I have said of the enduring character of marriage. I do not think so. No marriage that should be maintained will ever be broken by making divorce easy. It will add nothing to the sanctity of marriage to force those who are really unmated to remain mated by law. One marvels at the folly of such a view. I want people to enter into marriage and to remain in it, because they want to be there, not because they are forced.[79]

For I do believe that the great majority of women and men do really desire to live faithfully with one mate. Divided allegiance is possible only where love is of a slight character. If it is absorbing it cannot be diffuse, and the more diffuse it is the less the partners in such a union will be able to give or take from one another. It is impossible to be lovers and partners in the fullest and most human sense in several unions.

The real controlling power in marriage is our desire, though our acts may be, and usually are, directed as well by habit and tradition—a sort of conscience and feeling for the judgment of others. And divorce can never be easy while it at all hurts us to hurt one another.

I must, however, reaffirm my opinion that sexual relationships, whether within marriage or outside of it, whether legal or free, can never safely be unregulated, and will always be a difficult experiment. And experience has forced on me the knowledge that the most passionate union is often the one most likely to end in disaster. For Buckle is not far from right when he says we accumulate knowledge, but do not progress in morals, which depend on the unaltered heart of man.

Some characters are manifestly and essentially unfaithful, self-seeking, and regardless of the happiness of others in love and in all the affairs of life. Others again act unfaithfully through weakness or haste, or through the misfortune of circumstances. The mistake with many of these people is that they ever bind themselves in permanent unions. We should not condemn or deal harshly with them, for by so doing we drive them to undertake obligations which they do not, because they cannot, fulfil. In my opinion, it is foolishness to pretend that for the whole of sexual conduct there can ever be one fixed rule. We shall have more morality, not less, if we accept this.

It is for this reason that I am altogether persuaded of the need of much greater facilities of divorce than exist at present: divorce on the ground of mutual consent, and based on inability through any cause to maintain true partnership in marriage.

There are some men and also women unsuited for marriage and quite undesirable as life-partners; they are not, however, undesirable because of the legal bond, but because of certain qualities which as individuals they possess. And this wider facility of divorce would do very much to lessen individual hardships, and moreover it would cleanse, in a way not sufficiently recognised, the immorality which is present in many unions. Marriage, with its fixed duties and the restrictions it does impose, in particular, upon the woman, will always appear to some a bondage from which they will seek the quickest way of escape. If no honourable way is allowed to them, they will take a dishonourable course. This may be deplored, it cannot (at any rate under existing conditions of character and public opinion) be helped, and nothing but evil can follow by pretending it is not so.

Thus we find that the difficulty of divorce is the strongest factor that brings disgrace and immorality into marriage.

This matter of honourable divorce is, however, one only of the almost countless questions in the tangle of considerations involved in the difficult matter of any attempt to change sexual conduct. More important, perhaps, is the great disproportion between the two sexes in a country that calls itself and tries to be monogamous. In our society, where so many conditions and causes have corresponded to make marriage more and more difficult, there are a very large number of women and also some men, and will be for a long time, who, from necessity rather than from choice, have to seek to satisfy their sex needs and to find love in the best way that they can. I do not see that we can or ought to condemn without fuller knowledge than as a rule we can have, these breaches of the prohibitions and laws of marriage: I am very certain that no good can be gained by branding those who commit them as sinners. Rather the conditions that give rise to such conduct must be openly faced and wherever possible dealt with. War, acting as it must inevitably do in increasing these evils and making marriage more difficult for many women, perhaps will bring us to do this. Changes in our laws may be forced upon our acceptance. We shall have to be more careful to protect life and to prevent waste of the powers of life. We cannot, therefore, I think, go on, in this question of the sex needs that are not satisfied in marriage, with the old game of pretence, that no irregular conduct need be considered as long as it can be hidden, or at least not publicly acknowledged.

But of sexual relationships outside of marriage I shall speak in a separate chapter.[80] The question is too urgent to be dealt with hastily. I shall state what seems to me can be done to regulate these unlegalised unions so as to free them, as far as this is possible, from the secrecy and shamefulness which acts, I am certain, as the strongest factor in the distress and evil which they do almost inevitably bring, both to the individuals who enter into them and to the society which tolerates, but does nothing to protect, them.

In the past, we have failed sufficiently to recognise the immorality which is present in many marriages. Monogamy has in reality never been attained either by ancient civilisations or in the modern world. Thus, while accepting monogamy, we tolerate extra conjugal relationships, which can be regarded only as a hidden polygamy, and, indeed, from one practical point of view, it is even worse in its results than a well-understood and regulated polygamy, as these fugitive unions, being unrecognised, carry with them no obligations. And the action of this double standard of sexual morality, with its concealed element of lying hypocrisy, has brought, and rightly brought, into discredit legal monogamous marriage; it has led on the one side to the setting up of an ideal of marriage conduct which, as many in fact actually do not follow it, tends to become an outward form, and this on the other side leads to a concealed laxity in practice, which results only too frequently in irresponsible unions, hidden diseases and blasted motherhood, the most terrible of the evils in our disordered sexual life of to-day. Facts of daily observation may not be shuffled out of observation by any hypocrisy. They must be faced and dealt with.

The question becomes clearer, if we consider that some people, men as well as women, have a great desire for children; or possibly as the desire is not always consciously recognised, it would be truer to say that with them the sexual impulse is more deeply rooted. I mean, though it is very difficult in words to express this, that erotic desire is less personally overmastering, that they are in truer relation with the race—one link in the long chain of the generations. This being so, the getting of a child is the ultimate, though rarely, I think, the conscious, satisfaction of sex; while for others—and this is true of some women quite as much as it is true of many men—sexual relations are in themselves the final gratification of love. Children may come, but they are born because of the operation of this strictly personal impulse or need of the parents.

It is, I think, very necessary to distinguish between sex-passion and the desire for a child; they are not the same, though, of course, the one impulse may be, and is as a rule, involved in the other. We need more clear thinking and frank speaking on the two elements in the reproductive act. This is a human problem, one that belongs to mankind alone; moreover, it has greatly increased among civilised races, and is likely to become more, and not less, difficult with the advance of time. Animals have sex-passion, which is neither love as we feel it nor lust; with them, as also in some degree with most primitive peoples, this passion is seasonal, not always active, and is more or less closely connected with the obtaining of offspring. Far different and much more complicated are the conditions of love among us to-day. Men and women have a continuous desire for love, with sex-passion as its outward expression and children for its efflorescence. They also have lust, which is a comparatively new expression,[81] at least, that is my opinion as to what is true of the majority among us. I do not use the word "lust" here in any sense of contempt, but to express strong and conscious sex-passion, seeking its own satisfaction without connection with any possible result in a child. Then at a much lower level there is lust-desire without love, or clothed merely in a rootless ephemeral mimicry of passion—a libertinage having no law but curiosity in self-indulgence. And all passion is a very different thing from the serene considerations which, according to the Prayer Book, cause men and women to marry.

Now, it is because of what sex-passion has come to be among us—its variety in desire and in result—that we are far more remote than pre-human and primitive parents from having marriage and parenthood settled so as to meet the desires and sex-needs of every one, as would be easily possible if the reproductive act could be regarded as being solely, or even chiefly, connected with the birth of children.

I do not know if I have made my meaning perfectly clear, but what I wish to insist upon is this: It is necessary in all questions and judgments connected with marriage to consider the presence or absence in the partners of the wish to produce and possess a child. I propose to deal briefly with this question in relation to the character of women.

It is commonly asserted that the normal woman desires to be a mother. Now, this may be true, but what is forgotten is that all women are not normal, and thus there are many who not only have no desire to become mothers, but exceedingly dislike the idea of bearing children. You may say this is an unnatural condition; but such a use of the word "unnatural" is surely wrong; nothing is "natural" to the man or woman save what they have evolved, and by that I mean what they have come to desire to be; and my contention is that we have evolved a type of woman unsuited for motherhood because she does not desire it, and for such a woman it is "unnatural" to be a mother. Of course this turning away from motherhood is in numerous cases the result of wrong education, and is dependent on the weakened constitutions and shaken nerves of women, which forces them to fear the pains of child-birth, as well as inducing an increasing dislike to the restrictions and duties that the care of children will entail. These causes are strong to-day; doubtless they hold back many women from becoming mothers, but I do not think that they take us very far to the deeper hidden causes which are also present among us, nor can they be regarded as essential factors in deciding the question as to which women should be mothers. There is something acting much more strongly, a cause which must be sought in the character of woman herself, and one which, unlike those dependent on outside conditions, cannot, I think, be altered. You see, I regard the true instinct for motherhood as a quality directing all expression, something deep-seated in the nature, and therefore a quality that cannot be added to a character if the woman does not possess it.

And because I believe this, I regard any effort to force maternity, even as an ideal, upon all women as a great wrong. We do not expect all men to desire to be fathers, we must cease to expect all women to desire to become mothers. For by so doing we cause more evil than we know. And the hurt is not borne by the mother alone. The child born against the will of its mother must tend also to be without will; too weak to bear well the stress and struggle of life. This is no fanciful statement. I believe it can be proved by any one, with sufficient knowledge, who takes the trouble to investigate the facts. The child who is born through the physical mastery of the father and the physical subserviency of its mother, and against her desire, does pay the penalty in a heritage which lacks stability and harmony in character.

One of the many hypocrisies of our society to-day is the condemnation, still maintained by many who do not understand, of the use of the many safe artificial preventatives to conception. The mother must be given more control over the birth of her children. Personally I have not a strong feeling against the procuring of abortion, but perhaps the forbidding of it is necessary as a fence around the reverence for human life; but the prevention of birth is a different matter. And certainly each woman must be free to make her own choice as to whether she bears children or does not bear them; no man, and still more no social or moral compulsion, may safely decide this matter for her; she must give life gladly to be able to give it well.

Nor must we look with disfavour on those women who desire to avoid motherhood and its duties, or regard them as "unnatural"—this word, as I have just said, is used far too carelessly. It were well to remember that the parental instinct is not fixed and is dependent on causes that very few of us understand, that it is not present in all women any more than the fighting instinct is present in all men.

A vast amount of stupid confusion arises from our failing to accept the wide diversity in women's temperaments and characters in relation to this question of motherhood. Between the more usual type of woman, whose deepest desire and strongest instincts are fixed in motherhood, and the woman at the other extreme to whom even the thought of maternity is a terror, there are a wide range of intermediate types—women able to love and even in some respects markedly feminine, but with weak maternal feeling. Such diversity in the family qualities has always existed. We have seen in our past study of the family that the maternal instincts may be overlaid and even destroyed, being replaced by others more clearly masculine. Examples of this are found in the insect world, and striking examples among fishes and reptiles, where the father is the true parent and undertakes all duties connected with the young. The case of the phalaropes furnished us with a further remarkable instance of this reversal in the characters of the two sexes. Things are not quite as dramatic, perhaps, in the human world, but they are more fateful, more significant. And such changes in the expression of the emotions, dependent as they would seem to be on changes in the sexual character, can be effected, for every individual of one sex has in him or her the qualities of the other sex in a less degree; and any special circumstance or alteration in the conditions of life which acts on an individual or group of individuals in an opposite direction from the ordinary, may succeed in modifying and, in some cases, transforming the deep impulses of sex.[82]

I do not wish to follow this question here. It is, however, widely evident that in the society we have evolved to-day there are many women in whom, what I may perhaps call, an atrophy of the maternal instincts has taken place. This may be regretted, it cannot wisely be blamed, for it forms no solution of the problem thus to mark down for blame. There is one way, and one way only, as far as I can see, whereby this great evil that has happened and still is taking place might be stayed. The maternal women, the mother type, should be the only women to be mothers; which is, of course, the same thing as saying that every child should be born of passionate desire.

But this is not so simple in practice as at first sight it seems; it carries with it first the demand that women must be given the knowledge and means to prevent the conception of every undesired child; and second, and even more important, that all girls should be educated to understand something at least of their sexual nature so that they may know their own need and strongest instincts; then, does their desire turn towards motherhood, they will be better able to choose as the father of their children men who desire to be fathers as they desire to be mothers, so that together they may decide the number of children they will bring into the world and under what conditions. That is the only kind of motherhood that will endure.

I am prepared for an objection here. I shall be told that a woman, much less a girl, does not know whether she wants a child until she bears one; that it is then her maternal instinct will develop. I do not believe it. I find this is the opinion of men and of women who have failed to think straight; both judge in these matters too arbitrarily and with too little understanding. They forget how difficult it has been, and still is, for any one of my sex to be at all sexually truthful. Considering the folly of the education we give to girls, there is little reliance to be placed on what any woman says about sex. What we need most of all is the liberation of women's instincts through education in consciousness. Perhaps, then, we shall cease to expect the impossible, by which I mean we shall not hope to make good mothers of the girls who have no deep instinct to love children. I know, of course, that the girl who before marriage does not love children, may, and as a rule will, love her own child: but I am certain that in nine cases out of every ten she will do so in the wrong way; the child will be cherished only as a possession of herself, an extension of her own egoism, which is very far indeed from what I hold as the self-giving character of the mother-woman. Here is one reason why good motherhood is so rare.

One source of great error arises because of the hypocrisy that society still forces upon women in all questions of sex, and in particular on this matter of their wanting, or not wanting, to be mothers. You see, the desire for a child is allowed to them, but it is not yet allowed to them to desire love without the child. We are a strange people. And this belief, instilled into us by puritanism and a religion which denies simple human needs, that sex enjoyment is immoral without the purpose of procreation, has been a most degrading influence. It has done great harm. It has poisoned the lives of thousands of women and men; but the greatest of the evils it has wrought is that, under its influence, countless children have been born, both in marriage and outside of it, against the will of their mothers. Until it is openly recognised that women are not alike in their sexual natures any more than they are alike in their outward appearance, that they cannot all be classed together as the mother-sex, this evil cannot be changed; the old hypocrisy will continue and children will verily be born in sin, for they will be born without the mother's desire, and for this the race must pay the penalty.

We have, I am sure, to face the fact of the general occurrence among us of women of the siren type; they are the exact opposite to the mother type. With them the "pleasure factor"[83] in the sexual act is the aim and end of love: this results, as it seems to me, in an intensified egoism, which has far-reaching effects first in the woman's attitude to the man, as later in her attitude to her children. The siren woman is the property of all men, or rather it would be much nearer to the truth to say that all men are her property. I do not think such a woman can ever remain satisfied with one mate, though circumstances may hold her apparently faithful to her marriage vows. She is quite unsuited for monogamous marriage, unless, indeed, she finds a man of a similar type whom she has perpetually to reconquer. Even then there must be variety in each conquest to provide the excitement necessary with both to stimulate love. Such a woman, as, of course, also the man, is always unsuited for the selfless sacrifices of parenthood. She is the natural prostitute, who absorbs everything in sex for her own desire.

The case is quite different with the mother type, and her relation to the man is not the same; true, she also seeks and uses the man, the difference is not here. Woman is better equipped for the sex-battle than is man. There is nothing wrong in this. I hold that a woman should be able to take the man she loves as her right; she does take him now, but in ways that too often should make both herself and him ashamed. The mother-woman exercises her right of choice as the representative of Nature. She is the fount of the race, she seeks the man as her helper and because he will give life to the child she desires. Such a woman is not always faithful in marriage, but she wishes to be so, and she will be faithful in actual fact, if she is fortunate and finds in her lover the fitting father she seeks unconsciously for her children.

Of course, this is a purely arbitrary classification; the two types of character mingle in most women. There are traces of the siren in every woman, and no woman—though I am less certain here—is entirely devoid of the maternal instinct.

It is very difficult to know the truth. But it seems to me that, when from any cause the pleasure factor in sex becomes secretly over-accentuated, as it may so easily do under conditions where full sex expression is denied to many women, the normal sexual impulses are in some cases weakened or even atrophied through disuse, while in others satisfaction is gained in secret erotic practice, and by so doing the character and these deep impulses receive a twist in an unhealthy direction, leading or at least tending to an inflaming of the egoistical desires, which, if long continued, will increase to crowd out, like an overgrowth of some poisonous weed, the more tender plant of the parental instinct. While certainly not presuming to speak with authority on so difficult a subject, I think that the suggestion I have made may possibly afford an explanation of the poverty of the mother instinct in some women compared with its richness in other women. I plead for a patient recognition of the fact that in all these deep matters relating to sex we are still very ignorant.

Let me now give an example that quite recently came under my notice, of a woman who, though a mother, was without any glimmering flicker of maternal feeling. It seems to me to be worth recording as being the most striking case I have met of the siren type of woman, who, if I am right, is occupying a wrong place in any monogamous marriage. Facts speak more forcibly than any mere statements.

In a boarding-house at which I was staying there was a young and beautiful mother. She had borne seven children, of whom the two youngest were with her, a boy of about five and a baby a year old. She had with her also a young niece of about seven years of age. They were healthy and, I should judge, charming children. The mother apparently had no love for them whatever. It was a most extraordinary case. Physically this woman was fitted to bear children, but she was clearly without any capacity for caring for them. She reminded me of the phalarope mothers, who seek love adventures and leave the charge of their children to the fathers. In this case the father was not present: the guardian of the baby was the niece. I never saw a more patient worker than this tiny child. I do not know whether it was fear held her to her task. She did not play: all day she tended, and worked, and watched. Sometimes she was assisted by the tiny boy, her cousin.

Here is one out of many conversations that I chanced to overhear.

Harry, the boy, called to his cousin—

"Susie, I have washed baby's napkins, what shall I do now?"

She answered, "Begin to get the food ready; I will come in a minute to boil the milk."

This is no exaggeration, I state exactly what I heard.

Now, it is no use shrieking out that this woman's conduct is unnatural and a libel on motherhood. If the maternal instinct was a fixed instinct and bore good fruit only, this might be done. The objection to the wrong kind of women being mothers is precisely that it inevitably produces some such results. This woman simply followed the promptings of her own desires: the difference was that she did it much more frankly than is usual. She employed the days in playing croquet and tennis and in flirting with any available male. I do not think she knew she was not a good mother. At intervals, when she remembered, she scolded the children; but when she forgot them, which was frequently, she left them alone.

Often I talked with her, as she interested me very strongly. I wished that I could have known her early history, and especially some details of her sexual life. I could but guess, still I do not think I was mistaken. She told me quite frankly that she did not like children, though she added (clearly, though quite unconsciously, speaking conventionally), "Of course, I love my own children." Then (lapsing again into truth) she went on bewailing the length of the school holidays (the little boy and the girl were both at boarding-school) and her present position of being without a nurse to look after the baby. On the occasion of another conversation she told me that she did not care for men. I answered, "Probably not, but you like them to care for you." She laughed and seemed pleased, and asked me how I knew this.

Now, this woman was to me a most interesting study. A friend who was staying with me at the time blamed her very severely. I think this was unfair. What was clear to me was that life was demanding from this woman what she could not give. She was strongly sensual without being passionate; she was probably philoprogenitive or she would not have had so many children; but she was not at all maternal, and was quite unfitted to be entrusted with any child. She was not immoral—at least, I think not; probably she was faithful in the usual meaning to her husband. In her world the price was too high to make unfaithfulness worth while; but she was wholly non-moral. Such a woman should not marry; she should never be a mother. I would go even further and say her place was the place of the prostitute. This judgment may seem hard. Yet I know of no other remedy. You cannot alter these things by pretending they are not there. And the expression of sex is always a question of refinement and of character.

CONTENTS OF CHAPTER XI
SEXUAL RELATIONSHIPS OUTSIDE OF MARRIAGE

My purpose in writing on this subject—No desire to lessen responsibility—The great difficulties of such an inquiry—A return to the question considered in the previous chapters on marriage—

Some women and men unsuited for monogamous marriage and the duties of parenthood—The evils that must arise when those unfitted for true monogamy are forced to live under its cover—Sex subjects usually viewed either with false sentiment or with vulgarity—Shameful concealments and sniggering do not lead to true chastity—These bad conditions exert more influence on men than on women—Celibacy as unnatural and harmful in women as in men—One form of union can never be imposed for every one—Is secrecy advantageous to society—Effect of economic conditions and pressure of opinion—Without some change prostitution and the degradation of the more honourable partnerships outside marriage must be accepted—The position of the mother must always be secured—The war has caused increased independence of women—The war as well will cause a shortage of men and probably a period of poverty—These must act as further causes of avoidance of marriage—At the same time the nation will have an increased need for children—More than one form of sexual association required—The highest types of men and women should live in monogamous marriage—For others the sterile temporary union—The law should establish contracts providing for the woman in such relationships—Advantages of this procedure—Increase not hinder morality.

CHAPTER XI
SEXUAL RELATIONSHIPS OUTSIDE OF MARRIAGE

"All love must have its responsibilities, or it will degrade and dissipate itself in mere sentiment or sensuality."

I find this sentence written in an old notebook, one that for a long time I have not been using. I took the book up by chance, when my eyes lighted on this saying; at once I decided to place it at the beginning of this chapter on sexual relationships outside of marriage. I want to make it clear at the very start that it is far indeed from my purpose to make easy the way of irregular unions or at all to loosen the responsibilities that ought to bind men and women.

The difficulties of writing upon all questions of sexual conduct are very real. Almost always one is suspected of advocating license and of disbelief in marriage, so commonplace is it to misunderstand, so easy to misrepresent. For not only is there prejudice to encounter, which on no question is so obstinate as it is on this one that we are now considering of unregulated love, but we have to deal with so many different problems, taking account of many opposed facts, where threads are crossed and entangled and at best can be patched only roughly together. I plead for a patient recognition of the real seriousness of this problem, which, I am certain, will have to be faced in the near future if our sexual life and marriage are to be freed from secret disgrace that is unbearable.

We have found in the two previous chapters what all of us must know from our own experience of life, that some women and men are by their temperament unsuited for monogamous marriage and the duties of parenthood. Often, I would even say as a rule, these individuals are strongly sexual. They will not, because with the character they have, they cannot, live for any long period celibate. They will marry to gain permanent sexual relief or they will buy temporary relief from prostitutes, unless they are able to seek satisfaction in an irregular union.

Now I affirm it as my conviction that the first and second of these courses are likely to lead to greater misery and sin than the third course; and of the three, the first, in my opinion, is the worst. I have no doubt at all on this matter. No one, who is not blind to the facts of life, can close their eyes to the evil and suffering that a coercive monogamy forces upon those people who are unfitted and do not desire to fulfil the obligations and duties of living faithfully with one partner. And I would ask all those who stand in fear of any change or reform in our marriage laws or of any open toleration of wider opportunities for sexual friendships to consider this fact: the discredit which has fallen upon monogamous marriage arises largely from the demoralising lives lived under its cover by those unsuited for enduring mating.

Our moral code is, however, much less ruled by law than by custom and the united will of the community. It is for this reason that I want to force men, and even more women, to think practically on these matters. My own opinion is firm. Apart from the fact that the disproportion in the number of the sexes in this country makes marriage impossible for all and condemns great numbers of women to sterile celibacy (a question I have dealt with elsewhere[84]), I am persuaded of the need for much wider facilities for honourable partnerships outside of permanent marriage; such unions are, I am sure, necessary in order to harmonise our sexual life and meet the desires of a large, and I believe increasing, number of women and men, whose exceptional needs our existing institutions and customs ignore or crush.

Let us view these questions in the light of their results. Most of us fail to meet the facts. We never realise the evil of this hypocrisy—love everywhere carried on secretly, that is acting always as a disturbing force in our sexual life—it is a worm that gnaws unceasingly at the roots of marriage and destroys too often the most beautiful blossoms of love.

One great source of difficulty arises from the want of frankness in our thoughts. Especially is this the case with women, who throughout their lives have had the great fundamental facts of life clothed in euphemisms, until it seems as if they have succeeded, by the help of many fictitious aids, in concealing the natural outward signs of the existence of sex. And largely from these concealments our every idea of sex has become tainted with sentiment and vulgarity. We can hardly speak of the subject even to our children without an apology.

The actions and emotions of life undraped with lies seem to most of us anathema; we, who have so veneered our lives that we know no longer of what wood they are made; we, who for generations have been so covered with shameful concealments, deceiving even ourselves, and are impervious to the claims of that ill-bred creature—Life.

And how deep we have wandered into sin in seeking to escape from it!

Need we put up with this? Must we turn our eyes away for ever from things as they are—stifle our desires in fear of what we shall do?

The sex-needs almost always are dealt with as though they stood apart and lay out of line with any other need or faculty of our bodies. This is, in part, due to the secrecy which has kept sex as something mysterious. We have most of us been trained from our childhood into indecent secretiveness. But there is as well a deeper reason, and it will be a long time before we can change it. Sex is so powerful in most of us, and, when from any cause awakened into consciousness, occupies really so large a part of our attention, that we are afraid of ourselves, and this reacts in fear of any open acknowledgment even in our thoughts of our own sex-needs. Still less can we grant the sex-needs of others, perhaps stronger and different from our own need.

It is necessary to face very frankly this tremendous force of the sex-passion, for the most part veiled in discussion. Many women and some men do not realise at all the immense complications of sex, or understand the claims that passion makes on many natures. Almost necessarily in any inquiry into these questions of sexual conduct one's opinions are biased by temperament and personal experience. We are dealing with forces in which the individual element cannot be set aside. It is foolishness always to preach continence. Sexual abstinence is possible without great effort for some people, it is not possible for all. I am certain we have to recognize this fact, and to allow for its action. It is not what we want people to do, but what they will do, that we are considering.

If we look at the matter practically, it is of course necessary to remember that this question of the possibility of, as well as the advantage to be derived from, sexual abstinence is an entirely different one, as it relates to the time before, or after, the first experience of love. The sex desires are strong when roused, but when not definitely aroused, the ideal of chastity asserts itself, and for long periods these desires may not greatly occupy the conscious imagination. It is clear that the physical problem cannot be, and ought not to be, considered apart from the will. Great good in some cases may be done by establishing control over thought.

It is, however, idle to count on a course of thought and action being taken by the rough majority among us which so much of our civilisation and daily environment makes difficult and indeed impossible. A race of young men and women surrounded with shameful concealments and bred to a blind acceptance of wrong sexual conditions, accustomed to an atmosphere of sniggering and suggestiveness in connection with the central facts of love and life—such a race cannot have, much less practise, an ideal of true chastity.

These wrong and vulgar conditions without doubt have acted more strongly against men than against women. And I would note in passing, that here, as I believe, we find one explanation of the greater continence among unmarried women than among unmarried men. It is not because satisfaction for the sex-needs is more necessary for the health and well-being of men than it is for the health and well-being of women—a statement I do not believe; nor is it proved that this absence of conscious sex-desires necessarily implies the absence of unconscious sex-action; all that can be claimed is that the sexual impulses have been diverted into different expressions, and the explanation of such diversion is to be sought in the boy's and young man's education and life, which forces sex so much more strongly into the conscious thought and attention.

We are dealing with a question very difficult to solve. On this assumption that the sex-needs of the man are more imperative than the sex-needs of the woman, much that is false has been accepted as true; there are many who have advocated a "duplex sexual morality," and while demanding from the woman complete sexual abstinence until she marries, regard this as impossible in the case of men. Such a separation as this between the sex-needs of man and the sex-needs of woman is, in my opinion, a very grave error. Celibacy is unnatural and harmful in man, it is at least equally unnatural and harmful in woman.

Now, it is on this question of the sex-needs of women that I find myself, as I have suggested already, in such direct opposition to the great majority of women, numbers of whom do not, will not, admit to a consciousness of any kind of sexual need. I believe they are quite honest, but I know they are mistaken.

The doctrine of chastity being the natural and special virtue of women is entirely false. Complete abstinence from love cannot be borne by women through a long period of years without producing serious results on the body and the mind. And these results are by no means clearly dependent on a conscious knowledge of unsatisfied sex. The evil may be pronounced even when the woman herself has not the slightest knowledge of her real needs. In many women the penalty is paid in an unceasing and wearying restlessness of mind and body. We have also to face the fact that prolonged and enforced abstinence may act to cultivate a morbid obsession with sexual things. I believe that the celibate often is less chaste than the normally sexual individual. This may seem to be a wanton charge to some, but I am not speaking without due consideration.

I know well that some among my readers, and in particular women, will say that I am wrong, many will accuse me of exaggerating and complain that I see sex in everything; the few only will know that I am right. I would, however, refer all those who doubt to the researches of Freud and his followers, which have proved in the most conclusive way that the manifestations of sex may be concealed in numberless guises. Without some understanding of the "Unconscious" it is useless to attempt to deal with these questions. We need to realise that the fact of an individual, or group of individuals, being unconscious of the presence of sex does not prove that sex is not acting strongly and often harmfully within them. Nay, we may go further and say that could it be proved that desire was absent and no sex difficulties of any kind be discovered, this is no reason why we should necessarily be too satisfied. If no kind of action is apparent, it is very probable that some deep evil is at work, which hinders sex from a more healthy and open expression.

I am haunted by the fear that the careless reader will think I am writing against chastity. This is not so. I would affirm again, with all the power that I have, that compulsory sexual abstinence may not be confused with voluntary chastity. We must be very clear in our thought about this. We can never establish an ideal of true chastity until we have rooted out from our social life all the unnatural and empty forms of chastity. The long waiting for marriage which economic and other causes have forced upon us, more and more increases the difficulties of maintaining any true chastity. It is a great evil which almost always wastes the energies of life.

There are very many women (as also these are men) who are moral, because they are too great cowards to be immoral. The reasons for chastity must in many cases be sought in the poverty of experience and the difficulty of obtaining love, in the hard binding of circumstances, and, even more often, in the terror of being found out. Respectability is the strong moral safeguard of woman. The conception of faithfulness to one mate (the true chastity) is as strong in many men as it is in any woman, a fact to which I gladly bear witness, from my knowledge of the men I have known. It is too commonly taken for granted that sex-passion is less refined in men and different from sex-passion in women. I am sure in many cases it is not true. I am not going to discuss the question further, as it is one that cannot easily be proved.

It is, however, very necessary to break down the idea that for the impulses of sex, with their immense complications and differences, there is one general rule either for men or for women. In every case the element of personal idiosyncrasy must be taken into account, and, for this reason, the difficulties of these questions are enormously complex. Nor is it possible, I am sure, to make any arbitrary judgments. To me the man or woman who is able to live a celibate life is not necessarily better than the man or woman who is not. I may prefer one type, I may dislike the other, but this also is a matter of my personal idiosyncrasy. We cannot safely class those who differ from ourselves as wrong, and set them down as fit only for suppression and restraint. We have to put aside those shrieks of blame that are possible only to the ignorant.

It is all very well to preach the ideal of complete sexual abstinence until marriage, but there are the clear, hard conditions of contemporary circumstances for all but the really rich, who can marry when they want to do so without other consideration, and the very poor who marry young because they have nothing at all to consider. We have to face the presence amongst us to-day of an amount of suffering through enforced celibacy which is acting in many directions in degrading our sexual lives. Any number of these sufferers, both the unmarried and the married who are ill-mated, are everywhere amongst us. I need not say more to prove this: the facts face us all, unless, indeed, we are too ignorant and too prejudiced to know what is happening.

Many new lessons will have to be learnt. I would suggest as a first step towards honesty and health, that we ought to claim an open declaration of the existence of any form of sexual relationship between a woman and a man. We shall, I believe, do this, if not now, then later, because we are finding out the evils that must ensue, both to the individuals concerned and to the society of which they are members, by forcing men and women into the dark, immoral way of concealments.

It is ridiculous to say, as many do, that sexual relationships between two people affect no one but themselves, unless a child is born. The partners in even the strongest and purest mutual passion have no right to say to society, "This is our business and none of yours." The consequences may be so grave and wide for society that the deed can never be confined to the interests of the pair concerned. And the sexual partnership that is kept secret will work anti-socially just in the same way as any other secret partnership. Opportunity will be given to those who desire to sin and escape the responsibilities of the partnership, while other men and women, who wish to and would act honourably, find the way so difficult that in nine cases out of ten they fail in their endeavors. Many unions that now are shameful would not be shameful if the parties had not been driven into concealments, which cannot fail to act in a way that is immoral.

We must see things a little more as they are. We must accept ourselves as we are. We must do more than this, we must accept others as they are, and cease from blaming them when we find them different from ourselves. We must give up being hypocrites. To force every one to accept the one form of union is not the wisest way to deal with the matter. We must understand what is the result of our doing this. It does not prevent people from acting wrongly. Anything may be done, any sexual partnership be undertaken, however shameful, as long as it is hidden. We shall have more morality, not less, by an open recognition of honourable sexual friendships entered into outside the permanent binding of monogamous marriage.

I do not think we need fear to do this. My own faith in monogamous marriage, as the most practical, the best, and the happiest form of union for the great majority of people, is so strongly rooted that I do not wish, because I hold it as unnecessary, to force any one either to enter into or to stay within its bonds. I want them to do this because they themselves want to be bound. We get further and further away from real monogamy by allowing no other form of honourable partnerships.

Under present economic conditions and the pressure of social opinion, the penalties that the woman has had to pay for any sexual relationship outside of marriage are very heavy. This is manifest. Indeed, when we see the difficulties faced in these unions, that so many women do take the risks is another proof, if one were needed, of the elemental strength of the sex-passion in women. But mark this: it is only the woman whose social conscience is unawakened, or the few women strong enough and able to ignore the censure of their friends, who can enter into these irregular relationships—except in a hateful secrecy. And this has acted, as I believe, harmfully in a way not usually recognised, in so far as it has driven into marriage many who would have been better not to marry.

At present our monogamous marriage is buttressed with prostitution and maintained with the help of countless secret extra conjugal relationships, which thus makes our moral attitude one of intolerable deception. To this question I shall presently return.

Under existing social conditions the opportunities for sexual relationships to meet the needs of those women and men unable, or not desiring, to marry must, in almost all cases, entail the sacrifice of the woman. It is an unsocial, because an ostracised union. Our efforts at reform have so far been not only ineffective, but absurd. It is no use shirking it, if some change cannot be made, then we must accept prostitution and wild-love as well as the degradation of all the more honourable partnerships entered into outside of marriage.

I believe that many of these problems of our sexual life must remain unsolved; some of them, perhaps, are unsolvable, but certain of the evils are preventable. And first note this: there is one rule that is able and ought to guide us. I have asserted elsewhere,[85] what again I would affirm here: it is an essential fact of sexual morality, as I conceive it, that in any relation between the two sexes—I care not whether the association be legal or illegal—the position of the woman as the mother must be made secure. The immoral union is the union which results in bad and irresponsible parenthood.

It is because I believe this, that I wish to see saner, more practical, and more moral relations made possible between those women and men who live together but do not marry.

But before I attempt the difficult task of suggesting what seems to me the way in which better conditions could be established, it will be necessary to note briefly a few facts concerning changes actually taking place in the position of women, which it seems to me must be certain to affect profoundly the conditions of marriage and the problem we are considering.

The quite new importance as workers which women have now obtained will react inevitably on the relations between the sexes. In every sort of occupation, in clerking, shop-assisting, railway work, motor driving and conducting, police work, in labour on the land and in many more unusual capacities, they are being found efficient beyond precedent. And in the munition factories, in the handling of heavy and intricate machinery, their adaptability and inventiveness, as well as their steadfastness and enthusiasm, have surprised all those who are without knowledge of the bewildering resourcefulness of the feminine character. All the disengaged energy of women has been employed. They have gained a strong position in the economic world. This is evident, but what is not realised are the forces working beneath.

What is going to be the permanent result? Will all this energy evaporate after the war, will it be reabsorbed in the home and work directly connected therewith, or will this great force of women's work be still used in industrial and other employments? It is not easy to give a certain answer.

Leaving aside the question whether such work if permanently continued will be good or bad for women, a matter on which already I have expressed my opinion strongly,[86] I want to consider how these fresh and advantageous labour conditions have affected, and will, I think, go on affecting, women's own desires. The question is whether this change that war conditions have brought is one which the desires of women cause them to welcome, or whether it is an arrangement that has arisen out of necessity to which they are essentially antagonistic.

What, in my opinion, makes the present situation dangerous is, that long before the war women were forcing an entrance into the world of labour, and struggling in competition with men to gain the positions which now are being thrust upon them. And I do not believe that in the mass to-day they are doing their work temporarily and to replace men for the period of the war, but rather they are aiming to establish their own economic emancipation. Probably of the million women[87] who have plunged into new work in connection with the war, the great majority are much better off economically than ever they were in times of peace. War has brought more of gain than of sacrifice. The new thing is the opportunity that has come. Individually women were adventurous before the war; they have now become adventurous as a class. War has but accentuated and made obvious the change that for long had been taking place in the desires of women. This turning away from themselves, from their own lives and duties, to the world and employments and duties of men, is a thing that was going on before the war, slowly and against much prejudice, but what matters is that it was going on.

I shall make no attempt to deal with the serious economic results that are likely to occur should women, when the war is ended, struggle to compete with men in the labour market. The disasters that would follow such action are sufficiently plain. One result would certainly be a clash of sex, unavoidable in a work-struggle for the upper hand between women and men. The great temptation to women then will be to keep their positions by accepting lower wages than the men can take. No one can know whether they will do this.

There can be no question that the situation will be difficult. For the return of women to the home and what hitherto has been considered exclusively feminine work is going to mean much more than a change of occupation; it will be going back to the insistent duties of the narrowed woman's sphere with new ideas and a fresh command of life. It is useless pretending that this can be easy. For one thing, the great uplift in women's wages has given girls as well as women an independence, with a quite strange joy as spenders which they have not known before.

And this new power in industry has been associated also with many women with a new power in the home. The withdrawal to the war of the men of the family has left women with an opportunity to spend incomes over which hitherto they had no direct control. So that sometimes one wonders whether men will be allowed to re-enter their homes, if they come back, on the same terms as before they held. Will women again accept with contentment a position of economic dependence? This cannot fail, I think, to act directly on the conditions of marriage. The question would seem to be this: Will women come back to the home believing the home to be the central interest of their lives? Will they feel that motherhood, with the care of the little child and all the duties it should entail, is the ultimate joy, for the denial of which no personal freedom or success in work can compensate?

It is one of the unhappy features of our present condition of necessity for women to carry on the work of this country that the most deep and far-reaching issues are being decided in haste, and in many cases by young girls who have never been taught by any wise training to realise their own nature as women, or to understand their sexual needs with their immense restricting power. And my fear is that the things which matter most to life will be lost. I feel that almost everything in the future depends on the inner attitude of the thousands and thousands of girls and young women who to-day have gone out of the home. I wish I had the gift to make them feel the far-acting importance of their personal attitude. The root of all action is the will or desire. Yes, that is the danger. Our desires are the greatest realities that we have, and we should look closely to the direction towards which they are turned. Nothing but the strongest desire on the part of women will save the home. Many forces will be acting to make permanent conditions that cannot fail to act adversely to any right ideal of home life. My hope is that women in the mass will understand in time and resist these forces. Yet, I do not know, and sometimes my fear is more active than my hope.

At least, it is evident that in the immediate future the home is not going to be re-established without effort. Women will have to make great sacrifice to surrender in every direction the new power of controlling and spending money which now they are enjoying. And for this reason, even if for no other, many women almost certainly will seek to hold their places in the labour world and keep on working for themselves. Therefore, it is, I think, safe to expect that to some limited extent the present extension of women's employment outside the home will be permanent when peace is established.

Certainly it is unnecessary for me to say, after what I have written in the earlier chapters of my book, how exceedingly I regret the permanence of conditions that can seem good only in an industrial society. In my opinion the working of women will be the greatest of the many disasters that are likely to follow and remain from the war. I wish I had the power to prevent it. I do not, however, see any way in which this can be done. For one thing, if the desires of women are being set in a direction away from the home, this, as I have just said, must count as the strongest factor of all. What women want to do is what they are likely in the end to do.

So many women have been for long, and still are, suffering from the delusion that conditions which industrialism, with all its failures in the art of life, first established, and which war now has made necessary, are an advantage to be maintained after the need of war has made them unnecessary. This is the great mistake. I would emphasise again what I have shown in an earlier chapter,[88] that conditions which act against the home and marriage (always dependent on the individual home) are sure proof of social instability. Such conditions are centuries old; all this flood of change is bringing nothing that is new. In all periods of unsettled life the individual home and the family have been threatened. The primitive form of marriage, the maternal form, where the husband visited the wife in her own home, is very near to the most modern suggestions for the readjustment of marriage. And the heavy working of women is a further sign of disturbance and of primitive conditions of life. It is a step backward, not a step forward. Few women, however, realise that this is so. Perhaps this explains why so many among them are talking and behaving to-day as if no more babies were desired to be born.

How far this will be carried I do not profess to say. Women will have a fresh power to refuse the position of wife and mother; thus it seems likely that there may be an increased option against marriage in its true and binding form. And closely connected with the independent position of women will be the great shortage, for the next decade, of marriageable men, due to the killing and disablements of war. It will be a world in which the proportion of women will be very high. And although it would be folly to estimate precisely how this great numerical strength of one sex will act, whether it will strengthen women's position, or, as it equally well may, will lessen their importance in a society crowded with unwanted women, it is plain that it must directly affect the sexual relationships. Women, accustomed when young to control their own lives and able to be self-supporting, will not only find it much more difficult to marry, but they will be in a position to get along economically without marriage. To every married woman there are likely to be three or four unmarried ones.[89] It will also probably be a period of poverty. The economic stress which war causes will almost necessarily continue in the years when we shall all be compelled to meet the huge task of national recovery that peace must bring. It is possible that for some years it will be more difficult to maintain a family than it has ever been before. This will be a third factor acting against marriage, and tending to maintain as permanent the class of energetic, not strongly maternal and undomesticated women workers.[90]

In different directions also causes very much the same may possibly be acting to the same end. The desires of men as well as the desires of women may be affected, and be turned from marriage and the duties of the family and the home. Many men will not come back out of the hell of war the same men that entered it. It may not be easy to plan life on the old rules, the safe customs of civilisation may well count for less. Some men will not want to return to the posts kept open for them by women; to sell tablecloths to fussy women, or to spend dull days in offices adding columns of figures and addressing envelopes, may not appear "a man's job" to men who have met the stark facts of death and life. I doubt the zeal of the response of all these men to the binding ties of family life. And in this way, it may be, that many fathers will be cut off from the family and turned away from desiring the sacrifice and duties that children entail, which cannot fail to act as a further force in modifying marriage.

If we try to take an entirely practical view of the position, certain grave facts must, I think, become evident. For side by side with these forces acting against marriage, and the parental sacrifice necessary to maintain the ideal of the family, must be placed the nation's increased need for children —in particular for male children. The repair of the war drain on the world's manhood must fall heaviest on women. It is woman who has borne and bred and loved each life that has been lost by war. It is she who will have to make good the waste. This is her bill of compulsory service.

Never will child life have been so precious as it will be after this World War. Already in this country we are beginning to recognise this need. Excellent work for the restriction of infant mortality and the protection of child life is beginning to be undertaken, and these questions are receiving a practical recognition which they never gained in the days of peace. But much more drastic action than has as yet been considered will be needed. It is certainly not inconceivable that this need for children may lead to changes both in our public and private attitudes to many sexual questions. I am hopeful that it may force us to face squarely many problems that hitherto we have turned from in fear.

Speculations on all matters connected with marriage and the relations between the sexes are so hazardous that they are likely to be wrong. I do, however, think that, having regard to the direction in which so many forces are acting, the position in regard to the special problem we are considering has become clearer. Monogamous marriage and the home based upon maternity and offspring has got to be saved. And in my opinion this will be done most surely by a frank acceptance, under the almost certain conditions of the future, of more than one form of sexual association.

This proposal is not made lightly. I am not advocating such a course as being in itself desirable or undesirable. I am attempting merely to estimate the drift and tendency of the times, considering those forces that were beginning to act before the war and, as I think, must continue, even with greater power, after the war. I suggest, therefore, the one course that seems to me can in any practical way help us to be more moral. All the facts that we have found work out to force us to the realisation that an increasing number of women will not be able, and probably will not desire, even if they marry, to bear children. Now, I do not believe in changing the ideal of marriage so that its duties no longer bind women to their children and to the home. I think it better to make provision for other partnerships, to meet the sex-needs (for we can cause nothing but evil by failing to meet them) of the women and men who are not able or do not desire to enter the holy bonds of marriage and undertake together the duties and sacrifice inevitable to the founding and maintenance of a family.

I know the whole question is a very difficult one. Let me try to make my position somewhat clearer.

I am in one way in agreement with Roman Catholic Christianity (I use the phrase to make my meaning plain, and ask indulgence if to any one it seems in itself indefensible). The Roman Catholic Church admits the need of two standards of sexual conduct—some women and men are fitted for a religious life and should bind themselves to celibacy; others need to marry, and to them marriage is permitted. The difference between my view and the one just expressed is that, whereas it is usual to suppose the morals of the celibate monk or nun superior to those of the married man or woman, I should hold the opposite opinion; it is the highest types of men and women who would seek to marry and be best and happiest if living together as faithful man and wife, as devoted father and mother. I do, however, hold that there are others—women as well as men—without the gifts that make for successful parenthood or happy permanent marriage. I would recognise the divergence of these two roughly defined classes and let those who cannot marry be openly permitted to live together in temporary childless unions, destined, I hope, to show to the world the inferiority of every type of ideal of the sex relationships other than the monogamous union, which fulfils the completion of the woman and the man in the child created by their love. And further, these sterile unions would, by their childlessness, act to remove for ever from the world those unsuited to be parents. It is this last result that matters most. As long as we force those unsuited for faithful mating into marriage and hold them bound against their desire, children will be born who must pay the penalty in weakness of character of their parents' sins against love.

I believe if there were some open recognition of honourable partnerships outside of marriage, not necessarily permanent, with proper provision for the future, guarding the woman, who, in my opinion, should be in all cases protected, a provision not dependent on the generosity of the man and made after the love which sanctioned the union has waned, but decided upon by the man and the woman in the form of a contract before the relationship was entered upon, then there would be many women ready to undertake such unions gladly; there would be women as well as men who, I believe, would prefer them to monogamous marriage that binds them permanently to one partner for life. In this way many marriages would be prevented that inevitably come to disaster. And this would leave greater chances of marriage and child-bearing for other and more suitable types.

It is also possible that such friendship-contracts might, under present disastrous conditions, be made by those who are unsuitably mated and yet are unable, or do not wish, to sever the bond between them, with some other partner they could love. Such contracts would open up possibilities of honourable partnerships to many who must otherwise suffer from enforced sexual abstinence or be driven into shameful and secret unions.

By this means a solution might be found for conditions of dishonour in our midst that we all know to be there—dishonour that, as far as I am able to see, is likely to be increased, and not lessened, in the near future by the conditions left by war. Moreover, prostitution, and also the diseases so closely connected with prostitution, would be greatly lessened, though I do not think that sexual sins would cease. There will always be for a very long time men and women who will be attracted to wild-love. This we have to recognise. Men would not, however, be driven to buy sexual relief.[91]

We have got, I am certain, to recognise that our form of permanent marriage—the monogamous union—cannot meet the sex-needs of all people. To assert that it can do this is to close our eyes to the facts we all know to exist. The extending of the opportunities of honourable love must be faced before we can hope for more moral conditions in marriage. I must affirm again how necessary, in my opinion, is some kind of fixed public recognition for every form of sexual relationship between a man and a woman, so that there may be some accepted standard of conduct for the partners entering into them.

May not something be done now, when we are being forced to consider these questions, to make some such recognition possible? Partnerships other than marriage have had a place as a recognised and guarded institution in many older and more primitive societies, and it may be, as I have tried to show, that the conditions brought upon us after the World War may act in forcing upon us a similar acceptance.

I believe that, in face of the many past disorders in our sexual conduct, such a change would work for good and not for evil; that it would not destroy marriage, but might re-establish its sanctity.

The whole question of any sexual relationships outside of marriage in the past has been left in the gutter, so to speak, in darkness and concealment. This would be changed. It is the results that have almost always followed these irregular unions that have branded them as anti-social acts. But the desertion of women, which has arisen from the conditions of secrecy under which they now exist, would be put to an end. One reason why extra conjugal relationships are discredited is because the difficulties placed around them are so numerous that, as a rule, only the weak, the foolish, and the irresponsible undertake these partnerships. Make these partnerships honourable and honourable men and women will enter into them. I do not see how we can forbid or treat with bitterness any union that is openly entered into and in which the duties undertaken are faithfully fulfilled. It is our attitude of blame that has made this impossible.

I can anticipate an objection that will probably be raised. Why, I shall be asked, if sexual relationships are to be acknowledged outside of marriage, preserve marriage at all? I have answered this question sufficiently. Monogamous marriage will be maintained because the great majority of women and men want it to be maintained. I have affirmed before my own belief in the monogamic union: the ideal marriage is that of the man and woman who have dedicated themselves to each other for the life of both, faithfully together to fulfil the duties of family life. This is the true monogamy; this is the marriage which I regard as sanctified. But I, regarding it as a holy state, would preserve it for those suited for the binding duties of the individual home so intimately connected with it.

And I do disavow the sanctity of many professedly monogamous marriages that are maintained only with the support of prostitution and clandestine loves. Squalid intrigues have been the shadow of the old, narrow moral code. The contract-partnerships I have suggested will do nothing to change the sanctity of any true marriages. And the answer I would give to those who fear an increase of immorality from any openly recognised provision for sexual partnerships outside of permanent marriage is, that no deliberate change made in the future in our sexual conduct can conceivably make moral conditions worse than they have been in the recent past. As a matter of fact, every form of irregular union has existed and does exist to-day, but shamefully and hidden. It is certain that they will continue, and that their number will be increased.

I have sought to put these matters as plainly as may be in the conviction that nothing can be gained by concealment. Any one who writes on the subject of marriage reform is very open to misconception. It is not realised that the effort of the reformer is not to diminish at all the bonds in any sexual partnerships, rather the desire is to strengthen them, but the forms of the partnership will have to be more varied, unless, indeed, we prefer to accept unregulated and secret vice. Matters are likely to get worse and not better. We shall, I do most sincerely believe, gain more morality by doing what I am pleading for than will be gained in any other way.

The only logical objection that I can think of being advanced against an honourable recognition of these partnerships is that, by doing away with all necessity for concealments, their number is likely to be larger than if the old penalties were maintained. This is undoubtedly true; it is also true that recognition is the only possible way by which such unions can cease to be shameful. Prohibition and laws, however stringent, can do nothing. The past has proved their failure; they will fail still worse in the future.

Nor is the change really so great or so startling as at first it may appear to be. Our marriage in its present form is primarily an arrangement for the protection of the woman and the family. What I want is that some measure, at least, of the protection now given to the legal wife, should also be afforded to all women who in an open and honourable way fulfil any of the same duties. I am not seeking to make immorality easier, that is very far indeed from my purpose. These changes for which I am pleading will make immorality much harder, for it will not be so easy as now it is to escape from the responsibilities of love.

No one can suppose, of course, that these changes can be other than gradual. There will be no stage at which a large section of society will give up the accepted convention of concealments with regard to unregulated unions, and will stand perplexed as to how they may readjust their opinion and moral judgments on this question. What will happen is this. The slow abandonment by society of the old attitude of blame and fear, as experiments in sexual partnership are made, at first by the few, to be followed by an ever increasing number. When the need for change arises, then does a change come.

CONTENTS OF CHAPTER XII
THE UNMARRIED MOTHER

The law should help unmarried parents to give adequate protection to their child—Repressive terrors drive men to desert girls made pregnant through their lust—The penalty for illegitimate parentage should not be paid by the child—At present the child does pay—Figures to show this—Illegitimate infant death-rate—Unmarried mother not able to give proper care to her child—Some mothers unfit to care for their children—Different types of unmarried mothers—Four cases—Where both parents working-class least harm usually results from birth of a love-child—Enlightened legislation in Scandinavia—The law in England and in France—Good legislation in Australia and New Zealand—Other countries—Five proposals for reforming our law.

CHAPTER XII
THE UNMARRIED MOTHER

"The British Empire has invested thousands of its best lives to purchase future immunity for civilisation. This investment is too great to be thrown away."—Right Hon. D. LLOYD GEORGE.

One of the most pressing questions that we shall have to face in the near future is the attitude and practical action which, as a people, we are going to adopt towards the unmarried mother and her child. I have so far said almost nothing upon this problem of illegitimacy, though the whole difficult question is connected with, and is, in fact, closely dependent for its solution on, the conclusions we arrived at in the preceding chapter on Sexual Relationships outside of Marriage; we then realised the moral advantage that would result from an open avowal and the regulation of all sexual partnerships, with the fixing, as far as this is possible, of a standard of conduct to be expected and claimed from those who enter into them. I have left over this question of the child on purpose that we may give it special consideration. No other matter is of greater significance to my book on Motherhood than is this, and none is deeper in my own interest or, in my opinion, of more urgent importance.

It is really impossible to evade it much longer. There is obviously something ridiculous, at a time when the fateful importance of child-life is being forced more and more upon our attention, to repeat our conventional, unimaginative and inconsistent judgments.

We are learning new and sharp lessons. Terrific war losses are teaching governments to consider the necessity of preserving the new generation even to its last and meanest members. At last the movements to improve the condition of illegitimate children, for which many of us have for long struggled in vain, have received new impetus. What humanity has been powerless to do, the most ancient of all inhumanities—war—has suddenly accomplished.

And it is well. We cannot go on as we have done before. We call motherhood holy, and yet we have sanctioned the sacrifice of mothers, driving them to crimes, to abortion, to child-murders and to death; we have sent them into sweated industries; we have turned them out onto the streets, forcing them to choose between starvation and prostitution. We have permitted the yearly destruction of tens of thousands of little children, born into a hard and barren world without the slightest provision for their physical and mental needs. At the same time, the fact has been hammered into us of the declining birth-rate. This has gone on and on, but we have done nothing that the evils may be stopped and life take the place of unnecessary death.

I cannot understand an attitude which simultaneously condemns the non-maternal woman, who does not wish to be a mother, accusing her of sin in shirking the duty of bearing children, and then brands the unmarried mother to infamy. By the cruelty of our law and the short-sightedness of our "moral" attitude we have worked to make life a martyrdom for the unmarried mother, and for the children born out of wedlock, who are smirched by us with the shame of their illegitimate birth, and thus are forced downward in the hard struggle of life.

And such foolish and cruel action has all been done in the name of morality! Let us tear the mask from the lying face of our social conscience. We need a clean clearance of a moral attitude that really is profoundly immoral.

Let no one make a mistake. In pleading for these unhonoured mothers and their children, I am not advocating illegal parentage. There is a sin of illegitimacy, as presently I shall show. Irresponsible parentage must always be immoral. It is, however, the parents who behave illegitimately, not the child, since it can never be the fault of any child that its parents have brought it into the world. I would wish for every child that it should be born within the happy safeguards of a true monogamous marriage. But I cannot close my eyes to the facts of life. I know that we shall not be able to make it impossible for extra-conjugal procreation to take place: love-children will be born. And what we, in our curious moral muddle-headedness, forget is that by penalising the mother we cannot escape the penalty being paid by the child. Our attitude in the past has been a reproach to our social intelligence.

I am very far indeed from any desire to lessen parental responsibility. And if I want the harshness of our law and our moral attitude changed, it is first of all because I wish to make it possible for unmarried parents—the father as well as the mother—to give adequate protection to their child. If they do not do this willingly, I would use the pressure of the law and a strong public opinion to bring them to their duty. Under present conditions this can never be done. It is because our harshness does no good that I condemn it.

The iniquity of our bastardy laws and public opinion concerning illegitimacy both reflect the Anglo-Saxon habit of mind, which persists in ignoring all social problems arising from the sex relation. We have never yet squarely faced the question, we have just pushed it into the darkness, and pretended it was not there. It has even been a kind of disgrace to bring it forward; and the evil and the waste is so hidden up that most of us have been quite unaware of its immense existence among us. But we cannot thus escape from what we have done, or rather have left undone.

The fact is, that all our thought on these questions has been obscured by the puritan view of punishment, based on the assumption that harshness in the treatment of sexual offences will make for a higher standard of morality. Do we really believe this? Surely the underlying fallacy of our morality has always rested here—in our desire to crucify the offender. We forget that, by doing this, we but open the way to make easy, even if not inevitable, the committal of further sin. By our attitude we drive men to desert the girls made pregnant through their lust, and open the way for them to escape from responsibility for their sexual sins and to disown their fatherhood; we do everything that we can to encourage unfit parenthood.

Few people want to do wrong; they drift into wrong; the circumstances are too hard or their wills too weak to resist. We are suffering a great deal of confusion from demanding from men and women a rule of conduct in sex without taking any care that the conditions of life render such conduct practicable. In the last chapter I tried to make plain how short-sighted has been the attempt to force all types into a single mould. The plan I there outlined for an open acceptance of honourable unions outside of permanent marriage, would cut at the roots of many of these problems, and, in particular, by lessening the sufferings from enforced sexual abstinence, would render much less frequent those disgraceful and hidden unions which result in illegitimate births; it would also materially reduce the dire results of venereal diseases, and would be, in my opinion, more beneficial and far-reaching than anything that yet has been proposed. I would affirm again that I am not advocating license of conduct. It is necessary to proclaim allegiance to the God of morals, who has proclaimed for ever "thou shalt" and "thou shalt not." But it is necessary also to understand that repressive terrors may drive men and women into greater sins.

Our bastardy laws act directly in this immoral way. The child born of unmarried parents has been branded under Christian teaching as "the child of sin," and condemned from its birth as a member of an unclean caste. But, from the point of view of practical morality, this identification of the child with the sin of its parents is wholly unjustifiable.

The urgent duty that rests upon us all is the duty of taking action to prevent the penalty for the sin of illegitimate parentage being paid by the child.

It is common sense, after all.

We have to remember that the birth of every child—and it matters not at all whether the birth is legal or illegal—is always the introduction of a new individual into the community. Birth is not a personal fact only, but a social fact, in which the State cannot fail to be concerned.

The effect in increasing the infantile death-rate and the misery caused in physical and mental unfitness in the children who survive, are the result of our blind action. This is what we have to change. For it is such social waste that makes our cruel bastardy laws so absurd. After all, you cannot go on indefinitely encouraging the production of wastrels. It is the practical question of health and social well-being that we need to consider in reforming our laws.

The practical aspects of the question are serious. Illegitimacy has a far closer relation than is generally understood to the racial wastage which it helps to feed. Certainly it looms large as a factor in social disintegration—in the degeneration which leads to the streets and to the prison, and the ever-increasing hosts of the submerged. The Minority Report of the Royal Commissioners on the Poor Law 1909, for instance, estimates (no definite statistics having been kept!) that in the United Kingdom in each year are born over 15,000 children in the Poor Law institutions, and of these 30 per cent. are legitimate and 70 per cent. illegitimate. The yearly harvest of these shame-branded children appears almost incredibly great. Roughly estimating, in Great Britain (excluding Ireland) there are 50,000 illegitimate births in each year—that is to say, about one million of these children are born in this land in a single generation. Nor is this all. In England, unfortunately, still-born births are not required to be registered; were these recorded the illegitimate birth-rate would be much higher than the present statistics show. In those countries where the records are kept, the number of still-born illegitimate births is always higher than it is for children born under the protection of marriage.

And to this vast host of helpless children we, in this land, give almost no protection. In the English law they have no father. They are *filii nullius*—nobody's children; without kin; they have no rights of inheritance. All through life they are branded. The child in England is not legitimised even on the subsequent marriage of its parents. In Scotland this injustice is not found. The illegitimate child becomes legitimate by the simple and natural process of its father marrying its mother. Can the cruelty of our English law have any positive value? It is difficult to think so. Aside from sentimentality, aside even from the value or worthlessness of punitive measures, here is a law that stands as a direct obstacle against right and responsible conduct.

And what is the result? The infant mortality rate, high as it is for the children of married parents, is doubled and more than doubled in the case of illegitimate children. Three times as many children born out of wedlock die before reaching adolescence, as compared with those children born under the protection of the law. Think just a little of the real significance of this alarmingly high infant death-rate; these tell-tale figures are the proof of our failure. Do they not speak of a waste of infant life which, if for practical reasons only, we cannot suffer to go on? This fact of England's need for children should drive us on to action. Here, as in many other cases of indifference, we have failed to recognise that life—the one thing without which all else must perish—has been slipping from us by our carelessness, in a way that threatens the whole future and well-being of our race.

In many towns in England the illegitimate death-rate of infants under one year has increased, and still is increasing to an extent that ought to give alarm. In London the illegitimate infant death-rate is more than twice as high as the legitimate. The exact figures vary in different boroughs: thus in

Poplar the number of legitimate infant deaths per thousand is 121.5 as against 281.24 illegitimate, whereas Wandsworth has 97 as the death-rate of legitimate children and 276 for illegitimate. In the city of Manchester, where the death-rate of legitimates is 169, that of illegitimates is 362. In one division (Clayton) it is 583, in another (Blackley) it is as high as 667. Bristol, again, has a legitimate death-rate of 124 per thousand and an illegitimate of 349; Leicester, 130 against 377; Cardiff, 124 against 349; while Cambridge, with a legitimate death-rate as low as 81 per thousand, has an illegitimate rate of 276.

The meaning of these figures is plain: the unmarried mother cannot give proper care to her child, as a rule she cannot feed it, and, deprived of its natural nourishment, it is more likely to die, and, if it lives, it will be less strong to meet life. This is proved by the vital statistics, which show that the illegitimate babies, unlike legitimate babies, are not stricken with death in the first week of infant life; they die more frequently in the second month than in the first, and more frequently in the third than in the second month. Illegitimates at birth are equal to legitimate children; indeed, from these statistics they would seem to be born stronger. It is evident that the high death-rate among them is caused only by defective nutrition and want of sufficient care. In other words, these children are killed needlessly by our neglect. For the sin of their deaths rests upon each and all of us, until we rise up and refuse to accept conditions that permit children to be born only to die.

And while you grasp the offence of these facts, do not be consoled by thinking that this open infantile slaughter is the only or indeed the greatest, evil that follows from our indifference. No statistics can do more than shadow the extent of the wrong; motherhood brought to despair—the child-murders that fortunately remain hidden, the secret abortions, the concealed births, the still-born children who might have been born alive. We have suffered these things. But it is the race that pays and rots; the penalty for our sins of neglect is paid by these innocent little ones.

Let me at this place insert a brief digression to point out one particular that it is very necessary for us to remember. There are many types among these unmarried mothers, as many as there are among married women; and some would be good mothers did we allow them the opportunity, others would not be good mothers under any circumstances, because they are weak in character and are incapable of maternal sacrifice. Now, the problem of the saving of the child is quite a separate one in these opposite cases: in the one instance everything ought to be done to keep the child with its mother, in the other the one safeguard is to keep the child wholly out of the mother's power.

I will give the reader four cases from my own knowledge to make this fact clearer; they will, I believe, speak more forcibly than any mere statement of my own opinion.

The first case shows illegitimacy at its very lowest—motherhood made a crime. The facts were told to me by a doctor friend on whose word I can rely absolutely. A company of five or six men were gathered in some outbuildings of a country farm, among them was one who was half-witted. In an adjoining barn was a girl, also half-witted. The men joked one with another; a bet was made, and the half-witted man was sent to seek the girl. This he did, and as the result of this hideous act a child was born and lived. I do not know what became of it.

In the second case also the woman was quite unfitted to be a mother, though her character and the circumstances were as different as possible. This time the mother was highly born and educated. Though I knew her fairly well, I was unacquainted with her family history, which probably would show many features of great interest. She was of neurotic temperament, and belonged to the type I have classed as the siren woman. She had several lovers, as she was strongly sexual. By one of these men, and by mistake, a child was born. The father refused to accept the responsibilities of his fatherhood, though he did not deny that the child was his. The mother also had no love for it, and the little one would have been neglected and probably would have died. But, when about two months old, the child was taken from its mother and cared for and most tenderly loved by one of the woman's lovers. He left her, as her indifference to her child killed his affection, but he took her child to bring up as his own son.

The third case is more usual, and shows us illegitimacy as it most commonly occurs. The events happened in the north of England, where once I lived. The girl was well known to me. She was of respectable parentage, and very beautiful; she would have made a good mother. The father did not live in the same village, and I did not know him; but I heard he was young and strong; he was the gardener at the place where the girl was servant; probably the child would have been healthy. But the girl was sent from her situation as soon as her condition was known to her Christian (!) mistress; later she was driven from her home by her fanatically religious (!) father. Thus hounded to death and to crime she sought refuge in a disused quarry; she was there for two days without food. It was winter. When we found her, her child had been born and was dead. Afterwards the girl went mad.[92]

I will add no comment, because I feel quite unable to write calmly. I can only record my belief that under a more moral public opinion and saner social organisation such crimes of mothers against their children would be impossible. Infanticide is committed always, I believe, under the biting pressure of want and despair.

The last case is in sharp contrast with all the others, and shows responsible motherhood outside of marriage. The woman here is strong and passionate and deeply maternal, but, unable to marry the man she loves, because he is married already, but to a woman who has no desire to be a mother, she chooses, therefore, to bear his child. I know several similar unions. Some of these have been temporary, some have lasted, but in each case the woman has had strength of character and a social position which have made it practicable for her thus to assert her right to motherhood. Such cases we may leave alone. I do not think any one of us should condemn such action. The immense pity is that women of this strong maternal type should by any cause be kept from marriage. They are the fittest wives and mothers.

The relation between marriage and illegitimacy is a very close one; any cause that hinders early marriage must tend to encourage the increase of illegal unions.[93] The question is, however, a very difficult one. And I am not fully convinced of the wisdom of permanent marriage being undertaken at so young an age that chance births would be prevented; at any rate, the danger would be great until our young women and young men are more sanely educated in sex. The young have very little understanding of their own need, and no experience of life; and for this reason a way might be opened up that, after marriage, would lead to even more harmful looseness of conduct. Already numerous illegitimate births are the result of unhappy marriages. This happens, perhaps, most frequently among the working classes, though I am not sure, and it may be only that among them the facts of such births are more openly known. The fear of another child to the too-hard-worked mother is often very great, and this (when the means to prevent conception are not known) causes her to refuse to have intercourse with her husband, which all too frequently sends him to another woman.

Unmarried mothers are overwhelmingly preponderant among the economically weak, in particular, among servant girls, factory workers, laundry hands, waitresses, and all classes of day workers. This does not necessarily prove greater looseness of conduct among these classes, and the more numerous illegitimate births are, of course, explained to a great extent by the fact that among the better-educated girls means to prevent conception are used; illegitimate births are also very frequently hidden. This, in particular, happens where both parents belong to the upper classes of society. It is also frequent with the gentleman father and the mother of a lower social class.

And here, before I go further, I must again give warning against the over-hasty view, that men and their uncontrolled passions are alone responsible. This opinion, once held by me in common with most women, I have been compelled to give up. Seduction cannot, I believe, be accepted, without very great caution, as the chief cause of illegitimate births. It is so comfortable to place the sins of sex on men's passions. But I doubt very much if any woman can be made a mother against her own will. I am inclined to believe that excitement and escape from dulness, as also the joy in receiving presents, are the principal motives that at first lead girls into illegal relations.[94]

We find that paternity is acknowledged most frequently in those cases where the father belongs to a lower social level, where he loses less by open behaviour. In these classes the man, unless prevented by a pre-existing tie, usually marries the mother at a later period, and he does not despise her. The woman's sin is not as a rule taken too tragically. If the father of her child does not marry her, it is quite possible for her to find another husband, who, as a rule, acts as a father to her love-child. For these reasons the least moral and economic dangers, alike to the child and its mother, occur when both the father and the mother belong to the working classes. This is not, however, always true.

The whole question is a difficult one; the further we inquire, the more strongly does this appear. We learn that there is no one type of the unmarried mother, no one cause of the evil of illegitimacy, no one remedy that will cure it. We cannot wisely be too hopeful. But this is not an excuse for our indifference. Our system of ignoring this question and of forcing the unmarried mother into shame, with its incredible short-sightedness and culpable lack of help and discrimination, is proved out-of-date, because we now know that it is useless. It does not prevent illegitimate births, for no law can change the sexual nature of men and women. As things stand with us at present, honourable or even decent conduct in illegal sexual relationships has a poor chance of being cultivated; but those who realise that this is the case are still very few.

It is because I have come to realise this that I have urged, with all the power I have, an open recognition of these hidden relationships as the only way to save them from disgrace and shame. I hope to have made it clear that I am not thinking of lessening responsibility in asking for a change in our law. I am not at all advocating any sentimental legislation; we have had quite enough of that. It is an intelligent insight that considers causes and their effects that we need to-day in the administration of our laws.

All thinkers are coming to see the waste of the old system. The modern tendency is to place *remedy* in lieu of *punishment*. Thus, we need scarcely doubt that we are approaching the acceptance of a more truly moral code, based on the need of protection for the child.

It is this, and this alone, that should guide us in the reform of our laws. The life of every child must be safeguarded, not on sentimental or even on ethical grounds, but for the sake of the health and efficiency of our race. This practical morality is what we need. The State must have healthy children, and by any negligence in working to this end it inflicts serious charges upon itself, and at the same time dangerously impairs its efficiency in the future. The nationalisation of healthy children is of much greater importance than the nationalisation of education.

It has needed the catastrophe of War to force upon modern States a just recognition of their obligations to motherhood and the child-life upon which their very existence depends. To a surprising and gratifying degree the position of the illegitimate child is being discussed in all countries, and practical remedies are being found for some of the worst evils, by associations for the protection of motherhood and by changes in the law. Much wise legislation already has been passed by progressive States.

Among ourselves, however, little has as yet been done.[95] Why is this? I know that reforms that matter are not easy to make. Our legislators seem to me as blind fighters, dealing blows that sometimes hit the mark by chance, but more usually miss it. The difficulty of bringing about any change in our laws is certainly very great, for respect of the law is, perhaps, the guiding principle of English life. So far any movement towards reform has been in the hands of private individuals, and only the few have cared at all. And there the matter rests, and there it will rest, until our politicians are by us driven into action. It is this for which I am hoping. For I do not believe that great changes in things that really matter are often brought about by Acts of Parliament. Parliament may register the reforms, may try to modify or check them; it does not create them. It is public opinion that does this. When we really care for the injustice with which we treat the illegitimate child, our bastardy laws will be changed. Till then we shall go on as we have done, enunciating moral platitudes in which few of us believe and raising sentimental limitations, but we shall be content to muddle on, careless of the evils we are sowing by our carelessness.[96]

Yet I do not despair; a change is coming. The widespread interest, and also the more practical and moral view taken by the majority of people, during the agitation on the supposed existence of the "war-babies," were to me a very hopeful sign. It is true the agitation was short-lived: soon we were told it was unnecessary. Nothing was done. The lesson must be driven deeper and then public opinion will awaken to the knowledge that the conditions causing illegitimacy and its disasters are present in times of peace as well as in times of war.

In the meantime, it may be salutary for us to know the action that other countries are taking in this question. Certainly we have much to learn. Our law, in this matter of protection for the unmarried mother and maintenance for her child, lags far behind that of other countries, and is one example only, out of many, of our hide-bound attachment to ancient abuses.

For the most enlightened legislative advances we have to look to Scandinavia, the birth-land of Ellen Key. Surely it is due to her beneficent influence that the position of the bastard child and its mother has been faced with a quite new practical efficiency; and as a result constructive legislation has been wisely undertaken, which will fix the rights of the illegitimate child and enforce responsible conduct upon both its parents.

In Norway a bill, prepared by the Department of Justice, was laid before the Storthing in 1909, "whose simple but revolutionary intention was to give *every child two parents*. It aimed to equalise illegitimate children and legitimate children before the law: that is, to give the illegitimate child the right to a father."[97] This bill, as one might expect, met with opposition; it was adopted as law only in 1915.

I wish it were possible for me to give in detail all the bill's wise enactments. Even its title, *Law Concerning Children Whose Parents Have Not Married Each Other*, is significant. The unjust stigma "illegitimate," as applied to the innocent child, has been discarded. This gives the clue to the intention of the bill. It is concerned (1) with the welfare of the child, saving it from social disgrace and the position of legal disadvantage which hitherto has been the lot of half-parented children; (2) with the fixing of both parents' responsibilities, so that no man or woman may escape the results of their sexual acts.

Undeniably here is a law that at once is moral as well as practical in its aims. And the double accomplishment is not so difficult as might at first thought appear. No cumbersome rules are laid down, difficult of application and likely to fail in their working; indeed, what most impresses one is the obvious simple common sense of these measures. Were I younger, I should feel sure that now Norway has shown us so splendidly what to do in this matter, and how easily right can be done, England and all other countries would hasten to act in prompt and glad imitation; but life has taught me that it is just the very simple things to right what is wrong that as a rule we never do.

Let us glance at the Norwegian bill. I can give only the briefest summary of its principal clauses.

(1) A child whose parents have not married each other has a right to the surname of its father.

(2) The child is entitled to demand from both his parents adequate support and education. The amount to be contributed by each parent for support to be dependent on the economic position of the father and to be decided by the authority appointed for that purpose. The cost of the child's education to be borne as far as possible by both parents.

(3) On the death of the parents, the child to have full rights of inheritance.

By these means the child born without the protection of marriage is given special protection by the law, so that in general his position is the same as that of the legitimate child. And in this way the child is saved, while the parents are punished for their careless sin in the one wise way, by forcing them to undertake the same responsibilities they would have had to fulfil to their child if they had not acted illegitimately.

But more even than this is necessary; the child must be saved for healthy life before birth, as well as being maintained and educated after it is born, and this can be done only by taking care of the mother. The Norwegian bill, therefore, provides for this to be done; the father is to bear his right share of the responsibilities of the birth.

Thus, the man has to pay the expenses of the woman's confinement; his obligations in this respect extending to providing maintenance during three months of pregnancy and six weeks following confinement, which maintenance may be extended to a period of nine months if the mother keeps the child with her and nurses it for that length of time.

But the most revolutionary clause of the bill relates to those cases where, owing to the loose character of the mother, or for other reasons, paternity cannot be fixed. The promoters of the bill, knowing that it is just these children who most need protection, has provided for their fatherhood in the following simple, but wise, manner: Where it is not possible to fix with certainty the man who is the begetter of the child, the responsibilities and obligations of the father shall rest upon any man who has had sex relations with the mother at such a time that in the course of nature he might be the father of her child. In those cases where several men have had intercourse about the same time with the mother, then each of them will be accounted, in part, as the father, and must contribute to the child's support, the amount to be paid by each to be determined by the authority prescribed. And the same rule will hold with regard to the confinement expenses of the mother.

It would be difficult to over-emphasise the far-reaching effects of such an enactment. So far the plea, "There were others," what the law calls the *exceptio plurium,* has served to free men from all the responsibility for irregular connections. Under the Scandinavian law there is now no such way of escape. Anonymous parenthood at last is recognised as a crime against society. The only plea now allowed in Norway to any man is that he has had *no sexual intercourse* with the mother, otherwise he becomes liable for the child's support, which he may have to bear alone or in partnership with other men who are also adjudged to be possible fathers. Here is a law to re-establish the father's responsibility. It also closes one of the widest doors whereby profligacy has been made easy. Casual and transient unions will no longer be able to be entered into without any thought of the consequences.

Is an act of such clear morality as this one impossible for us in England? I fear that at present it is.

What, then, have we done in this Christian land for the unmarried mother and her child? It is little enough that hitherto has been held to be necessary. The father, if he can be caught and his paternity proved, may be compelled to pay a few shillings weekly to the mother for aliment. Under no circumstances can he be made to pay more than five shillings; this sum is deemed to be sufficient whatever his financial or social status. Moreover, the payments for the child cease when it reaches the age of sixteen; and the law makes no provision that the child must be trained for a livelihood. No help whatever is claimed to ensure for the mother proper conditions during her confinement and the necessary rest before and afterwards to enable her to nurse her child. Further trouble arises for the mother from the costs and difficulties of the law. Improvements have of late been made in this respect; but much more waits to be done.[98] The difficulties that have hindered moral and responsible conduct are really little short of comic. It would seem that the object of our bastardy laws was rather to protect the father and to render profligacy easy than to aid the child or its mother. I ask, Is this justice? Is it even common sense?

One plain result is that a small percentage only—it is stated by some to be as low as five per cent.—of unmarried mothers ever apply to establish paternity and claim alimony from the man. It is much easier for the woman to go on to the streets; the army of prostitutes every year is recruited by many thousands of these girls. The punishment for the sin of an illegitimate birth falls on one partner in the act; the man escapes his payment.

The barriers that have been placed in the path of the unmarried mother afford certain proof of how greatly we are in need of further changes in the law. These should be made at once. Other countries are realising this and are not failing to act. Take, for instance, the lands of our Allies, where, in France, action at last has been taken regarding the famous Napoleonic edict, *La recherche de la paternité est interdite*. In 1913 this prohibition was quietly expunged; and, in certain cases, the child born out of wedlock now has the right to its father's name and nationality, and to half the property which would have descended by law to a legitimate child. Again, a law has just recently been passed by the Russian Duma by which the father of an illegitimate child is made responsible for the birth: he must keep the mother until such time as she is fit to earn her own living.

In Australia, where women possess a larger share than elsewhere in making and administering the law, much practical attention has been given to these matters and a number of reforms have been made which act directly in helping the child. Thus, in South Australia, paternity may be proved by the mother *before* the birth of the child; when this is done, the father must furnish security, by order of a magistrate, that he will find lodging for the mother for one month before and one month after her confinement, as well as pay the doctor and the nurse, and provide clothing for the child. After the child is born, the father pays a weekly sum, at the decision of the magistrate, to the mother for its maintenance. Children are legitimised on the marriage of their parents. In New Zealand (again a land where women's influence is strong) an illegitimate child is now registered in the name of the father, where paternity is proved.

Changes in the law, all favourable to the legal position of the child, have been made in Denmark, in Sweden, and in Switzerland. In this last country the bastard has all the rights of a child born in marriage, when once paternity has been recognised. And if the mother fails to find the father, the child himself, or his guardian, can take proceedings. A similar law, recently enacted, is now in force in Sweden: in Denmark the father supports the child up to the age of eighteen; he provides for the mother for one month before and one month after the birth of the child. The money for such help is paid to the mother by the authorities, and is afterwards claimed by them from the father. This may seem of small importance, yet it is our carelessness in such details that, in great measure, causes the utter futility of our laws.

I would ask you to consider very carefully these different wise and practical measures. Do they not show more common sense than our methods? Are they not more in line with the modern spirit—the spirit, that is, of intelligent seeking for the advantage of the child? And here at length do we not see the way that in the future may lead us to more moral action and greater justice in the framing of our laws? A wider knowledge has grown with our inquiry and an understanding of what we have to do.

The welfare of the child is the one consideration that matters.

I must drive this fact home again, even though I risk wearying my readers with repetition: our present immoral laws are practically equivalent to freeing the man from his obligations as a father; they drive unmarried mothers to death and prostitution; they are the direct cause of infanticide. Again I would urge practical and prompt action, which alone can bring us nearer to moral conduct by making responsibility a necessary condition of all sexual relationships, however carelessly and transiently they are entered into.

First, and I think most important of all, the law should take notice of the desire of the parents. In all cases where parenthood is acknowledged openly by the father as well as by the mother, and guarantees are given that the duties of the parents will be fulfilled, the child should be legitimised, receive the name of the father and be qualified to inherit from him, even if the parents are unable, or do not wish, to marry. This opportunity of right conduct once given to the parents by the law, I believe that many men would voluntarily take this course and gladly acknowledge their fatherhood.

In all other cases in which paternity is not voluntarily acknowledged I take the first and most important duty of the law to be the appointment of guardians. I believe that nothing else is quite so urgently needed to safeguard the fatherless little one. I do not think the illegitimate child safely can be left without supervision in the care of its mother. Those who talk here of the mother's right to her child are being misled by sentiment. These mothers are, as a rule, incapable of giving adequate care or any form of training to their children. I would go further than this and say that, in entering into such a union with a man, and thus depriving their child of a father willing to acknowledge his fatherhood, they have proved already their unfitness for motherhood. But this is not to say that the mothers must be punished, rather it is the more necessary that they must be helped, supported, and guarded, just because of and in proportion to their weakness, *for this is the only way of salvation for the child*. And, for this reason, the law, as it affects the unmarried mother, must be made easier in its working. All artificial difficulties preventing the mother from obtaining alimony must be removed. No longer should the law make it easy for any man to escape his sexual responsibilities. It is immoral to countenance laws that make profligacy easy.

We must, therefore, claim—

(1) The removal of the present limit of the father's payment to "an amount not exceeding 5*s.* per week." The alimony paid should vary according to the means and social status of the father: in all cases it should include some kind of training to enable the child to earn its own living; until that time the payments of the father should continue. And if the child should be physically or mentally deficient, so as to be unable to support itself, the father must continue his aid for all its life.

(2) A further charge should be made upon the man for the support of the mother for a period, certainly not less than one month before and three months after the birth of the child. He should be compelled to pay for a doctor and a nurse for the mother, and provide clothes for the child.

(3) The father's responsibility should be truly recognised so that, if the mother is driven to commit any deed of violence against the child, he must be held accountable with her and punished, should he have known of her condition and refused to help her.

(4) In the case of the death of the mother, it should be possible to bring an order against the father or the supposed father. The mortality in childbed in these cases is much higher than among married women, and it is clearly unfair that the mother's death should leave the child unprotected, without

any power on the part of its guardians to compel the father to fulfil his parental responsibilities.

(5) The father against whom an order has been made must be prevented from leaving the country unless he has first paid a sum sufficient to discharge his obligations or has made suitable arrangements for payments during his absence.

Probably all these conditions could better be secured if paternity was proved before, instead of after, the birth of the child. Registration on the part of the woman at the time of conception would be the best way to prevent the crime of anonymous paternity.

There is much more that ought to be done. We shall still be far behind the reforms of Norway. But the carrying out of even these simple demands will lead us a great step forward in practical morality. Can we, I ask myself, who in this twentieth century no longer are quite ignorant as to the factors that act in the making of fit citizens, who know that of all causes tending towards degeneracy, bad ante-natal and early life conditions are the greatest, can we pursue our policy of carelessness as if this knowledge were not ours? A recognition of the claims of the child is being forced home by our need. No longer can we afford to be careless of the life of the future. A new sense of our responsibility—a responsibility not to punish sin, but to prevent sin—is surely dawning on our social conscience. And as soon as we understand, we must hasten to reform our inhuman bastardy laws.

CONTENTS OF CHAPTER XIII
THE DANGER OF SECRET DISEASES

Extent of the evil—Why these diseases are not treated—Need for secrecy prevents those afflicted from obtaining the best treatment—Recommendations of the Royal Commission—Enlightened interest in the subject needed—Desire to punish men prevents wise action—If men fear to tell the truth they are more likely to infect their wives—Three attitudes towards the evil—Bad effects on both boys and girls of too romantic views of love—Woman often to blame for cleavage between husband and wife—The wife's responsibility for the husband's unfaithfulness—The art of love—Certain reflections.

CHAPTER XIII
THE DANGER OF SECRET DISEASES

"The abolition of prostitution and the suppression of venereal diseases would be almost tantamount to the solution of the entire sexual problem."—Iwan Bloch.

So far in writing of marriage and of the irregular partnerships entered into outside of marriage I have ignored the question of venereal diseases and of prostitution, so intimately connected with them, but to continue to do this would be to make my inquiry useless, as, properly speaking, they constitute the central problem of the sexual relationships. There are no other factors of the same importance to motherhood and to the life and health of the race.

Without doubt the subject is eminently complicated, while the problems involved are so immense, far-reaching and perilous, linking themselves with the deepest interests of the race, that I hesitate almost in making an attempt to discuss so wide a subject briefly, and necessarily inadequately, in the short space at my disposal. Yet it is clearly impossible to take the easy way and pass these matters over in silence.

On the question of prostitution I have written already in my earlier book, *The Truth about Woman*, where I stated as truthfully as I could some facts I had come to know about the prostitute class, as well as my own opinions on this very complex social phenomenon. I shall, therefore, now as far as possible leave this side of the problem without further comment. It must, however, be remembered that the problem of prostitution and the problem of venereal diseases are inseparably interconnected, the former evil being the chief cause of the latter. Indeed, if prostitution could be ended venereal diseases would of themselves disappear.

And here we touch at once the grave difficulty of the position. These diseases are set apart from all other sicknesses of our bodies. Moral considerations become confused with practical values. I do not see that this in itself can be wrong. For there can be no greater ideal than that of removing the poisonous sting that with such abundant activity has worked evil in our midst.

There is, however, danger in too much and wrongly directed moral enthusiasm. It is of vital importance that a contagious disease should be isolated and cured, and if moral condemnation acts to defeat these objects, it cannot but be a danger. A contagious disease that must be kept secret cannot be properly dealt with and healed.

I hope I made my own position clear when I wrote on prostitution, where I tried to avoid a purely moral and idealistic treatment of the subject.[99] I shall follow the same plan here. I shall limit myself to the aspects of the question that to me seem to be of special importance, choosing by preference facts about which I have some little personal knowledge, or a fixed opinion of my own. In this way I may be able to contribute a word or two of worth to this difficult question.

The Report of the Royal Commission on Venereal Disease brought the subject before a reluctant and apathetic public. It was time. According to the Commission one-tenth of the city population is infected by syphilis. The number of those affected by gonorrhœa is much larger. The latter disease is the more terribly injurious to women and children, because it is often considered a triviality by men. Syphilis serves as the origin of many functional and organic diseases, and its hereditary influence is truly disastrous. Blindness, deafness and insanity, as well as a weakened nervous resistance, are the inheritance handed to the children of the syphilitic. Gonorrhœa is the chief source of sterility in women, probably accounting for one-half of all cases.

At a time when infant life is of such supreme value to the nation as it is to-day, it is impossible to exaggerate the importance of these facts. We have to realise that could we act strongly and wisely so that in one generation we grappled with this great evil and cured it, we could make good the suffering and waste of life caused by the war.

Is it not worth while to do this? It can be done. There was a time when syphilis did not exist in our civilisation. It cannot be traced with any certainty in Europe before the fifteenth century, although its origin is involved in some controversy. The attempt to suppress venereal diseases by proper treatment is of less than twelve years' duration. Three men—Wassermann, Ehrlich and Noguchi—have supplied the knowledge and given the means whereby the evil may be attacked. Up to the present little use has been made of the effective means of diagnosis and cure that we now possess. The cure has been left to private doctors. No general hospital would treat these diseases, and the special hospitals are few in number. Benefit societies and insurance commissioners have refused to grant the usual benefits to patients suffering from these diseases. The inoculations are very expensive, and many patients, even among the wealthy, have not used them, as they have feared to discover the truth. The desire for concealment has done everything to make cure difficult.

I must emphasise constantly the danger of secrecy. We have to face the facts as they are, not as we wish them to be. And for this reason, because the results are what we now know them to be, we must demand the clearing away of the moral stigma that has been placed as a ban upon the infected. It is so plain. Until every one attacked by these diseases seeks the best remedies, there can be no cure; and they will not seek the remedies while the presence of the diseases is considered as evidence of sin. In the past we have relied on fear as a deterrent and ignorance as a safeguard. They have failed. Let us now try practical cures. A pharisaic attitude is so highly mischievous that it becomes immoral.

The Government has taken prompt and fine action. It has removed one great difficulty, and effected all that can be done without fresh legislation. A comprehensive scheme of free diagnosis and treatment in general hospitals is to be organised by local authorities, who are to receive a grant from the Imperial Exchequer amounting to 75 per cent. of the cost. It is to be hoped that this admirable action will counteract the evils due to the increase of venereal disease certain to accompany the war.

The chief recommendations of the Commission other than those connected with direct immediate cure, which the Government has been able to carry out by an administrative Act, are as follows—

(1) The presence of infective venereal disease should be a cause for the prevention or annulment of marriage; further, the process of annulment should be made available for all persons, however poor.

(2) A communication made by a medical practitioner to a parent, guardian, or other person directly interested in the welfare of a woman or man in order to prevent or delay marriage with a person in an infectious condition should be a "privileged communication." It should not, in such circumstances, be libel or slander to state that an intending husband cannot safely marry.

(3) It is further strongly recommended that better instruction be given on sexual subjects. "The evils which lead to the spread of venereal diseases are in great part due to want of control, ignorance and inexperience, and the importance of wisely conceived educational measures can hardly be exaggerated."

There should be no delay in dealing with the last recommendation. A strong President of the Board of Education could, by an order of his pen, give instruction in an afternoon, and start arrangements which could introduce such teaching in all schools. It is, however, another matter whether there would be teachers capable to give the instruction. It is doubtful also whether sex teaching, introduced in this way as something apart from the usual educational course, could ever safeguard from sin.

I need, however, say little in this chapter on the important and difficult question of sexual education, as the whole of the last section of my book deals with that subject. I shall there try to show that the greater number of the evils connected with marriage and motherhood are due to false ideals and wrong methods of training in early life. I am, in particular, convinced of the mistakes we have been making in the education of girls—mistakes which prevent them as young women from having any clear aim to guide their lives, and act, as I believe, disastrously on their whole nature as well as spoiling their happiness. This public recommendation for a recognition of the sexual life and the problems connected with it as being of vital importance in the training of the young generation fills me with strong hope. But everything will depend on how such instruction is going to be given. Unwisely undertaken, it may easily lead to more harm than good. To be really efficacious it will need a sweeping change in the home and a revolution in the school. Now is the appointed time to act; if the opportunity be allowed to pass, it may not come again. The force of tradition and the convention of silence has been broken as it has not been broken before. We are all convinced that the time to change has come and to do something; when so many are agreed upon what ought to be done, the danger lies chiefly in the dispersion of energy by the weariness brought on by endless discussions on the way to give the education—a subject which unfortunately lends itself to much talking and disagreement.

But to return to the Royal Commission Report. Recommendations (1) and (2) cannot be carried out without special legislation. To obtain the support of the House of Commons for measures which would necessarily be opposed by some persons in every constituency, which have no vote-catching value and have not been chewed to pulp by long-continued party platform oratory, is a difficult task. The ordinary member of Parliament feels afraid to have convictions which are unsupported by powerful organisations; convictions which may cost him much opposition at election times. Probably such a measure to safeguard marriage could be more easily initiated by a vigorous and fearless member of the House of Lords. The House of Commons at the present time, even apart from the Great War and its urgency, is often busy for months with intricate Government measures, which take up nearly all the time available. Marriage laws cannot be dealt with in half an hour on a Friday evening.

This need not discourage us too much. It will not serve to leave matters to official action alone. If the victory against venereal diseases is to be won, strong signs of general interest must be shown. More even than this is necessary. The interest shown must be of an enlightened character. I feel it is urgent to emphasise this need for wise, and not hasty, action. Women have of late been taking a quite new concern in sexual questions, in particular in venereal diseases, so intimately connected with their interests. This is as it should be. But I have been forced to the knowledge that this interest, unbacked by wide knowledge and still more by experience of the facts of life, often leads them into folly. The possession of the vote by women has been expected to achieve immediate magical effects; it has been forgotten that women voters would be neither united in their aims nor possessed of the political capacity which would enable them infallibly to gain all for which they wished. Women ought not to hope to solve the ancient, fierce enigmas which have vexed mankind in every modern civilised society.

In my opinion, the greatest cause of error in women's judgment arises from the tendency (doubtless due to what their sex has suffered) to throw the whole blame for sexual sins on men. Some women carry sex antagonism like a flag, which they flourish in every wind. These are, of course, a small minority; but the majority of women fail to take a wide, sane view of both the question of prostitution and that of venereal diseases.

Let me give an illustration. I recently attended a meeting where a paper was read on the Report of the Venereal Disease Commission. The reader of the paper, being a woman doctor, took the wise view that the most important matter was the cure of the disease. In the discussion that followed, it was plainly evident that few of the audience agreed with her. These were women who had read about, and to some limited extent thought and studied these questions. Yet the general view was that *the men ought to be punished*. One speaker, who stated that she was married, said that *no true woman could or ought to forgive a husband who had become infected with venereal disease*.

Now, it is this view, here so crudely expressed, that I am writing to combat. Such an attitude of blame and unforgiveness has to be changed, or no legislation or public action will effect a real cure. *Women are really responsible for the secrecy of these diseases.* And what is the result? *Because these infectious diseases are secret they are largely uncured.*

I hasten to say that I am not taking an unfair view of the position. It is, of course, easy to understand the attitude taken up by women. Blame is not easily avoided. I would, however, ask them very earnestly to consider whether there is not some confusion in their minds.

The sin that the man commits against his wife is being unfaithful. Having caught the venereal disease is a misfortune. The effect must not be blamed by itself. Let me illustrate this point of view by considering a different case. Your child gets scarlet fever by an act of direct disobedience or sin. He goes to play at a house he has been forbidden to enter. Would you, because of his sin, refuse to pity and nurse him? Rather would you not forget his disobedience and desire only to help and to heal him?

Do you see what I mean now? It is not that I uphold immoral conduct in the husband or in the lover that I plead thus for pity and understanding on the part of women.

Few men are intentionally evil. They do not even act foolishly in this question of infectious disease because they are wantonly careless. Often they are fully alive to the danger that may result to their wives from their own infection. I repeat they are not necessarily bad men, and they may love their wives and children; but they are cowards. All men are cowards when it comes to facing their wives with their own wrong doings. If they cannot rely on the pity of their wives, few men will dare to tell the truth. If they cannot tell the truth, they cannot avoid infecting their wives. This may lead to the birth of infected children, and who may say that in this case the crime is the man's alone? It is to prevent this crime against the child and against life, that I urge upon women a wiser and more tolerant attitude.

For greater clearness, I may state the matter thus: there are three attitudes that may be adopted towards sexual disease. First, that of the pure moralist, who says only, "This is a sin to be punished." On the opposite side is the purely utilitarian, who says, "This is only a disease to be cured." But both attitudes may be alike wrong, or, more correctly, the truth lies midway between the two. The disease, as a disease, needs to be cured. This is the first step with which nothing should interfere. But far different and much more complex is the treatment required to alter the actions that lead to the disease.

As a first step, public opinion ought to condemn too late marriage, instead of recommending it on economic grounds. The mania for making economics the centre of life should now surely cease: the falsity of this view has been exposed by many great writers, but much stronger is the condemnation that must be given to it by all who can understand the evils that it has wrought in our sexual lives. Late marriages must be one of the causes contributing to men's use of prostitutes before marriage. This subject has been dealt with already in Chapter XII.

A natural division of the subject here presents itself. The problems of venereal infection are different before and after marriage. A practical knowledge of the physical facts of sex should be the possession of every girl some years before the age of marriage. Sex must cease to be a subject on which it is not decent for a girl to speak. Until this has been achieved, it will be impossible to have that frankness between lovers which will make certain an acknowledgment being made of infection, if it is or ever has been present in the man, so as to do away with the dangers of concealment and further disease. In my opinion, this openness is of necessary importance to the wise choice on the part of girls of the men they are to marry.

Our whole attitude towards youth in relation to sex is mistaken. And some of our worst mistakes take a direction not usually recognised. We often over-emphasise the possibilities of romantic love and chivalrous devotion, or we leave our children to gain this false attitude from the books they read. This is bad for both boys and girls. To personify all inspiration and nobility as Woman often but acts to make unknown vice attractive to youth. The unknown is almost always desirable. It is probable that times and places where excessive respect for women has been expressed in poetry and romance have been distinguished by looseness of sexual habits; just in the same way and for the same reason that extremely vulgar behaviour between the sexes is compatible with the strictest physical chastity.

In the case of girls, the evil that may be done by over-exalting romantic love is a different one. To idealise the male virtues of courage, adventurousness and self-confidence comes near, in many cases, to teaching the girls admiration for the calm, reckless Don Juan. This is the man who is likely to have been infected by venereal diseases.

In the story of the *Beauty and the Beast* we have material out of which part of the great sex difficulty can be explained. In the fairy story, the husband before marriage looks like a beast, after marriage he becomes a prince. In real life, the story is inverted. There is a deluding force in the mere skin and limbs of those of the opposite sex at the time when maturity is reached which may give princely attributes to those who would be seen as beasts at other times. The prince seen as a beast after marriage is a tragedy into which the romantic, ignorant girl must beware of drifting. The man who most boldly plays up to the romantic part expected of him—reciprocating to the perhaps unconscious encouragement of the girl—is not the man who will be the most agreeable to live with. I believe there is real danger in the sentimental view of love that is common to most girls. They do not know the poverty of feeling that loudly expressed sentiment may hide. The defect of many unfaithful lovers is not sensuality, but sentimentality. The lower types of lovers are strangely, almost incredibly, sentimental. Such teaching as this about the danger of an over-romantic view of love will not safeguard from all evils, but it will at least give knowledge that may protect in some time of peril.

The problem of the wife infected by a husband, who becomes diseased after marriage, is one that is different and more complicated. I have spoken already of the urgent need on the part of the wife that she should feel pity for the husband, even if she does this as the only means of protecting herself and her children. Without this pity, men will not dare to tell the truth. And even against their judgment and their wish, they will have sexual intercourse with their wives to prevent suspicion.

There is a further question that must be placed before women, and it is necessary for me to speak plainly. There is a question which I would ask the wife whose husband has become infected since marriage with one or other of the two forms of venereal disease: What is it that sends the man who is married to seek sexual satisfaction with the prostitute? It will not do to dismiss this question with the old, unreasoning condemnation of the male and his brute passions. In the case of the man of average decency, it is not deliberate choice that first sends him to dissipation.

Let us look at the matter a little closer and with greater truth. In marriage the woman dominates more often than usually is known. She has the children on her side. Undeniably the greatest function of any man in the life of the average woman is to be the father of her child. All other things that he means to her are secondary to this. For this reason, after the birth of her children she frequently ceases physically to desire her husband. Thus the position arises that many husbands, after some years of marriage, find themselves in a condition of loneliness in their own homes. And the cleavage is wider than the physical needs, and extends to the mental and spiritual plains. The woman's life is filled with her children; she ceases to belong to her husband as completely as he belongs to her. She holds back more and more of herself—the vital part that he wants. The man feels that he is losing, and, after some bluster and conflict, he begins not to care.

This, I believe, is the history of many marriages that started with love. The result in the end is almost certain. The lower types of husband from time to time will break away and seek distraction in wild love. Other men of more refinement will suffer much more, till they seek to find love with some woman in a permanent union outside marriage.

It may, and I expect will, be said that I am looking at this question from the man's side only. This is not because I do not feel the woman's position, but because the facts I am trying to state are so often neglected, in particular by women themselves. Women have been taught to believe, and do really feel, that by sexual unfaithfulness a husband does them the cruellest possible wrong that a man can do to a woman. But is the man ever wholly to be blamed? After all, he has given away only what his wife has shown him she does not want for herself. Most English wives always are acquiescent rather than passionate in the sexual embrace. Even when in love they are unresponsive, hiding what they feel, and rarely showing their husbands that they want them with any real desire. After a few years of marriage, his embraces are suffered as a duty. And here I would re-state an opinion given in an earlier chapter: I do hold that man is by his nature faithful. If he has once loved a woman, he does not cease to desire her until after she has ceased to desire him.

This brings me to the last question I want to consider. Why does the desire of the wife so often cease towards her husband? It is a difficult question to answer. One reason has been given already in the false attitude of the woman, which in so many cases makes her ashamed of expressing openly the passion that she feels. Yet there is, I think, another and much deeper part of the truth that is fairly clear. Each man is able to enforce his sexual desire upon his wife at a time when she feels no desire, whereas she cannot gain her desire unless he gain his. We may perhaps trace back to this cause the feeling of disharmony and waning of desire which injures the woman's power to love. Of course, this disharmony is not always conscious even to herself, and the man is quite unaware of the evil. But his acceptance of the woman's subordination, however gladly given, does exhaust the passion in her.

This difference in the power for sexual sacrifice between the two sexes is, I have frequently thought, one of the gravest causes of our misery. It will take very long to overcome it. Only as we advance in refinement and knowledge of love can this antagonism in the sex act lessen, as the woman gains in frankness and the man comes to know how to arouse and keep aflame her desire.

And there is here a question I would put to those husbands who are suffering to-day from the sexual coldness of their wives. I would ask them: Have they taken sufficient trouble to understand, both on the physical and psychical side, the sexual nature of woman, which is much more complex and difficult than their own? The art of love is not understood by Western people. If we paid more attention to this subject marriage would be freed from the greatest cause that brings it to disaster. Greater openness and sexual confidence between the husband and the wife is the first necessary step. But we shall never have this until we have rooted out of our moral conscience the idea of "the body as the prison of the soul." I have often asked myself if this misconception of love is not the real cause of all sex trouble.

And the remedy? Yes, that is the difficult matter. We cannot alter these evils by any cut-and-dried plan. The expression of sex is a question of refinement, and its regeneration must begin with a movement towards consciousness.

It may seem that we have reached no very definite conclusion. We have not solved the problem of venereal diseases. There is nothing to be gained by denying the difficulties that visit us in our sexual lives, or in talking, as many do, as though there were an easy way out. There is not.

I hold preaching on all these complicated questions to be quite useless. No platitudinous formulæ, no recrimination of one sex against the other sex, will do any good. The wrong is deep down in our attitude towards love, in our system of education, and in the very prevalent vulgarity of our surroundings. It is there that we must seek for it and destroy it.

I dare to think of a regeneration of our sexual lives through education and a fuller understanding of the meaning of love. By education must be understood all that influences the desires and imaginations, so that our children shall be turned to seek health and clean living.

Yet it were unwise to be too hopeful. We cannot be architects of life. Our sons and our daughters will make new mistakes, even should they escape our follies. We can see a very short way along the path of life, and often we are confused. The wisest amongst us are only as bricklayers, and the best can but lay two or three bricks in a lifetime. Our work is to do that if we can. We can guess very feebly at the whole design. Many mistakes must be made by us, as they have been made by those before us. And it may be the duty of a new generation to pull down the work that in sorrow we have toiled to build up.

PART V
SEXUAL EDUCATION

Wendla. I have a sister who has been married for two and a half years, I myself have been made an aunt for the third time, and I haven't the least idea how it all comes about. Don't be cross, Mother dear, don't be cross! Whom in the world should I ask but you! Please tell me, dear Mother. I am ashamed for myself. Please, Mother, speak! Don't scold me for asking you about it. Give me an answer—How does it happen? How does it all come about? You cannot really deceive yourself that I, who am fourteen years old, still believe in the stork.

Frau Bergmann. Good Lord, child, but you are peculiar! What ideas you have! I really can't do that!

Wendla. But why not, Mother? Why not? It can't be anything ugly if everybody is delighted over it!

Frau Bergmann. O—O God protect me! I deserve—— Go get dressed, child, go get dressed.

Wendla. I'll go. And suppose your child went out and asked the chimney sweep?

CONTENTS OF CHAPTER XIV
THE MOTHER AND THE CHILD

A tragedy of childhood—*The Awakening of Spring*, by Frank Wedekind—How we have ignored the need of the young for sexual enlightenment—The old method of silence a fatal mistake—Our fear of sex—The question of the sexual education of the child—Conflicting opinion—The twin causes of our civilisation prudery and prurience—The manner in which parents shirk and evade the natural inquiries of their children about birth and the facts of sex—The inevitable harm of this action—The early activity of the child's intelligence—Foolish stories and lies—Stimulate instead of quiet curiosity—Sex knowledge gained from servants and vicious companions—This danger from servants greater in the case of boys—Many young boys seduced by women—The duty of the mother to instruct her children—The difficulties that hinder parents—The child and the sexual impulse—The teaching of Freud—The danger from mistakes in the early training of the child—No age too young for education to begin—Mistakes that may be made—Our unconscious teaching stronger than anything we say—The mistake of set lessons—Sex not a subject to be taught like arithmetic—What is necessary is to tell the child the truth—Its questions must be answered as soon as they are put—The importance of not arousing curiosity —The child, not the mother, to be the guide—Cases in which we must be prepared to fail—The mother cannot always help her child—Recapitulation—The real difficulty in sexual education arises from our treatment of sex as something apart from the rest of life—We are afraid— Nothing worth doing can be done until this is changed.

CHAPTER XIV
THE MOTHER AND THE CHILD

"The child at its mother's knee is not too young to hear from her lips the sacred facts concerning his own origin; in a few years, indeed, he will be too old, for he will have learnt those facts from a worse source, perhaps in the gutter; and instead of being beautiful to him, as they might and could be, they will be merely dirty."—HAVELOCK ELLIS.

The quotation I have placed before these three chapters on Sexual Education, which form the fifth and final section of my book, is taken from the play, *The Awakening of Spring,* by Frank Wedekind; he calls it a tragedy of childhood, and dedicates the work to parents and to teachers. The play deals with a group of school children, just entering the age of puberty, and consists mainly of their conversations one with another. These imaginative young souls speculate about the mysteries of birth and sex in a manner that is typical of all children, not mentally inert. Herein rests the great value of the work: we come to realise the terrible darkness surrounding the sexual life of the great majority of boys and girls, with the resulting tragedies that may, and often do, destroy health and even life. Unable to explain the forces germinating in their nature, these children are hindered and crushed by the sham decencies and complacent morality that greet their blind gropings. Never was a more powerful indictment made against the sham of our educational system as a preparation for life.

The manner in which, up to the present time, we have ignored the need of the young for enlightenment and guidance in questions of such elemental importance to health and well-being is at once remarkable and difficult to understand. Under the influence of the idea of the sinfulness and radically evil nature of the sexual life, we have stood helpless, as if we were faced with a mysterious and malignant power; we have left the development even of our own children to the blind hazard of chance. Those among us who were wiser were not heeded. Celebrated pedagogues of a hundred years ago, such as Rousseau, Salzmann, Jean Paul and others, expressed themselves strongly in favour of the early sexual enlightenment of youth, and gave many valuable suggestions as to the methods of such teaching. Their wise recommendations remained for the most part without practical results. Only in recent years, in connection with the question of the protection of motherhood and the campaign against prostitution, has interest in the matter been reawakened. A heightened sense of responsibility has been quickened amongst us. An increased knowledge, gained by the patient work of investigation of the sexual impulse, is proving the immense importance of its right direction in the individual life. This would seem to be forcing us to act.

To-day it is conceded, even by many who are conservative in their attitude to sex, that the old plan of silence and leaving this matter to chance, has been a fatal mistake: we are coming to understand that every child has a sacred claim to wise training in sex knowledge.

There can be no doubt of our past guilt. The proof rests in unnumbered and needless disasters in the lives of almost all of us—sufferings unendurable and maiming; hurts to our deepest selves, that we have come to understand only when our thoughts have been liberated by knowledge.

From our fear of sex, we have become the victims of sex.

What can save us? It is women—the mothers who hold the future in their keeping. The answer rests with them. Liberation from the manifold problems of our disordered sexual life depends largely on a right transmission of knowledge to our children, so that they without harm may become wise. Such teaching must be given first by the mother. In this way only, through a trained and wiser motherhood, making possible the unhampered unfoldment of the children of the future, can humanity come into its heritage.

This is my firm conviction, my profound belief. And for this reason, in my book on Motherhood, I have placed the question of sexual education last, because I hold it to be the most important of all—the foundation necessary before other changes or reforms can be of any avail.

There is much that gives me hope. This question of the sexual education of her children has begun to stir in the conscious thought of countless mothers. The days of folded hands are happily over. Mothers of all classes desire knowledge for their children because they want to save them from suffering and from falling into the mistakes that they, through want of knowing, have themselves made.[100]

While, however, mothers, as well as the great mass of educationalists and reformers, recognise more and more the need for this knowledge for all children, they are yet uncertain as to how and when sex teaching should be given.[101] There is too much hesitating so that often cowardice prevents any action being taken. And the question, "What shall we teach our children and at what age ought we first to speak?" is one to which few have as yet found a certain answer.

The truth is, the vast majority of mothers and teachers are themselves amazingly and perilously ignorant on the whole subject of sex. The ban of silence has worked untold evil in our thoughts, and what makes the difficulty even worse is that we are so very much afraid of sex it is impossible for us to learn. Hence we go about seeking mysteries and hunting lies, and completely lose sight of what should be as clear as daylight—the need of the little child.

The twin curses of our civilisation that fetter the spirit, prudery and prurience, acting together, have drawn sex into the darkest, unwholesomest corners of our minds, so that few of us mention the subject even to our own children without a feeling of shame. So pitifully afraid are we of the facts of life that we invent fables and lie to them as to how they were born.

Parents shirk and evade the natural inquiries of their children; very often no kind of answer is given to their young searchings for the truth. In other cases foolish fictions that outrage even a child's intelligence are repeated, and falsehood piled upon falsehood. For it is one condition of a lie that it can never stand alone; and when a mother has lied to her child once, she is compelled to weave a network of falsehood to sustain her first false statement. She must go on from one foolish evasion to worse untruths to keep up appearances. Every story which, like that of the stork or the gooseberry bush, rests upon a lie, is an outrage to the child. And the mother's authority stands upon a veritable quicksand, for the day will come when the child will not believe her. A careless word may be spoken by a servant, a companion, or some other, and, if the mother has not saved herself in time, she will be discovered by her child as a liar. The whole structure of her pretence and shameful evasions will totter and fall to ruin. And with it must go her power to influence her child. Barriers of doubts and silence are raised which, as time goes on, more and more will separate the child from the parent. And such barriers once set up can hardly ever be broken through. An embarrassing sense of shame, rising like a poisonous gas between mother and child, will work death to any confidence. How many mothers have been forced in bitterness to cry, "I lied to my child. I concealed the truth year after year. Now my child turns from me, and no longer has faith in me or in my words."

And this failure of duty on the part of the mother works unknown harm to the child. That is the essential point. Do our children remain in ignorance of the facts of sex which we, in our fear, fail to teach them? No, they do not. Girls and boys in tens of thousands take the course of action threatened by the child Wendla—they go and learn from others what their mothers have refused to tell them. Few children fail to discover, either through their own intelligence or by some information they gain at school or from servants, some kind of sexual information. Thus too often they glean their first knowledge of sex from the vulgar, ignorant lips of the prurient.

I marvel at the blindness of parents, who seem unable to approach this question with even common understanding. Nine children out of ten gain information upon the relations of the sexes in the worst possible way. Fortunate is the child who escapes the contamination of ignorant indecency.

It should be remembered that in children the activity of the intelligence begins to work at an early age. Curiosity is very prominent: all children want "to find out." And their activity will certainly tend to manifest itself in an inquisitive desire to know many elementary facts of life, which are dependent upon sex. The primary and most universal of these desires is the wish to know where babies come from. The degree of curiosity differs, of course, in different children; I do not think it is absent from any normal child. If they do not question their elders, they certainly will talk with one another. And the shy child, or the child who is kept from other companions, is not saved from these curiosities: I am inclined to think that the interest is strengthened and made more dangerous by repression.

Many foolish stories are told by mothers, in their blindness and lack of faith, to put off the child's natural desire to learn its origin. There is a curious illusion that children accept these fables, and really believe that the baby is found in the garden under the gooseberry tree, or brought by the stork, or by the doctor in his bag. But the child's perception is more acute than is believed, and very rarely is any one deceived. And the mother forgets that by puzzling the child's mind with these foolish stories she defeats very surely the object for which they are invented. The greater the mystery about sex matters the more will childish curiosity be aroused. We cannot escape from this. *The child thinks much less of what it knows and is sure of than of what it does not know, but wants to find out.*

And the same objection, of stimulating instead of quieting curiosity, applies to the plan adopted by many parents of telling the child when it asks these questions that it is too young to understand and must wait until it is older. This postponement is better than inventing foolish fables and telling lies, but I am sure it is unwise. The mother thinks the child is satisfied and forgets. Very rarely is this the case; the child puzzles alone, its curiosity only quickened by the hurt that has been given to its sensitive young intelligence. A wide experience has taught me that the only children who do not talk or think much about the origin of babies are the children who know how babies are born.

The silly stories told by parents are supplemented by equally absurd and often seriously injurious conversations with other children. Many servants of both sexes are addicted to idle and irreverent, even if not vicious, talk upon this subject, and by this means the views of many children, and even their whole future outlook, upon sex are distorted and besmirched. This is particularly the case with boys, where any intimacy with servants is much more dangerous than a similar intimacy in the case of girls.

I must follow this question a little, though it leads me aside from the main subject of this chapter. Young boys at school and elsewhere are in constant danger. It is rarely that girls are placed in a position of intimacy with an adult male, except their father or their brothers. The very reverse is the case with boys: they are tended, and when young are washed and bathed, by women servants, their clothes are looked after by women, in sickness they are nursed by women, and in innumerable cases they are brought into much more intimate relations with women than girls are ever brought into with men.

I would like to say a great deal more about this danger. The part played by servants in the sexual initiation of boys carelessly left in their charge, and often when they are still children, is much larger than usually is credited. It is folly to close our eyes to the evils that may, and often do, arise. Perhaps in no other matter has the ignorance of mothers worked greater evils or been more culpable than it has been here. Nor is it servants alone that have to be feared in this connection: many boys have been seduced by women, who would be least suspected of such an act. I could give cases from my own knowledge: men, at least, will know that I speak the truth. The facts are ugly, but they may not be overlooked. No mother should be ignorant on these matters. For myself I would trust my little adopted son—he is twelve years old—with no servant and with very few women. This may seem a hard saying, but it is based on a wide knowledge of what happens to many boys. We expose our children to manifold dangers which only now are we coming to understand. We have to accept these things unless we are ready to act.

Even if no such great evil happens, much harm may be done by vulgar speech. Beautiful and sacred emotions, marvellous processes of nature, legitimate and essential longings, become associated in the tender expanding mind of the healthy boy with the unseemly, the shameful, and the unclean. Where the child should learn to wonder, he is taught to know shame and to deride. The results are terrible in many cases.

It is the mother's duty and privilege unceasingly to watch her child, but this she can do only if she has knowledge and is wise.

It must not be thought that I am unmindful of the many and great difficulties that hinder the actions of parents. Under our present conditions of almost universal concealments, the sexual education of our children is, indeed, so difficult a problem that I am conscious of all manner of obstacles as I attempt to suggest a solution. Of one thing only am I certain: we can no longer leave this matter safely to the hazard of chance.

I know well that there are many parents who, fully recognising the importance of safeguarding their children, yet hold back in fear of what they think may be the danger of bringing the sex impulses too early into the child's focus of consciousness. It is also thought, though less often said, that in previous generations boys and girls got on very well without this fad of sex-instruction. But the question is whether they really did. The widespread prevalence of sexual troubles (which are only now beginning to be understood and to gain the attention that for so long they have claimed) is to a large extent the corollary of our hypocritical or cynical attitude as adults to the difficulties of youth. We ourselves have "muddled through," and we placate our consciences with the whisper, "What we have done, the youngsters can do also. Let them alone, it's a beastly awkward subject to tackle."

It would be waste of time to answer such arguments. I would point out only one result of such criminal and cold-blooded indifference: it is generally the most promising children who are destroyed through sex struggles. The coarser-fibred children may escape and come through without great hurt: it is the sensitive children—who fight and recoil and thus suffer—who are sacrificed by the total lack of appreciation on the part of their elders of their difficulties and blind gropings for light, sacrificed sometimes to the slaying of the body and the soul.

The first objection needs more careful consideration. Here, as I have pointed out already, the greatest difference of opinion arises in connection with the questions as to when and how sexual instruction should be given to children. Some, like myself, plead for the enlightenment to be as early as possible, in the first years of the child's life, so that never may there be a conscious period in which the child *does not know*. There are, however, many who disagree and hold it better, for the reasons I have shown, to defer sexual instruction till the child is older, to the onset of puberty, or even later. Perhaps the attitude common to most parents is one of hesitation, that may be expressed in the question: For how long can we safely leave this matter alone?

No one will wisely give a dogmatic answer to this question. Yet I think we can come to a better understanding if we at once put out of our minds any idea of formal instruction. Sex is not something outside of life—a subject that we can teach or not teach to our child, like arithmetic, for instance. This has been our great mistake. And we shall see our folly more clearly, if for a little time we focus our attention on the child, and stop our rather useless discussions.

Now it is part of the popular belief about the sexual impulse that it is absent in childhood, and first appears in the period of life known as puberty. This is a serious error and one that has brought many evil consequences, not the least of which has been our failure to understand the nature of the child. We are now reaping our mistakes and finding out that the exact opposite of this is the truth. The remarkable work of Freud, that has opened up a whole new field of inquiry, has shown us that the sexual instinct is never absent in the normal child. "In reality," he states, "the new-born infant brings sexuality with it into the world, sexual sensations accompany it through the days of lactation and childhood, and very few children can fail to experience sexual activities and feelings before the period of puberty."[102]

Possibly there is some little exaggeration in this view, for the basis of our knowledge is still very narrow; but it seems certain we must accept Freud's view as in the main right, as, indeed, any one of us who has had any experience of children may prove for ourselves by our own observation. Have you ever considered the games of your young children—the way in which they imitate father and mother, play the game of the family, and delight in being the parents of their dolls? Your child is being taught by Nature, and the first appearance of sex in its heart occurs as simply as the fall of the dew upon the flowers. It is we, their elders, who in our blundering too often break in and sully this beautiful unfolding. Sex is not something to be escaped from. This never can be done. We have, even if against our will, to accept its presence.

Freud—and his opinion may not be put aside—holds that in all young children there is present a sexual life more or less subconscious, which may be exaggerated and even perverted by any carelessness, neglect, or repression. It is believed that certain manifestations of infantile activity, notably the excretory functions and feeding, as also the common habit of thumb-sucking and biting of the nails, are closely connected with the sexual impulse.

In normal children the sexuality of this infantile period, which lasts until the third or fourth year, then passes into more or less complete oblivion.

There follows a happy play period during which sex is latent, and this lasts until puberty approaches. It is during this period of sexual latency that the psychic forces of the child develop—forces which, in later years, act as inhibitions on the sexual life and narrow and direct its expression like dams. But in nervous children, where frequently there is sexual precocity, this order is very likely to be disturbed. And the danger may be increased by the over-fondling of an unwise and voluptuous mother, by an ignorant nurse, or the suggestion of an older and vicious child, with very detrimental results. A wrong direction may most easily be given to the child's sexual development in its earliest years. Neurotic manifestations such as hysteria, obsessions, and many sexual perversions, are traced back by Freud to the influence of the wrongly directed or repressed erotic experiences of childhood. It seems to be quite clear that any repression of the instinctive and subconscious infantile sexuality makes for evil; that the only safe course to follow is the culture of a healthy and right expression. Freud goes the length of saying that obsessions are in every case transformed reproaches which have escaped from the attempted repression and are always connected with some pleasurable sexual feeling aroused in childhood.

Now, before I go on further to point out the line of action, and the change in our attitude to this question, that must follow inevitably from our knowledge of the early existence in the child of the sexual impulse, I would wish to underline as strongly as I am able the facts that we have learnt: (1) *Every child is born with a sexual nature*; (2) *this infantile sexuality furnishes the groundwork of the later sexual life*; (3) *and the individual's sexual conduct and health will depend, in part at least, on the peculiarities of this early period of infancy and childhood*; (4) *therefore, the sexual desires and instincts with which the child is born cannot safely be left alone; they must be dealt with in some way*; (5) *for a wrong direction to these instincts may most easily be given by any mistake or neglect on the part of the mother or those connected with the child*; (6) *lastly, and most important of all, repression of sex is always dangerous; any efforts made in this direction are very likely to lead to evil in the later life of the child.*

We have found now the answer to the question we were seeking: *the sexual education of the child should begin in its earliest years, since there is no age too young for harm to be done by our neglect or mistakes.*

The first teacher must, therefore, be the mother, who is with the child and should watch over and direct its unfolding nature, by unceasing and selfless care, in these early years when care counts for most. And I would state in passing, that here is another reason—and I hold it the strongest reason of all—why no mother, who is not forced to do so, should leave her home to work and have thus to delegate her sacred duty of caring for her child to another.

But again we are faced with difficulties many and various that will have to be overcome. For while every one must agree that a wise mother is incomparably the child's best teacher, it is equally true that the unwise mother may do incalculable harm. And when we face, as I am attempting to do, the conditions of the ordinary home, as we all know it to be under the present guidance of ignorance and prejudice in these questions, it seems certain that few mothers can wisely carry out this teaching. Not much hope for the child until this is changed. Thus, it is clear that the sexual education of the child will have to begin with changed conditions in the home and sexual education of the mother.

This is going to be a very difficult task, and I speak here of good mothers, not of bad ones. It is a painful fact that many mothers, who are keenly conscious of their responsibility and most anxious to train their children aright, are too shy to be of much direct use to them in their sexual education. They cannot free themselves, even when they wish to do this, from the vulgarisation of the idea of sex that has resulted from their own training.

There can be nothing gained by pretending that this question of sexual education is going to be an easy matter. It may be so in theory, it will not be easy in practice. Sometimes, indeed, I am so filled with doubts and sadness, that, if doing and saying nothing were working well, I might be tempted to think that to establish sexual training under present conditions was even a worse course than to go on leaving the matter alone. But I know that all is not well. By continuing our policy of negligence and cowardice we are holding open the way to disasters in the future, the far-reaching evils of which we are only now beginning to understand.

It is obvious that sex instruction may be given blunderingly even with the greatest good-will; I am, indeed, exceedingly doubtful of the efficacy of any kind of formal teaching. Certainly set lessons, or even "arranged talks," should not be given to young children. All children harbour curiosities regarding their bodily structure and the basis of life. In an atmosphere of trust, sooner or later they will express these natural curiosities in a tentative, haphazard way. This is the psychological moment for the mother's teaching. The question asked must be answered truthfully and in terms simplified to the comprehension of the child. The reply must have the air of being both candid and confidential: that is to say, it must satisfy curiosity and at the same time leave the impression that such subjects are to be avoided in general conversation, not because they are "nasty," but because they are so sacred and intimate that they should be mentioned only to those the child loves and respects. The ideal must ever be to educate through love, to avoid always repressive measures, and to aid the expression of the normal sex instincts: let the child establish its own psychic individuality.

Our unconscious example must always be far stronger in its result on the child's mind than anything we can say. Of what use can our teaching be, if, through our own want of purity, the concealments that breed curiosity and shame, are evident in all our attitude to our bodies and to the physical facts of our being? The child is not shown the duty of reverence for himself; he is not taught the beauty of all the processes of his young life; the sex organs are left without proper names, and the child is told that it must not speak of these parts. We are continuously careless in our conversations and in our acts before our children. We take them to see picture plays and allow them to read books and tell them stories in which love is vulgarised, and all kinds of false statements are allowed. In these and in numerous other ways, weeds are caused by our folly to spring up in the child's mind. We can never undo by any teaching a sense of shame in sex and love that our actions and thoughtless words have revealed to the quick intelligence of the child.

It is entirely false to think that the facts of sex plainly and simply told will shock and seem strange to the young child. It is to the prurient only that there is anything ugly or disillusioning in birth and love. The child will receive your information with wonder and guileless delicacy. The mother need have no fear of her child, only of herself. The error in all these cases is the error of our own impurity of thought; the hateful idea that the facts of sex are ugly and disillusioning. Here we have the key to the whole problem: it explains the utter helplessness and weakness of our attitude. It will be very long before this can be changed; the evil is rooted so deeply in almost all of us.

A child of four and even younger will begin to ask questions of its mother. As soon as the questions are put they should be answered in such a manner that the child's curiosity is satisfied. And this brings me to what I hold to be more important than all else. In this difficult question of sexual enlightenment, *it is the child who must be the guide of the parent.* I regard this as the most urgent rule for every mother. *Never arouse sexual curiosity in the child, either directly by offering instruction on the subject or indirectly by careless speech or action, but always be ready to satisfy such curiosity at once when it is present in the child's consciousness.*

This is, of course, to say that every question of the child must be answered by the truth. It goes without saying, that the mother must give her answer just as if she were talking on any other subject, or explaining the function of any other organ of the body. This course can be adopted only where adults are able to talk of these subjects without shame. There must be no hushed voices, no special manner in speaking. Any hint of such feeling or hesitancy on the part of the mother will communicate itself at once to the quick consciousness of the child. Here again I am driven back to the difficulty of our own fear of sex: this is the stumbling-block that hinders the right teaching of our children.

I know there are many parents who will fear this openness of speech and action, holding that it is dangerous to break through the mystery and reserve with which we have surrounded the physical facts of love. This danger is felt to be specially great in the case of girls. I am certain this is a very deep mistake. Show the child that the mystery of sex rests in its sacredness: teach it that, for this reason, we do not speak of the subject lightly, holding it in too great reverence for common speech; but never let it be thought of as a subject tabooed, one on which openness of thought is not nice, for thus it will become shameful, and uncleanness and not mystery will keep it in the dark places of the child's consciousness.

But here I would give a further word of warning to the mother. She must not expect or desire from her child a continued attention to her teaching, nor must she force by over-emphasis or any kind of moral warnings a false sentiment in her teaching. I believe this to be very important. The child, at the age when such questions first will be asked and should be answered, will tire very quickly of any information that the mother gives. It will break off to run away and play, or will interrupt the most beautiful and carefully prepared lesson. But if the mother is wise, she will never go beyond the interest of the child.

Facts communicated in this way and at such natural opportunities are subconsciously noted and swiftly dismissed from the consciousness of the child, who soon becomes interested in something else after the disconnected discursive fashion of childish thinking. And, when so treated, it will be found that children are not inordinately interested in these questions; they will break off from what they are asking you about birth or the procedure of the sexual act to talk about toy soldiers or dolls. This very carelessness in attention is, indeed, the immense value of this form of teaching: the child has the information and yet does not trouble about it, and ignores it when it is not to the point. Such can never be the case when the information is given in the form of a set lesson and interconnected with moral teaching. So important is this that I think it better and safer for the mother to err on the side of saying too little than saying too much. All that is essential is that the truth should be told.

Now this is not going to be easy. Above all else, it is necessary to establish, as far as is possible, feelings of openness and sympathy between the mother and her child. And for this it is essential that the mother must herself have the most absolute faith in the purity of sex, and in her own physical relationship to her child and to its father. Without this nothing that is worth gaining can be gained from any form of teaching. The slightest doubt or uncertainty on the mother's part is fatal; then, at once, shame will begin to creep in to hurt the young and sensitive life.

There is another matter that must be considered. It is often stated, by the most careful parents as well as by those who are careless, that complete and perfect sympathy exists between them and their children. "My child tells me everything" has been the thought to bring comfort to many mothers. But is this true? For myself I have wondered if such an ideal can ever be attained fully. Nor am I certain, if we think of the child only, whether it is an ideal really to be desired. We have to remember that we—the parents—belong to one generation and the child to another. And this barrier of age is felt in nothing more strongly than it is in sex. The intense and complicated forces that have moulded us are but awakening in the young life. We can, at best, hope only to guide our children; we can give to them some little knowledge gained by the experience of our mistakes, but we cannot give them the knowledge they can gain only from life, nor can we save them from making their own mistakes.

Idle curiosity is banished by simple honest teaching, and much evil is thereby prevented. But the boundless curiosity of the child is not and, indeed, should not be satisfied. The boy or the girl, as he or she grows older, will have to experiment, to find out for himself or herself. To ignore this need is, I am certain, to blind ourselves to the facts of life. We must be prepared that, with all our care, our most loving efforts to gain the confidence of our children will be met by refusals.

And although this failure may, and, indeed, must sadden us as we watch the child of our love passing out of the protective circle of our power to help, we need to know that this is a natural process—a step forward that should be taken by the boy or girl; we even fail in our duty do we try to hold them back and refuse to loosen the cords of guidance. The child is fulfilling his or her own needs in turning from us. Age cannot always help youth. In the early years the child desires and should have the very individualised and binding relation with its parents, but when he is older he ought to free himself from the old bindings—from the covering protection of the mother and father—if he is to establish his own character and suitably adapt himself to the world outside the home.

Our children will turn away from us in their search for knowledge and experience. All that any mother can do is to establish a relationship of openness and confidence in her child's early years, for if it is not done then hardly ever can it be done later. But even when this has done, there will still be needed the utmost care that what has been gained may not be used for the mother's own satisfaction and against the good of the boy or the girl.

All the wisdom and patience and tenderness and sacrifice of the parents will be needed after the epoch of puberty and in the difficult years of adolescence, to know when it is wise to give advice and claim confidence, or when the harder duty must be done of pushing the boy or the girl away to experiment and live upon their own responsibility.

Here, again, I would give warning: in these later adolescent years it is always the child—boy or girl—and not the parents who must be the guide. The mother and the father must be ready at all times, but their task is, I think, one of very patient and loving waiting: it is the child who must desire to give the confidence. It is true that the wise parent may create opportunities of confidence; to these the boy or the girl will respond readily; at least this will be so when the early training of the child has been without any hateful sense of shame.

Such are the facts as they present themselves to me.

The real failure in sexual education arises from our treatment of sex as something apart from the rest of life. We have got to change this, if we are to help our children. Sex must cease to be a forbidden subject. Label any natural function as improper, not to be spoken about and repellent, and at once you set up an abnormal curiosity, and open a way for almost every evil. We must cease to be afraid.

There is, of course, a very deep reason for this fear of sex. The sex impulses are not often realised and understood in the conscious life of men and women, and although they can be caught up and fused into all that is best in the individual character, they remain in most of us unrecognised and untamed. You will see what I mean. The sex instinct has retained its wildness, and we must, I think, face the fact that there is in all of us a volcanic element in sex, underlying and influencing all the rest of our nature, and, for that very reason, shaking the individual character from its foundations with tremor, if not with catastrophe. This distrust of the dynamic force, which so often we have found difficult to control in ourselves, causes us to fear for our children. We are afraid that many growths we do not like may spring up in them. And the immediate result in us is an inhibitory awkwardness—largely an effort of hiding—in the face of everything that comes within hailing distance of the sex passion.

Until we have cleared our thoughts from this confusion of fear, very little good can be done. Let us purify ourselves and re-establish our own faith. When once we come to understand, we cannot go on leaving our children to be sullied, and in some cases—and those not a few—even crushed and destroyed by our mock modesty, sham decencies and complacent blindness.

It is my firm conviction that most of the perversions of sex, a whole list of diseases, the almost countless number of unhappy marriages, many of the existing social evils—may be traced back to this cause. It is unsafe to prophesy, yet I think much of the misery would be remedied, if once we could dispel the unwholesome mystery with which we, in our timidity and uncleanness of mind, have enveloped the facts of birth and the relations between the sexes. Such mystery is really nothing but shame; much of it may be dispelled by the wholesome light of simple and wise teaching. So only can we hope to guide our children's natural and beautiful unfolding. We must inculcate in them from their earliest years respect for their own bodies and for the reproductive act.

Reverence for sex as something holy should be part of every child's education. The eternal hymn of Love is the noblest strain in the universe, and the young should be taught to heed it reverently. There must be no false valuation of the impulse which unites men and women, if we wish our daughters and our sons to fulfil worthily the high duties of parenthood. We cannot teach unless our faith is great and we also practise. We must plant deep in our children's fresh natures a desire for beauty, not alone in outside things, but in all thought and in every deed relating to the Life force, which is Love.

You will see now the scope of the claim I am making for sexual education: it is to be the means whereby concealments are to be broken through and shame in sex is to be destroyed.

CONTENTS OF CHAPTER XV
SEXUAL EDUCATION WITH SPECIAL REFERENCE TO THE ADOLESCENT GIRL

Our very limited powers—Our children have to experiment and to learn life for themselves—The theoretical teacher who reforms the world on paper—The hindrances placed in the way of the sex emotions—We educate girls and boys as if they were sexless neuters—The folly of this denial of sex—The origin of our fear—An attempt to express the psychological meaning of the combination of the man and the woman—The differences between the boy and the girl—An attempt to follow this dissimilarity—The evils arising from the modern tendency to ignore sex differences—This the real weakness in the position of the modern girl—She has a profound distrust of herself as a woman—Our schools and educational system founded on the needs of boys—This a great evil—The development of the girl at puberty more difficult than the development of the boy—Every girl lives a hidden life of her own—The conflict in the sensitive soul of the adolescent—This the age of romance and idealism—The danger of sudden and wrong knowledge of the physical facts of sex—Full instruction of girls more necessary even than the instruction of boys—The immense danger of repression—The transformation of puberty—Painful experiences of youth act harmfully in the later years—Our deadly silences and sham presentation of life—The injury we do to the girl by ignoring her sexual life—Induces sexual coldness—This the great cause of unhappiness in marriage—Our fear and denial of love—This what is wrong with life.

CHAPTER XV
SEXUAL EDUCATION WITH SPECIAL REFERENCE TO THE ADOLESCENT GIRL

"But, alas! a hindrance ever lurketh in our way; it is the leaven in the dough, the deadly flies that invert the sweetness of the fragrant wine; … Thus … the wrongful thoughts ferment. Evil plougheth in and urgeth as a task-master. He wasteth and destroyeth, and, lo! we are taken captive in this thraldom; he giveth over the innocent and pure to death; defilement spreadeth, and of joy there is naught left."—(Eng. trans., *Jewish Prayer for the Day of Atonement*.)

Now, because I desire sexual enlightenment for all children, and, in particular, for all girls, and seek as a reformer the re-shaping of education in the home and in the school, it does not follow that I am so over-presumptuous as to believe it possible in this way quickly to remedy all sexual mistakes, or that I do not realise how our policy of muddle and leaving these matters alone has not always been as disastrous as, indeed, we might expect. I know that in many cases and among numerous young people the sexual life follows a healthy and beautiful unfolding, in spite of anything we may do or may leave undone. And it needs but a cursory view to see that all is not confused and an aimless conflict of waste, but that the wonderful beauty of youth often will triumph over the meanness of our fears, our subterfuges and blind blunderings. One perceives something that goes on, something that is continually working in the child to make order out of our muddle, beauty out of our defacements: to force light, frankness and purity in place of our shams and our lies.

Doubtless to the theoretical teacher eager to reform the world on paper, it seems a very easy matter to lay down rules for mothers and teachers regarding sexual instruction—new finger-posts to conduct, whereby the young generation may be guarded from making the mistakes that we ourselves have made. But can we do this? For in sex we have as yet learnt very little, and I doubt sometimes if we can ever learn very much, except each one of us for ourselves out of our own experience. We of an older generation cannot save our children very far, or hold them back from life. And it may be well that at once we realise and acknowledge the very narrow limits of our power.

But this is not to say that we are to shirk and continue to act as if all were well when we know that it is not so. The manner in which, up to the present day, we have completely ignored the very fact of sex in our educational system is almost incredible. There has been in many directions a vast range of betrayal and baseness in our treatment of youth.

No other emotion is so hindered, opposed, and loaded with material and moral fetters. We know how education makes a beginning in this way, and how life continues the process. Perhaps some of these hindrances are inevitable; but many are the direct result of our adult stupidity, and the way we have failed in training the young. How can you expect the primitive powerful sex impulse not to suffer? The sex emotions are among the deepest, if not the deepest, of our nature; they exercise an influence on every phase of development, and, in one form or another, direct the entire being of the individual. We know this. And all the time we continue to educate girls and boys as if they were sexless neuters. Could folly be greater?

By our teaching and our example we are destroying for the young the harmony of Nature. We ourselves are shame-faced because we are still savages in sex. If not, why this awe and funk, these taboos and mysteries, all the secretive cunning with which we hide from the young facts that we all know, but pretend that we don't know?

And it cannot be overlooked that this fear of sex is of very ancient origin, which makes it the more difficult to eradicate. We have, I believe, to allow for an ages-old, and therefore strongly rooted, sense of separation, causing an often unconscious antagonism between the two sexes. We see its unchecked action in many examples in the animal kingdom, though not in all—it is quite absent, for instance, in the family life of certain insects and in the perfect loves of many birds, whose life-histories we examined in the first section of this book. We see the same antagonism acting continually among primitive peoples in the elaborate and sacred system of taboos which separate the two sexes. Indeed, the beginnings of the marriage system can be traced back to a primitive conception of danger attaching to the sexual act. I am not very hopeful that this sex separation that is a kind of antagonism can ever be wholly eliminated; I am not even sure that it is well that it should be eliminated. May it not be that love itself would be withered did we take it away? I am not certain at all; I know, however, that this fear of sex has led us into great folly.

What is the psychological meaning of the combination of man and woman? It is the union between opposites, which, perhaps, I may try to explain further as the union between consciousness and unconsciousness. The man is essentially conscious, the woman essentially unconscious; the man is concentrated in his intellect, the woman is concentrated in her senses. These, at least, are the nearest words in which I am able to express it. And of one thing I am certain: the modern way of mixing the qualities of the two sexes acts directly for unhappiness and in harm to the race. I did not always think this: I did not want to think it. I have come slowly to be convinced and against my own will. And I am glad to take the opportunity now, as I near the end of my book on Motherhood—the subject which ever has been deepest in my heart—to state this as my later opinion, which has been made clear to me by the experiences of my life.

There is no use in saying there is no difference between the girl and the boy when human nature keeps asserting that there is. There is even, as I have been forced into accepting, a natural tendency between boys and girls to draw away from each other. You may see this separation in every co-education school where the children, led by deeper instincts than we have understood, bring our wisdom to foolishness. They unconsciously feel that separation which we have been trying to pretend does not exist. Each sex, at the very dawn of the teens and before, is unfolding interests, tastes, plays and ambitions of its own.

It would be interesting to follow this dissimilarity as far as it could lead us. Sometimes it would seem that we had got to the bottom—to what is common to the girl as to the boy; the qualities that both sexes share as human beings, where the ties of similarity seem to link their characters. But wait! deeper than this we must seek for the truth. Even in this likeness there is an all-pervading unlikeness. And it is just this: the differences, which cannot, I think, be expressed, but which do exist—differences in souls, in minds and in bodies—as well as a separation in the habits, the desires, and attitude to life, that makes for such harmony in the elemental depths.

The influence of sex extends in mysterious ways that as yet we do not understand. And the variation between the girl and the boy is far greater, I believe, than has ever in modern times been recognised. The longer I live, and the more life teaches me, the more strongly I am convinced of this fact: you do not make the girl into the boy by ignoring her special functions; you do not lessen sexuality by pretending it is not there.

From the start of puberty this difference between the girl and the boy should be faced; great is the harm that follows from our pretending it is not there. And the hurt suffered in my opinion, is almost always more serious to the girl than to the boy.

Many women are blindly prejudiced on this question as, indeed, I myself once was. The reason of such mistake is plain. This breaking down or lessening of the differences between the two sexes may be, and is, possible. By means of education and the action of habit a child may be impressed with characteristics normally foreign to its sex, qualities and tendencies are thus developed which ordinarily appear only in a child of the opposite sex. I would refer the reader back to the early section of this book for examples, most curious and suggestive, of such complete transposition of the female and male characters.[103] Things are not quite so obviously plain in the human world, but they are not less fateful, less significant.

We touch here the real weakness in the position of the modern girl: the profound distrust that she has of herself. I do not mean, of course, intellectually or as a worker, but a distrust of herself as Woman. I believe it results directly from educational influences. All our effort is directed to repress from the consciousness of the girl the realities of her own sexual nature; and what we do is to hinder her deepest instincts so that often they fail in finding a healthy expression.

In our schools the educational system is founded on the needs of boys and not on the needs of girls. I regard this as a great crime. For one thing, the development of the girl is more obscure and difficult than the development of the boy; in her sex-life there are finer balances, which opens up the way to greater evils. There is every possibility of morbid disturbance from any mistakes in the training. The girl has more that she needs to learn to establish her health and sexual happiness than has the boy; the pubescent period lasts longer with her and is more unsettling; while the greatest difficulty of all, perhaps, arises from the fact that her conduct is more ruled by deep unconscious instincts. Every girl lives a hidden life of her own, and it is within this shrine of her individuality that the primitive and fierce instincts of her sex struggle to find expression; and though always unacknowledged and often, indeed, unrecognised, alike by the girl herself as well as by her elders, it is these instincts that direct her growth and are the determining influence of her life, far more important than the actions directed by her conscious self, which is occupied in learning lessons, in play, and all the outward interests of the daily life.

And it is this deeper ego that suffers from our educational system and the elaborate ingenuity with which the facts of life are hidden and glossed over. Girls in our schools, and also in our homes, are trained to become secretive about themselves, treating their special sexual functions as a mystery and a shame. Truth-telling is inculcated in all matters except sex, and here there is an unceasing evasion, which prepares disharmonies at the very dawn of sexual consciousness.

Let us understand what harm we are doing. Do we know? Do we care? We have, I suppose, a certain vague ideal as to what Woman should be, but as far as I can see we give no kind of training to help a girl in any way to live healthily and fully her life as a woman. As it is, one is tempted to say that it is rather in spite of than by means of her education that any modern girl arrives at any conception of her womanly nature and her tasks. We really seem to be proclaiming a sense of injury because there is such a fact in the girl's nature as sex.

Again I assert that our crime is manifest. We have set up an educational system that is blind to the needs of girls and the facts of their sexual life. How many among us women of this generation have suffered hurt—thousands of women defrauded of happiness and of health, bearing with them year after year the mark of lost instincts, stifled desires, and natures in part murdered. Do I write strongly? Yes, I do; but I write of what I know to be true.

Mothers, wrapped in the long trance of complacent living, remain indifferent, or are themselves too ignorant and dead to life to give help. As their daughters come to consciousness, as they begin to suffer their own fulfilment, they can do nothing and they cast them off. Hard shut down and silent in themselves, how many girls suffer the anguish of youth reaching out for the unknown ideal that they can't grasp, can't even distinguish or conceive. What we call education helps them not at all, for how can any educational system succeed when it runs contrary to nature? All the larger intimate problems that encompass life are neglected, while the intellect is crammed with a store of quite useless facts. Real education would lead to emancipation, but instead we prepare girls for examinations.

And what we have to fear is a deadening of physical and spiritual response that must tend to follow from this suppression. For what is a girl's life? She works and rests from work, eats, and sleeps, and plays, and all the while she remains wrapped in the closest egoism, her strongest instincts smouldering beneath the dull weight of an education that is not an education, but an unstimulating and conforming pretence, and not fitted to the needs, of living. Even when she is free and is turned out at last, apathetic and obliterated, she carries with her vague dreads of positive acts and new ideas. How seldom does she succeed in urging out of herself the inmost vital part she has stifled. She is compacted of numbed faculties and inhibited desires.

The inmost Self yearns to get out and away, to spend itself, to find its due share in the ever-creating life. But the confidence and possession of the Self has been destroyed; the ego is left alone with its dread, with the distrust of desires not understood and instincts thrust back within.

And do you not see the result of this conflict to the sensitive soul of the adolescent? The terrible evil of disharmonies first started during these pregnant and inceptive years that should be the infancy of the higher powers of womanhood? Robbed of a just confidence and pride in her sex, her own stifled instincts become to a girl hateful and as something of which she should be ashamed; she begins to chafe against her womanhood and spurn it, bemoaning the limitations of her sex. She lapses into boy's ways, methods of work and ideals; she comes to live gaily enough and to laugh carelessly, not knowing what she has lost; to care nothing to be herself—content to choke the vision in her own life.

So it has been with you, with me, with all of us. Are we content that this blighting shall be suffered by our daughters?

The evil is happening for want of a generous guidance from us who have gone before. I write of what I know. Great and unending is the misery that we make possible by our folly, sickness of body and soul, so that the repressed nature rots away and doubt eats into natural faith. Nature is violated at every step, and *after we have educated her*, in nine cases out of ten, the girl emerges a mere residuum of decent minor dispositions. There is need to change.

Much that is said or done, both consciously and unconsciously, by the adult will torture the adolescent's sensitiveness much more than is conceivable to any one who has no insight to the curious psychology of girls in these difficult years. There is as a rule at this period of life a painful dualisation of the soul; thus, while seeking to know about sex, many girls will turn violently from the truth, so that any guidance we may give now will be very likely to arouse anger and disgust. And I know of no safeguard except a full knowledge of the physical facts of sex—of begetting and of birth, that has been gained earlier in the play period of childhood, in years when such knowledge can be assimilated unconsciously and its deep significance causes no response of personal disturbance.

We have to remember that these are the years of romance and idealism, when the always strong tendency among girls to sublimate and spiritualise love is at its highest. Sex knowledge could not possibly be given at a worse time than now, when the young soul is passing through its difficult birth and the conscious self seethes and teems with emotional ferment. If at this period the physical side of love is brought for the first time into notice there will be a withdrawal of the girl's ever-sensitive confidence, and worse, an ebb of the nerves, caused by distrust liberating the demon of fear; an almost certain reaction of incredulity and disillusionment will follow, with after results that may prove to be deep and far-reaching in their danger to healthy life.

We find then, contrary to the usual opinion, that an early and full instruction in the physical facts of sex is more necessary for girls even than it is for boys. The dangers of ignorance, or of sudden and too late knowledge, are greater. For any primary reaction of aversion, which is rarely absent, will in many cases strengthen into disgust and a curious horror that is partly fear and partly strengthened desire. For at the same time there will very likely be a strong attractive element in the form of intensely excited curiosity, which may be active and experimenting, but more often and with even greater danger is kept hidden, but yet spies and clutches for new evidence. Such unhealthy curiosity, remaining for long unsatisfied or insufficiently satisfied, almost necessarily sets up morbid reactions, causing many sexual evils.

You may say, of course, that I am mistaken; that these things do not happen—at least, not in the case of your daughter or of any nice girls. I can answer only, that it is you—the mother or the teacher—who, I fear, are wrong, living in the paradise of the fool. I am not exaggerating at all. I have tried to show how serious is the shock and how severe the disillusionment that may follow to the adolescent on a too sudden meeting with the physical facts of sex. It is time for us to cease pretending. We must realise that the mutilating or slaying of sex is followed always by disaster.

Instincts which have been prevented from their natural expression must tend to escape and find expression in abnormal forms that may, and often do, give rise to greater devastation. We have to face these things: there is no use in turning from them because they are horrid and in fear of giving offence.

Let me take but one fact. Masturbation is of very frequent occurrence among girls and among women, and this form of erotic indulgence acts directly in lowering sexual sensibility, and not only limits the desire for love, but prevents a right physical response so that satisfaction may be gained from the normal sexual act.

Is it not time that we women began to be frank? We have pretended to ourselves, and argued away from these questions far too long. Love cries out against our denials. Extreme passion may work ill, but the opposite extreme of the sacrifice of healthy natural instincts is as great an evil.

I am driven back always to this: the immense danger of repression. For our hindrances lead inevitably to repressions, always dangerous; and these tend to set up deep indwelling disharmonies, and then the way is opened up to manifold evils that may be traced into many by-paths of the after sexual life. And though I know there are many among my readers impatiently exclaiming that I am constantly dragging sex into everything, I assert that I do not drag it in: it is there. And for this reason alone it is certain that to formulate a system of education which ignores sex must lead to disaster.

I would call attention again to the fact noted in the previous chapter that the sex impulse is never absent in any child, however young. The transformation of puberty is really a co-ordination of the individual sex-life that already exists. With the development of the bodily structure and the marked changes in the sexual organs, there takes place a psychic growth which causes a perfectly natural seeking out of the young soul for experience and love. There is every possibility of morbid disturbance should this new order of development be hindered and not take place. And if this beautiful natural transformation is to succeed there must be no forcing back of the nature upon itself. The period of adolescence should crown and complete every organ and every faculty. No over-emphasis can be laid on the fateful issues that may follow to each girl from any mistakes in training at this period of adult birth, when the nature must find its new expression in the right direction of health or in the wrong direction of the abnormal.

We are deceived so often by the outside appearance of things. The painful experiences of youth may disappear from the conscious memory, but they do not thereby cease to act as an influence directing the after life.

Every mother and every teacher ought to understand this. Any hurt now done by our folly can never be undone. No experience is entirely lost. What seems to have vanished from the consciousness has really passed into a sub-consciousness, where it lives on in an organised form as real as if it were still part of the conscious personality; and although any experience may lie dormant, unknown to the conscious self, it may, and almost certainly will at some time, cause emotional reactions that continue without a known reason to excite and direct the outward ordinary life.

Our easy, complacent and devastating folly in ignoring the special physical nature of girls, and the elaborate ingenuity with which the facts of life are hidden from them or glossed over by unhealthy sentiment, is the true cause of the physical and spiritual etiolation of womanhood. There is, I allege, murder to the girl's power to be herself—to fulfil her woman's destiny—in our evasions, our deadly silences, and sham presentation of life, conditioned in all cases by theory and never by the act of living.

It is because I believe this that I am writing with all the power that I have against our schools which show the most coarse lack of understanding of the nature of the girl. I want new schools fitted to the needs of girls. The aim of education should be a general cohesion in all the different elements of the personality. And if the method is right, it will prove a way to greater happiness and fulness of growth. No longer will sex be held as a hindrance to life. I believe that almost everything in the future depends upon this.

Life would be liberated. An instinct that continually is hindered and denied cannot easily develop for health; and often, owing to these hindrances, the sexual life is stunted; then later the right and simple impulse to the performance of the sex act and its final consummation and enjoyment may be interfered with for ever and even prevented. Will you think what this means. In plain words, we are, by our false ideals and the wrong attitude towards the sexual life which conditions our system of education for girls, doing all that we can to prevent them from being women. I am not exaggerating; I am trying to make you see what it is that is wrong with life.

Every one who refuses to blink facts knows that the vast majority of marriages are unhappy owing to the coldness of the wife. It is certain that sexual anæsthesia to-day is present in many women, and there would seem, indeed, to be an increasing diminution of the strength of the sexual impulse.

Any number of women are unable to give themselves up to the sex act in such a way as to derive from it real satisfaction and the gladness and health that it should give. This is a very grave matter. The evil would be less if these frigid women did not marry, but as a rule they do marry. It is a curious fact that women who sexually are cold are sought as wives with greater frequency than are more passionate women, probably because their easily maintained reserve acts as a stimulus to the man. Men are persistently blind in these matters. They want response to their own desire in their wives, but most of them are very much afraid of any woman who possesses the strong passion to enable them to give such response. The woman gains her fulfilment from the man when he gives her his child, but when she turns from him she leaves him unsatisfied.[104] The drama and the novel are burdened with this problem, which, indeed, intrudes itself on every hand. We are, by our wrong ideals, inducing an entirely perverted view, which regards physical desire as something of which women should be ashamed, and the sex act as a thing in itself degrading and even disgusting—the nasty side of love; something to be submitted to, indeed, in order to bear children, or for the sake of the loved man, whose passions must be allowed, but not for the health and desire, the delight and perfectment of the woman herself. This false view, I affirm again, is the blight that has been, and still is, the destroyer of woman, and through her, equally the destroyer of man.

And this fear and denial of love, this separation between the sexes, is the serious side of the problem of marriage. For the hideous disguises and constant lying often made necessary to the husband, owing to the wife's entire failure to realise the physical necessities of love, makes domestic life an organised hypocrisy. We fight, and fight to be free, yet ever anew the antagonism lays fresh hold, it crops up in many and curious ways, imposing its poison and destroying love—the deep, deep-hidden rage of unsatisfied men against women. The need for love will not often allow itself to be inhibited without claiming payment. And if desire so frequently manifests itself in abnormal forms of the coarsest and commonest dissipation, this is almost always to be explained by some hindrance opposed to its normal expression. When women face facts and realise this truth, many things in men's conduct will be clear that hitherto have been hidden from them.

Again it may be thought that I am exaggerating; and there are, I know, other aspects of this question which just now I am neglecting. But the unreal and abysmal misconception into which one sex has fallen with regard to the other—this horrible, grasping, backwash of shame—is, in large measure, the result of our pretence and the way in which women have been kept living with blinds drawn down upon most of the unruly turbulence and elemental forces of life. It may also be held mistakenly that in what I have said I am writing against women; that I am raising a belated cry for masculine prerogatives and standards of sexual conduct. But that is not so. I am, it is undeniable, writing against the attitude of the modern woman towards marriage, her coldness of response to passion and her suppression of the realities of sex; an attitude I deplore and hold to be destructive alike to the happiness of women and men and to the health of the race, as also to any practical moral life. But such coldness and atrophy of instinct, I believe, has been imposed upon women by wrong education, the conditions of ignorance under which they marry and become mothers, and all the hindrances set around them, preventing them living out their lives from a sexual point of view.

It is example and the ideal set before us which produces the formation of opinion and of character, and few mothers remember the inner discord which exists between what they teach their daughters about love and what they act themselves in the daily life. And if the home is wrong, the school is, I think, much worse. In olden times, and still among primitive peoples—whose unconsidered actions are in many directions so much wiser than is our knowledge—girls were early given by matrons all the gathered wisdom of their sex pertaining to wifehood and motherhood; just the knowledge that we make it hard for them to gain. Could folly be greater than this?

With the decay of the specific traditions of the ideal of womanhood the idea of a general culture, neither male nor female, has tended to prevail. We touch here the deep roots of the evil. And what I wish to make plain is the inevitable failure of an educational system which makes no kind of arrangement for the special care and training of girls during the most critical years of their growth. There is, I allege, in all our educational establishments a strange and most culpable lack of understanding of the nature of the girl and her functions as a woman. They model brains without proper consideration of bodies, and with frightful convention repress from the seeking young the realities of love, and treat as secret, almost as something to be ignored, the functions connected with a girl's sexual life.

The mistake here is so far-reaching that I find it difficult to write calmly. For again I must assert that what we are doing is really to teach our girls a shameful denial of their womanhood. I wish that the power of my pen was stronger, so that I might bring a stinging consciousness of all the terrible mischief that is being done to the knowledge of every mother and every teacher.

How many of us have ourselves suffered? But our memories are strangely short. We forget, in our complacence and lazy, vicarious optimism, the dark places that imprisoned our young growing souls, haunts of gloom and despair that were never lit by a ray of sympathetic enlightenment from our sadder and wiser, but so forgetful, elders. We forget the grievous wounds to our self-respect. We forget the duality of soul; those oscillations between fear and disgust and curiosity and desire, with, perhaps, furtive trembling concessions to a power we did not understand, to be followed by morbid reactions of loathing, both of the mysterious impulse and of ourselves, that survive in those deadly disharmonies that are beginning to engage the attention of modern psychologists, and act to-day in our adult consciousness to war with the sum of unity which is happiness.

Yes, we all have forgotten. Yet none the less has this shameful early struggle left us fettered and seeking, and we have no window to inform us we are in prison. It has warped our natures, till, when in after years we look at Love, we behold, not the shining impersonation of the Life-force, but seeing double, view a monstrous Siamese twin of two figures, Lust and Sentimentality, a satyr bound to a wan angel by a navel-cord of procreative necessity. And often there is no rest, no cessation from a conflict that has left us helpless, so that for us love is moulded round a core of diseased desires.

It makes us examine our hearts. Is it to be so for ever?

We forget that perhaps four-fifths of the misery that follows in the train of sex-fulfilment is due to this mental and moral "diphobia" acquired in the days of adolescence in the unassisted struggle with the awakening and entirely misunderstood sex-impulse. We may forget, but few and happy are they who escape the effects of that encounter. According to our temperaments it has made us sedulous puritans and unconscious hypocrites, passionless neuters, or careless cynics and voluptuaries. And we are all of us to some extent marked and dirtied for ever. Deep and ineffaceable in us are the records of our disastrous early grapple with a great organic impulse which no one taught us to understand.

I am strongly of opinion that the tendency, so prevalent among women, to regard love as a twofold thing, one part of which is physical and evil and the other part spiritual and good, is almost diagnostic in an individual of a disharmony arising from an ancient reaction against sex, caused by some hindering influence or shock, encountered at the opening of the conscious sexual life.

The tremendous force that awakens in soul and body in these early years, and that with wise control and comprehension might be tended till in due course it flowers into Love, is early shorn of its splendour. Its whispered intimations of wondrous things to come fall on deaf ears. Taught to regard it as a malignant enemy that may destroy, instead of the most sacred and wonderful agency in human life, we enter into a hopeless struggle to eliminate the most basal part of our nature, or fawn before it in furtive and shameful surrender.

So most of us, embittered by the degradation of this struggle, *whether it be won or lost*, grow up to view with distrust what we absurdly call the "physical side of love." We, and especially women, accept it resignedly as an unavoidable baseness in the grain of Love. We forget that the baseness is in us and not in Love. *Love has no physical side, or mental side, or spiritual side.* It is a unity upon which we lay sacrilegious hands when we make an artificial separation into physical and spiritual.

We do this because of our own impurity, and because of the hurts we have suffered. We can no longer look at Love without furtively scanning his garments for the stains of Lust. We have created Lust. Lust is a morbid by-product in the evolution of Love.

It is this that we have suffered.

CONTENTS OF CHAPTER XVI
A CONTINUATION OF THE LAST CHAPTER, WITH AN

ATTEMPT TO SUGGEST A REMEDY

An attempt to find the remedy—What is the real root of the evil—The young woman of the new generation—The years since the war began—An examination of present conditions—What is likely to happen when peace comes—The independent woman—The Commissioner's Report of the National Birth-Rate Investigation, 1916—The failure in our lives—Where is the real root of the evil—The whole educational system of girls in our homes and in our schools is wrong—The importance of menstruation—Influence of conventionality—Wrong ideals set before girls—The destruction working in our midst—Fear of sex directs our educational system—The remedy to begin in our schools—We must educate girls to be women—Menstruation and the girl's special sexual life must be emphasised and not as now ignored—Adolescent schools—The sexual life of the adolescent girl—The difficulties that must be faced—Opposition on the part of women—Motherhood to be saved—Regeneration of the girl's instincts through consciousness—The hope with which we may look to the future—Motherhood will triumph.

CHAPTER XVI
A CONTINUATION OF THE LAST CHAPTER, WITH AN ATTEMPT TO SUGGEST A REMEDY

"With fear and trembling take care of the heart of the people; that is the root of the matter in education—that is the highest in education."—K'UNG FU 'TZU.

It is, of course, easy to write of these evils, the difficult thing is to find the remedy. And the question I now wish to put squarely is this: Where is the real root of the evil, what is wrong in our educational ideals that accounts for our failure to develop the best and happiest type of women? You may, of course, deny this, and assert that we do not fail, but that will not alter facts. I say we are creating a race of work-efficient and highly educated, but unsatisfied women, whose very independence betrays their sorrow. This is a very serious matter. It would seem that our young women have now for the first time realised their power in outside things. War has acted quickly in facilitating their economic emancipation. But I find it hard not to think that this may involve a cost which their womanhood will not bear without injury more or less profound. Women are being sold to work in the same way that formerly men were sold. And though no one can know the results, I am very far from sharing the sense of satisfaction expressed by so many to-day: I fear for the girls I see in such numbers in every place of work a deadening of response to life—a further clog and degradation of womanly feeling and instincts. And as I have said again and again, my fear is much deeper, because this externalisation of life is no new thing. I could add more, much more; but words—what are they in the face of facts! Last week I was in conversation with a young and comely tram conductress. She was married: I asked her if she had children. She answered me: "My goodness, No!" and then added, "One doesn't want babies on this job." One dares not generalise too largely, yet for so long women, in this industrially blinded land, have been struggling to gain the world at the payment of losing themselves.

The young women of the new generation are full of distrust, the most demoralising of influences. By this I do not mean that they distrust themselves; they do not. What they do distrust is instinct and emotion, with a corresponding over-valuation of intellectualism and of marketable work-power; and from this distrust there has followed necessarily a breaking away from fixed standards, with a loss of any steadying ideal. This, I think, is the essential trouble, sending them very far astray from the facts of life.

Look at the women you may see in all classes of society. You may see them hastening to and from their work; you may see them in the streets each evening or in every place of amusement. How many bear upon their brows this stamp of a nature unfixed of purpose, in the expression of their face as well as the body movements, in their restlessness and noisy happiness is the sign of disharmonies aroused, a nature strained and failing in the fulfilment of its functions. One feels that as women these young girls of the present generation have lost something, lost it so completely that they know no longer what they desire.

I should, however, like to make it very clear that I am not disparaging women, nor do I fail to admire all they have achieved in difficult positions. There is no need to re-tell the oft-told and much praised facts of what they have done in these years since the war began. There can be no shadow of doubt as to the efficiency and value of the work of the thousands of women at present engaged in many and varied branches of labour. But what I fear is the waste of the struggle should it continue for any period of years. Let us except this hard working of women as a necessary evil of warfare, demanding at the same time special protection and special provision for child-bearers. But do not let us fall into the error of regarding such conditions as in themselves good and desirable, leading, as I believe must follow, to a further obliteration of sex, with its differences and wise separation.

Difficult as at present is the problem, we need to understand that we cannot afford to be wasteful of the strength of women. We are being wasteful. The physiological life even of the unmarried woman ought to handicap her in almost every kind of work. Long hours of standing, the lifting of heavy weights, any kind of drain on the nervous power, cannot fail to do harm. There are days when every young girl and woman who may have to bear children, however strong, ought to release tension, to step aside from work to maintain full health. I am filled with impatience at our pretence on this question of women's health. There is a difference between the work capacity of the woman and the work capacity of the man. Sex must play a far larger part, making far stronger claims on the strength of the girl and the woman than it ever does in the lives of boys and men. It is vain to assume that because women are willing, and apparently able, to do the same work now as men in the past have done, that, therefore, it is wise to allow them to do it. The price of the violent energy, so wastefully being poured out, will have to be paid. Countless women and girls are using up now the nervous energy and strength of which they are merely the pilots and guardians; the health and calm of spirit which should be stored and transmitted to generations to come.

The increased activity and exertion daily demanded from child-bearers must be anti-social in its racial effects. Either these girls, constantly stimulated, over-excited, and robbed of the tranquillity they need, will bear enfeebled children, or, what is more likely, through the direct premium placed on childlessness, fewer and fewer children will be born, and from this there may tend to follow a further deadening and even a crushing out of the maternal instinct. Children will not be wanted.

I pointed out in the earlier chapters of my book[105] that such a transformation of impulse may take place. The parental instinct is not fixed, and disuse is the swiftest way to decay. Think what this must mean to the life values of the future. I believe it is not possible to estimate how far-reaching may be the results of what is now being done so quickly and so recklessly. By our absurd denials and our ignorance we shall have brought down upon us this evil—our punishment for conceiving sex in women as something too terrible to be faced in its reality.

Let us understand what it is that we shall be doing. We are built up of habits just as a house is built up of bricks. And what motherhood is going to be in the future depends on our desires and our action to-day.

A sound nation has for its essential condition healthy children—yes, and many of them—and healthy mothers to bear and to rear them. We know this. But what are the facts? We find more and more young women turning away from motherhood. They are marrying in larger numbers just now, for war has turned men into heroes and this has made marriage popular. But we may not count too much on this, for no longer does marriage mean the bearing of children and the founding of a family. The wife no longer is comparable to the fruitful vine, no longer are children like olive plants about the table of the house. The blessings of the old sweet poem fail to stir our desires. Babies are not wanted.

The volume of evidence and the observations made by the Commissioners' Report of the National Birth-Rate Investigation, 1916, which lies upon my desk, cannot be read without a sense of almost hopeless depression. A dark picture is revealed of men and women harried and driven by the sex instinct within them; the relation of the husband and the wife made hateful from a perpetual fear of the natural consequences of birth. The struggle is but too clearly apparent in every section of society. The evidence discloses that the prevention of conception is growing steadily and rapidly, for though it began with and, for a time, was practised only by the well-to-do, it is now spreading downwards to the poorest, amongst whom the practice of abortion has for long been extensively used. Dr. Mary Scharlieb, whose report is, perhaps, the most interesting of all the Commissioners, states that in the working classes there are five abortions to every one live birth.

What sordid facts this Report reveals! What a failure it proves our life! Is there any use in talking of raising the birth-rate until these things are changed? Is our land fit to receive the children? Has not the child the right to demand from its parents that its birth shall be looked on as something more than an unfortunate mistake?

I know, of course, the difficulties which face the parents, among which economic difficulties are important, arising from the competitive capitalistic system by which all our lives are entangled. Yet I feel that these considerations, though they cannot be neglected and increase the evil, alone are not responsible; that the cause lies deeper and is dependent on the desires of the mind; that apart from any economic causes, and even assuming that every child could be better born and with a happy life secured to it, there would yet be much of the problem that would remain unsolved. And what I am trying all this time to make plain is this: If we wish to get rid of the atrophy that is increasingly present in the instincts of our young women, and quicken their response to passion, with its desire for motherhood, we must first get rid of our wrong values of what is good in life and makes for enduring happiness; and to do this we must change our educational methods, the training in the home and in the school, and conditions of work that are their parent. There can be no help and no change, at least I cannot see any, except to alter our ideals. Nothing else of any wide value can be done until these are changed.

In the name of common sense and of sanity let us get to the real bottom of this matter. To do anything at all we must begin at the beginning, where the wrong is started. It is absurd to go on crying out against the shirking of motherhood, while at the same time, in the education of our girls and afterwards in the arrangements we make for their working life, we show a complete evasion of the function most intimately connected with motherhood. That is where the clue to the trouble lies. The whole educational system in our homes and in our schools, as well as the conditions in our workshops and houses of business, is wrong. It discourages motherhood very heavily. And the rational thing for us to do in the matter is not to grow eloquent about a declining birth-rate, or to blame women for not desiring to be mothers, but rather to make intelligent changes so as to minimise to the young the discouragement that by our teaching and our actions we have hitherto given to motherhood.

And the first step towards this must be, I am certain, to banish from the consciousness of every girl all feeling of shame, and all concealments connected with her function of menstruation. In other words, we have to face the facts of a girl's sexual life. This is not going to be easy.

In the immediate past our attitude of hiding on these questions was due to reasons of prudishness in regard to all natural functions, and notably menstruation—the rubicon in the life of every girl, which first brings or, I ought to say, *should bring,* full realisation that life for her is separate and needs to take a different course from the life of the boy and the man.

This truth has been disliked so much that in practice it has been disregarded. The wrong is started early and is continued throughout the sexual life. The real controlling force in the education of the girl is the mother; and motherhood has failed. Girls, with an almost criminal neglect, have been left without any wise preparation for the first menstruation, upon the regular establishment of which function their health in the future must depend. Many girls, being seriously frightened or stirred to rebellion and anger, have done foolish actions, and through neglected hygiene evil is begun that never can be undone. This is no over-statement. The first few menstruations have a far greater influence not only on the body, but also on the brain and the soul of a girl than do those that follow later when the sexual health is better established. Every mother and teacher ought to know and heed this.

At best, and even when instructed by their mothers, girls have been taught to regard this function as a troublesome illness that must be suffered with patience; such a view, of course, being a relic of the supposed curse laid upon the woman's sex. Nor can it be said that even to-day there is any improvement when quite different ideals prevail regarding woman's place and her vocation. For the new emancipation has brought with it a false view that girls should be educated in the same way as boys, and should be brought up in the pretence that it is right and possible for them to work and play at all times like boys and to be as independent of their sexual life as boys can afford to be.

Now, it does not need much imagination to understand the harm of such teaching. The menstrual function—which really marks the sex of the girl and fits her for motherhood—is ignored as if its occurrence were of no importance. And such an attitude of dislike and hiding necessarily causes a feeling of shame, more or less deep according to the temperament of the girl. From the very first sex is presented in the shape of something to be despised and desperately fought against, something secret and disgusting. Even at this early stage disharmony enters into the young and sensitive soul.

Some girls revolt in the very depths of their being, while the common feelings aroused are expressed by such words as aversion and dislike, anger and shame. Do you not see now the harm that is done? How sadly we are sowing for the future. For what can be the result except to teach our girls a shameful disrespect for themselves. What wonder is there that many girls are stirred to rebellion which takes the outward form of resolutely ignoring their monthly periods, and the fact that they are girls. And the immediate result is a general lowering in the standard of sexual health.

I shall be told that this is not true. But I am writing of what I know. Menstruation is a perfectly natural function and every girl should be taught so to regard it. But at its start it does exercise a very disturbing effect on the whole system and character. And the folly that pretends that in these early years special care is not required at the monthly periods cannot be too strongly condemned. For the harm is deeper and further reaching than the physical hurt, though certainly in our folly we are making invalids of the future mothers of the race. Harm in many cases is done to the after sex expression; harm which probably is never recognised, and about which the ordinary parent and teacher are densely ignorant and optimistic. How little do we consider the consequences of our acts? I say there is no limit and no end to the evil that we are permitting. And the most fearful thing about it is that it all seems so wantonly needless.

The always difficult passage of the girl into the woman is alarming only to the girl who knows nothing about herself and her sexual life. Just as far as she understands does recoil and resentment and shame become needless. Rightly taught, she will learn to regard her special function, not as something to be hidden and ignored, but as the sign of the changes that now are taking place in her body—healthy natural changes that will fit her one day for love and wifehood and motherhood. Then, indeed, her shame and her aversion will be converted into pride. Understanding, she will have a fitting reverence for herself. She will now know why she is under certain restrictions, and has at the times of her monthly periods to refrain from overwork and all strain, and to give up some pleasures and excitements; she will do this gladly in order that her development into womanhood may be without pain, healthy and complete.

I believe firmly that this change in our attitude to menstruation—a change that will emphasise its importance to health and its connection with fit motherhood—a change that must start at the beginning of the girl's conscious sexual life, is absolutely necessary to the development of a higher motherhood. At least, if it does not come, I can have no hope at all. You cannot gather fruit from a tree that is unhealthy at its root. And you cannot have glad motherhood while you start out by despising the function most sacredly connected with motherhood. We must understand this. Until we do understand it, and then act in the practical way that will cause us to change our teaching to all young girls, we shall find women in ever-increasing numbers turning away from motherhood, and wasting in external things the realities of love and life.

How can healthy womanhood be possible within the limits and wrong ideals of our present system, and how can they fail to give rise to continuous restlessness? I declare once more and plainly that we are raising a generation of girls—those with whom the duties of wifehood and motherhood should reside—who have instincts atrophied by dull studies, to be followed by deadening work. I hold that this is a matter of the gravest concern, not only for women and men and their individual happiness in union one with the other, but is also what will decide the future of this land and empire.

But few among us understand the destruction that is working in our midst. We do not recognise the symptoms that mark the disharmony in the lives of the great majority of the girls and young women of the present generation. War has but increased the mischief. Independence in material things has given triumph to that rebellion which our mistaken training and wrong ideal had started long ago smouldering in the souls of our daughters. To-day youth is in demand; the young girl can fill every place. And youth has risen fearlessly and splendidly to every opportunity, but so quickly as not to have time to consider how much is being trampled underfoot. The danger of speed—the filling of every moment of time, always a mistake made by women—has been intensified by the war. The war race has provided the opportunity to live riotously and wastefully.

Of course, it is we of the older generation—the mothers—who are to blame. We have left our daughters in a dangerous position; we did not see where modern education, with its effort to obliterate sex, must inevitably lead.

Education may be either a most helpful or a most dangerous process. And what is most to be feared is the shut-in instincts that tend to twist the nature from its simple fulfilment. There is something essentially harmful in any failure or wrong expression of a special function. Now, we have insisted upon repressions, and what we believed to be a high moral and efficient working character for girls, not knowing that what we so mistakenly were straining for was really something very like an entire absence of any kind of womanly character. The real nature of girls is wild, and our fears have been very great. And for this reason have we held that the nakedness of the adolescent's new-born womanhood must be clothed with conventionalities and draped with culture.

It is this fear of sex that directs our educational system: there is too much drill and too much strain. Girls' schools are governed too much, for girls need, not less, but more liberty than boys. The teachers are dull and narrow in their own outlook and in their experience of life; they are not trained to understand the needs of adolescent girls, only to teach them facts that as a rule are of no real service; they do not trouble to train the inner and hidden instincts that really form character, they do not even look for them; they reck nothing of early development or late, of the presence of strong passion or its absence; they have no kind of understanding of the unceasing action of sex, forcing its expression in unconscious acts, which alone give the clue to character; of all this (the only knowledge that matters) the teachers are profoundly ignorant; but they measure out girl-humanity for the conventional standard of efficiency like a dressmaker measures out her material with a yard measure. There is no thought, at least none is betrayed, that the school is a preparation for living. No kind of training is given for the part the girls will have to play in the life of sex for their own health and happiness and the regeneration of the race. The sexual life is persistently ignored.

I recall reading somewhere—I do not remember the exact connection—how an official of a college for girls was questioned by a visitor as to the advantage gained by the students in their after life from a university training. She answered: "One third of the students profit by it, another third gain some little good, while the remaining third are failures." "And what becomes of the failures?" was the question asked, while the answer given was this: "Oh, they marry!" Now, I do not know if this excellent story can be accepted as a fact, but it does point to a contempt for marriage and its duties—a contempt for woman's sex and for her own work—which I believe is present in the thought and attitude, even if not acknowledged openly, among the majority of educationalists. This is a very serious matter.

The remedy, then, has to begin in our schools. We must control education with a finer sense of its value to life. And to do this we must accept the extreme importance of sex, and guard those differences which separate the girl from the boy.

As a first movement of reform, I would recommend one to three years' rest from the usual school work for every girl, during the period when her sexual life is becoming established. This is not, of course, to advocate idleness. I am not upholding any form of invalidism for girls; the adolescent always should have plenty of healthy occupation, but that is a far different thing from the strain of the ordinary school course, foolishly arranged for girls on the same lines as that for boys, and without any regard to the important function of menstruation. There should be attached to every school for girls a special class for adolescents, and this should be the most important class in the school. At the onset of puberty the girls would enter this class, in which they would stay for two years or longer. The sexual life would not be, as now it is, ignored; rather the chief work of the school would be the healthy establishment of the menstrual function, upon which the future well-being of the girl depends, and to the interests of which everything else should for a time be secondary.

There must be a new valuation of education, with an entire change of attitude, which will make possible more openness between the teacher and her pupils. The difficulties here will, I know, be great. If the mothers do not know how to help their daughters, and usually they do not; if the girls do not know how to help themselves, and dumb and untaught they are helpless, the task of the teachers cannot fail to be hard. And especially will this be the case wherever the mother has failed in her duty and a girl has received no kind of sexual training in the home.

I know of what I am writing here, and how real is the prejudice that will have to be overcome. In my own school I was met with this trouble again and again. The girls resented any mention of their menstrual function, and expressed often real anger and disgust when I required them to tell me the dates of their monthly periods, so that I might see they had extra food, more rest, and lighter studies. The answer that usually was given to me was this: "My mother never wanted me to tell her; I took no notice when I was at home." What an unconscious indictment of the mothers! Often it was after long and patient effort only that I gained my way, and brought my girls to speak to me naturally about this function. I had the very hardest work to free their thoughts from the deeply implanted feelings of shame and disgust: in many cases I failed altogether, and I cannot, indeed, be sure that I ever fully succeeded. Of course, my failures were the result of harm that had been done much earlier in the home.

It was at this time of my life, now long years ago, when these considerations were forced upon my attention by my failures with my elder pupils, that I was first led to desire special classes for girls to enter at the age of puberty, where the life, the work, and the aims were separate and quite different from the ordinary school. It is so much easier to do the wise thing, if what you are doing is a matter of course, and not something you start for yourself.

I am convinced of the value that would be gained for life from the plan I am advocating. I would begin with these special classes, but I want more than that to be done. A much better course would be that separate adolescent schools should be provided, preferably in the country, where all work as well as play could be done out of doors. All girls would enter before the commencement of puberty, and would stay in one of these special adolescent schools for two or three years or longer. The work would be organised entirely to meet the needs of the individual girl; there must be no set courses of study, no hide-bound rules, and above all no examinations to be crammed for. In my opinion, which was formed from my own experience in my school, girls should do hardly any steady work for one year before and two years after puberty; they cannot, I am certain, work continuously without peril. Mental overwork or any kind of strain destroys the nervous resistance and tends to that irritable weakness which makes the rankest ground for all sexual ill health, and may work to establish evil habits in ways not yet openly recognised. The kind of work done should be chosen by the girl herself; there should be far more opportunity for rest and for play, and, while guarding against opportunities for harmful idleness, any kind of mental or bodily strain must be avoided. Hard study, if this is necessary, will come later at the close of this special school period. But I plead for all girls during the difficult time of their metamorphosis from the girl to the woman to leave them much more largely than we do at present to nature and to themselves.

The adolescent girl often is thought to be lazy, and when called upon to work she shows an exasperating dulness and inattention. This is a natural condition when the girl is passing through the langour of physical growth; she is overcome, not by listlessness, but by the strain of her awakening senses, and the inattention of the mind is, as a rule, but a symptom of the mysterious and difficult maturing of the brain. The apparent apathy is not real: all the girl's power, all energy of body and mind is being consumed by the overwhelming force of the half-conscious life of instincts that are ripening within. The young girl for the first time feels, though very rarely does she understand, the power of her nature stirring her soul. And any seeming backwardness in studies during these years, as should be known by the wise teacher, leads afterwards to finer progress, if only the right opportunity of unstrained development is given. But it is this harmony of growth that we have been disturbing as with persistent zeal we have educated from the outside. Little wonder that we have failed. I have spoken before of the wide difference that is present between the nature of the boy and that of the girl, and though I speak with hesitation on a question that is too complex to permit dogmatic assertions, the boy has, I think, a much more healthy and conscious knowledge of himself; a girl understands herself less, and has a very dim notion of the motives of her conduct. This leads to very certain danger. The thoughts of most girls are occupied with vague and romantic longings, much heightened by the nonsense written on love in the books girls are allowed to read, stories from which every hint of wholesome reality has been omitted. Such false feelings, dominating the girl's mind at the time of the adolescent crisis, work grave evil.

While always thinking of love most girls know almost nothing of what love really is; and certainly the strain of any sudden chance investigation of the physical facts of sex is a very near danger.

That is one reason why, in a previous section, I have urged so strongly that sexual enlightenment be given to the girl while she is still at the age when sex has no strong personal significance.

The importance of early knowledge is not sufficiently recognised. If from childhood there has been frankness between the girl and her mother, and they have spoken together openly of sex and the facts of birth, it will certainly have happened that the chief emphasis in the mother's instruction will have been placed upon the relation between the child and herself.[106] Such teaching may well prove a great safeguard. The personal, or "pleasure," element in sex will in this way not be too soon forced and stamped on the girl's consciousness; it will be, as it should, deferred until the age of passion comes. Even then the result of the earlier teaching will be present to direct the desires. Love and marriage will not be divorced entirely from the thought of motherhood, as so disastrously happens with many girls to-day.

It is a question I must leave, though it is one on which much more might be said. For I believe we have here a further explanation of the triumph of the egoistical sexual desires over the parental instincts of sacrifice. I am altogether convinced of the deep and wide-reaching harm that is done, in ways that have never yet been recognised, from the sexual ignorance of girls and our shameful concealments and untrue education. And I have felt often that the brutal frankness of boys in sex matters, bad as certainly it sometimes is in its after coarsening effect, in many ways is better in its results than the confused silence and sentiment with which most girls are surrounded; it is, at least, in nearer touch with the facts of life.

I have had considerable experience with adolescent girls. I am sure that their thoughts are more occupied with sex than they know themselves, or is recognised by the adults who are with them. I am speaking here of the normal girl in whom the sexual impulse takes definite form during the early years of puberty. It will need all our wisdom and patience to be able to help the girl now, if we have left her in the darkness of her soul before. She is suffering the anguish of youth, reaching out for the unknown ideal, which she cannot grasp, cannot even distinguish or conceive. There are, of course, other types of girls—girls of delicate and sensitive temperament in whom sexual development for long may be delayed. This may be due to various causes, but is most frequently a result of excessive mental strain from over-pressure or unsuitable work at the onset of puberty, tending to de-normalise the sex-life.

Now, to some parents and teachers, not understanding the results, it may seem that this is an end to be desired, and that such a postponement of the sex-life to the years when the girl is older will be a safeguard against evils. This, I believe, is a mistake. The sex feelings are not absent but hidden, and the result too often is a profound melancholy and a dull heaviness which may continue to spoil life. And when the time comes, as come it must, and the long-repressed feelings force an expression, the sex-strain is often very great, and troubles frequently arise that could not have happened except for our interference with the right process of nature.

Of course, whatever we do, we must expect often to fail. We are not dealing with anything that can be fixed; and our methods as well as our success must vary with each individual girl. It is this personal element that has not been considered. And this is why there is such need for a higher and different standard in our schools, and of more knowledge and understanding on the part of all who are connected with the training of girls. I know of nothing that can prepare the girl but the early teaching of the mother, but I think in the later adolescent years it is the wise teacher who can better carry on the work.

The task of the educator ought to be plain: to encourage all girls in their natural reaching out for experience and knowledge of themselves, not to smother all that is individual in them under set lessons, necessary perhaps and helpful at other periods of growth, but now I am certain harmful, dulling the character with falsehood and the bodies with constraints, and wearying the minds with overstrain through long hours of drudgery into a dull acceptance.

The worst influence of the school is its isolation from life. Consciousness, not instruction, should be the aim of education. Yet in all directions our girls have been led and forced into following material consciousness, and, at the same time, they have increasingly lost consciousness of themselves. Realisation of one's own being—how to produce this by means of education—that is the question. What answer are we going to give?

Such a rest period in specially adapted schools as I am here advocating would serve not only to establish the health of adolescent girls and fit them for vigorous womanhood, it would, as I believe, change their ideal and remake life. In such surroundings fitted to their own needs, and with a different valuation of the future set before them, they would have a truer sense of self-consciousness; they would come to understand in quite a new way the responsibilities and high glory of being women.

The difficulties, of course, are numerous. And, first of all, it will not be easy to find the right teachers for these adolescent schools. They will need to be specially trained; but training alone will not serve. The teachers must have had a much wider experience of life than is usual to women; they ought to have genius and a passionate love of children: they need to be mothers in spirit.

Necessarily, the expense of such teachers and of these special schools, which should be established in great numbers and with no thought of sparing the cost, will be heavy. It will be thought, I know, by many that this fact alone makes the plan impracticable. I can answer only, that any expenditure that will produce fit and glad mothers for the future is an expense that will be met by a wise nation.

I would urge that this question be approached from a practical attitude. On all sides concern is being felt at the decline in the birth-rate, which has fallen one-third in the last thirty-five years. The Royal Commission that I have referred to already has made its investigation and issued its report. Much has been written on the problem, and many guesses made as to the vaguely understood causes. The economists find all the evil in economic conditions; the religious say that it is our morality that is at fault. Many are the remedies suggested, a few of which are practical and good. And so urgent is the matter felt to be, now that war with its destruction of life is teaching us a little more the value of life, that changes, long called for, but hitherto seemingly unattainable, shortly may be made in our divorce and marriage laws. The sharp and cruel line drawn between the married and the unmarried mother will at last waver and break on its rotten supports. Already the saving of child life has become a matter of such urgent need that much necessary reform is being accomplished. There is little doubt that these valuable movements will go on.

Yet, I think, we are failing to attack the real cause, and unless we do attack it there, right at the beginning, we shall go on as we usually do, experimenting in this way and in that, doing one thing and leaving another undone, and we shall only tinker and fuss and then wonder why we fail. Blind and fools! we fail, and shall go on failing, because we do not educate our girls and act in life in such a way as will encourage motherhood.

I have put out my idea: I have tried to be as explicit as possible in suggesting the remedy. I am conscious now of opposition that will be raised. I shall be told that my plan, which seems so simple, of educating girls to be women is not practicable. And then I shall be reminded of the immense surplus of women in this country who are unable to marry and live a full and healthy life—a surplus large before the war, enormously greater now.[107]

Let me state at once that I am very far indeed from forgetting this great host of enforced celibate women. I have spoken more than once in my book about them, and I am not now concerned with their position. What I want is to save the future. Many girls and women to-day are finding their work and the fresh excitements of independence sufficient to gladden life. They do not claim pity; yet this satisfaction that women are feeling is the danger that threatens the future. It is just because these women, whose desires will be fixed on work and away from motherhood, must be here among us, in every place, especially in our schools and in our factories—everywhere in contact with youth—that I am pleading with all the power that I have for a quite changed training for the young girls of the coming generation of women. I fear greatly the influence that I believe must grow up if industrial values of what is good in life are unchecked, and the desire of women is turned more from motherhood and the life that matters to the outside details of existence.

Life must be re-shaped, and the first step is the perception of an idea. We want belief, for life must have a structure—the scaffolding on which we may build. And each individual woman among us may not be trusted to make her own structure—to convey and carry whatever it may be that she desires. Such selfishness makes any permanent building impossible. That is why in this generation we have lost our ideal.

The previous age fixed its attention on the reform of injustice in the outward relations of men and women, on the regulation of capital and labour, on the equality of the sexes and the improvement of the conditions of life—efforts which culminated naturally in socialism. My work is one dealing essentially with an attitude towards life. I would protest against the want of respect for the ultimate emotional aspects of life, the love of man for woman and of woman for her child—a want of respect which makes it impossible to tell a young girl openly the reason why she must not over-exert herself at the time of her monthly periods. I confess to little patience with this effort to escape sex. Everything connected with birth and maternity has to be hidden and mentioned only in whispers. We have forced the attention of girls away from motherhood, fixing their desires on work and independence. Obedient and inexperienced, they have followed our guiding. We have taught them to regard the physical attraction which they ought to feel towards men as *not nice*, thereby associating in their young minds all sexual feelings without distinction as *not nice*. We have left them ignorant that sex feelings may be good or bad according to their associations. Harmful emotional repression has been inevitable, with a result in the after years of distaste for motherhood and passionate marriage. We have made love unclean and separated it from their lives. And, where love is not, all else is barren. I must speak strongly, for very great is the evil we are countenancing.

The attitude of woman herself is the deep secret of this question; and by attitude I mean something more than the desire of the individual girl or woman, I mean the collective spirit in which life is approached. That is where we have been wanting. We, the mothers and teachers of this last generation of women, have failed to grasp life and all that it means.

What we have most dreaded in education is sex. We can control this attitude only in our schools. Emancipation can come through a regaining of consciousness. Get this right—let our girls feel that their education *because they are women* is the most important work of the nation, more, not less important, than is the education of their brothers, and the rest will follow.

We have by our whole attitude shown the most coarse lack of understanding of the needs of girls. Instruction has been the sole effort of our schools. This has hampered the perfection of life. Our daughters have but accepted and abandoned their bodies and their souls to the rollers of that crushing machine we have called education.

All of us are responsible, for our thoughts and our desires affect the universe and our neighbours. Neither can any repentance that may come late, nor any wailings of dismay, stop the consequences of our sinning follies.

I cannot lay too much stress on this sense of women's desire, for it is this that will direct action in the future. If we cannot have a fundamental change of desire, a fresh view of what is a sane, complete and profitable life; if we cannot cease from our fears of sex; if we cannot alter the ideals we place before girls and work a revolution in the practice of our education, we shall do no good. There will be endless talk of advancement—of higher motherhood, of economic emancipation and freedom in marriage; there will also be continued tinkering legislation, with many timid experiments in mother-training and child-rearing, and underneath the spirit of motherhood will be dying, dying all the time.

But the unbeliever will cry out: All this is utterly impossible; this is the old clog and degradation for women, limiting her to the single function of her sex. My answer is this. Even so it was from the beginning of time. Nature has so planned it, fixing the maternal instinct deep in the mother, and claiming from her the payment that must be given. Woman can only bow before the Throne of Life. She is entrusted with life's supreme mission, that of transmitting the sacred torch of life to future generations. She belongs not to herself but to posterity. She must not squander her gift. She must store her energy that she may give life to her child.

Woman, all-containing, universal—how should she be limited to herself? This is my deepest belief.

Woman is the giver, the interpreter. Freedom for her never can be identified with self-assertion. Great elementary truths to-day have acquired an intensified significance. Oppression stretches like a rod over the earth, the world is ploughed with swords and reaped in blood. The echoes of slaughter reach from land to land. The cataclysm, with its immense appeal to terror and love and hate and pity, has acted to stir us profoundly and quicken our response to the emotional aspects of life. Old prejudices are rooted up; institutions are in the melting-pot. A people habitually resistant to emotion, we have been awakened to reality. I cannot doubt that we shall profit. We were occupied in intellectual pleasures and energies, but now our souls have been harrowed. This is the great opportunity if we have the will to use it.

Fear has been in us the folly irredeemable, planted like seeds of the wild weeds among our wheat. Even in our childhood doubt has slept with us in our cradles, as verily we have been conceived in sin, being born without passionate joy. And this disharmony has followed us up and down in the home; doubt was our schoolfellow, ever following our steps in our work and in our play, until fear has become our perpetual companion. I see the past, the present and the future existing all at once before me, and I know that as soon as fear is conquered redemption is ready.

Then no longer will the blessings of the Psalmist be changed by our faithless folly into cursing, but again the wife shall be as a fruitful vine by the sides of the house and the children like olive plants around the table. Behold, thus shall the woman and the man be blessed together, and they shall see good all the days of their life.

But this regeneration will come only through the creation of our wills. Without unceasing desire nothing can be done. Desire is action. If you leave off desiring salvation you are lost.

I tell you no virtue can be found apart from our desires. Life is the struggle everlasting, unceasing sacrifice, constant aspiration.

What is the secret, if it is not Love?

The spirit of Life is Love triumphant, the immortal force which incites the struggle, makes glad the sacrifice, which stirs the desire to achieve. And the law of Love is as easy to state as it is difficult to apply: it is the transforming of the will which says "mine" into the will which says "thine." It is a law that can be comprehended only by living it.

I shall be called old-fashioned. Yet, perhaps, after all, I see further, deeper, and more surely than those who call me so.

The union of the man and the woman cleaving to each other can be the wonder of life. Marriage should be a blessing of the senses, a kindling of the spirit, a mutual surrender, and a new creation.

Creation is not accomplished; it is continuous and unceasing, and in its work every living thing has its share, destroying and creating.

What is it that I desire? What is it that I expect? What is the change of whose coming I feel as assured as of the rising of to-morrow's sun?

I look for a regeneration of woman's instincts through consciousness. She, who has conquered the world, will then renounce the world. The old corruption will be swept away. Woman is the keeper of redemption; it is her work to lead man back to the gate of his being.

We are waiting in pain for the new liberation. Love alters everything, it melts the whole world and makes it afresh. Love is the sun of our spirits and the wind.

Is there, indeed, this glad hope of things changing? Changing? They have got to change. The weeds of our mistakes have so grown up that they are choking us. Yes, whether from inside or from out, I do not know yet, but there is change and awakening coming. Motherhood will triumph. Life is going to be made new before long.

www.ingramcontent.com/pod-product-compliance
Lightning Source LLC
Chambersburg PA
CBHW081615100526
44590CB00021B/3452